Climate Change and Power

The Sustainable Development Programme is the new name (from February 2002) for the Energy and Environment Programme of the Royal Institute of International Affairs at Chatham House. The Programme works with business, government, and academic and NGO experts to carry out and publish research and stimulate debate across a wide variety of energy, environment and business topics with international implications, particularly those just emerging into the consciousness of policy-makers. Research by the Programme is supported by generous contributions of finance and technical advice from the following organizations:

- Amerada Hess Ltd
- Anglo American plc
- BG Group
- BP Amoco plc
- British Energy plc
- British Nuclear Fuels plc
- Department for Environment, Food and Rural Affairs (UK)
- Department of Trade & Industry (UK)
- ExxonMobil
- Foreign & Commonwealth Office (UK)
- Osaka Gas Co. Ltd
- Powergen plc
- Saudi Petroleum Overseas Ltd
- Shell UK
- Statoil
- Tokyo Electric Power Co. Inc.
- TotalFinaElf
- TXU Europe Group plc

Climate Change and Power

Economic Instruments for European Electricity

Edited by Christiaan Vrolijk

THE ROYAL INSTITUTE OF INTERNATIONAL AFFAIRS | Sustainable Development Programme

Earthscan Publications Ltd, London

First published in the UK in 2002 by
The Royal Institute of International Affairs, 10 St James's Square, London SW1Y 4LE
(Charity Registration No. 208223)
and
Earthscan Publications Ltd, 120 Pentonville Road, London N1 9JN

Distributed in North America by
The Brookings Institution, 1775 Massachusetts Avenue NW,
Washington, DC 20036-2188

A catalogue record for this book is available from the British Library.

ISBN   1 85383 822 5 paperback
           1 85383 821 7 hardback

The Royal Institute of International Affairs is an independent body that promotes the rigorous study of international questions and does not express opinions of its own. The opinions expressed in this publication are the responsibility of the authors.

Earthscan Publications Ltd is an editorially independent subsidiary of Kogan Page Ltd and publishes in association with the WWF-UK and the International Institute of Environment and Development.

Typeset by Denis Dalinnik
Printed and bound in the UK by Creative Print and Design Wales, Ebbw Vale
Original cover design by Visible Edge
Cover by Yvonne Booth

Contents

Part I
Climate change and economic policy instruments

Part II
Case studies of European electricity sectors

Part III
Interactions, implications and conclusions

List of figures, tables and boxes

Figures

Tables

Boxes

Foreword

Charles Nicholson

Three important forces are at work on the European power sector, shaping its long-term future. First, energy market liberalization has introduced competition to the sector's traditionally monopolistic companies. The first steps towards market liberalization were taken several years ago in several countries. However, the process of liberalization and indeed privatization is spreading to many more countries. Second, technological progress has made a substantial impact on the production technologies used in the power sector. In particular, gas-fired power plants have become much more efficient and cheaper, leading to a substantial shift in fuels used. At the same time renewable energy technologies are maturing rapidly, with declining costs and higher efficiencies, and are gaining market share. Third, environmental and social responsibility issues are becoming more important to the public, policy-makers and business alike. In particular, climate change issues have come to the fore with the Climate Convention agreed in Rio de Janeiro in 1992 and the Kyoto Protocol in 1997.

In this book, Christiaan Vrolijk and his co-authors explore the interaction of these three forces, focusing on the climate change policies in six European Union countries: Denmark, France, Germany, Italy, the Netherlands and the United Kingdom. These sectors are diverse, and so are the climate policies proposed in these countries. The focus of the policies ranges from taxes to emissions caps and emission trading to fuel switching and promotion of renewables.

In a rapidly changing sector with such diverse forces shaping it, a comprehensive overview is key for all the stakeholders, industry, government and observers. The book attempts to shoot a moving target: since the text was completed, the European Union (EU), for example, has agreed to ratify the Kyoto Protocol before the start of the World Summit on Sustainable Development, in Johannesburg, South Africa, in summer 2002.

The power sector holds the key to meeting the targets of the Kyoto Protocol. It both emits a substantial share of greenhouse gases and has significant opportunities for substantial reductions. Electricity companies have already played a key role in the emissions markets, invested in renewables and achieved substantial reductions – in particular in the United Kingdom.

The power sector will have to look closely at climate change policies, which drive a market in greenhouse gas emission reductions and create their purely policy-based market value. Good risk managers will have to take into account the costs and opportunities of the greenhouse gas markets, and will have to prepare their companies for a 'carbon constrained future'. This book provides an essential guide to these challenges facing the power sector, but is equally enlightening to other industrial emitters, policy-makers and non-governmental organizations (NGOs).

Charles Nicholson
Group Senior Advisor, BP

Preface

Early in the morning of Saturday 10 November 2001, in the Palais de Congrès in Marrakesh, Morocco, parties to the Kyoto Protocol agreed on the remaining issues, making the protocol ready for ratification. The Marrakesh Accords finally finished the work on the Kyoto Protocol, fulfilling the plan of action agreed at Buenos Aires in 1998; they include legal text on the various parts of the protocol, including both the mechanisms themselves and procedures to ensure compliance.

Surprisingly, perhaps, after the failure the preceding year of COP-6 (Part I) in The Hague, the home town of my family, this agreement seems to be robust. Compliance procedures are in place, and eligibility for the Kyoto mechanisms is restricted to parties to the protocol that have the proper systems in place. Only the relatively wide definition and allowed wide use of sinks could be seen as reducing the environmental integrity of the protocol. However, this is only a small sacrifice compared with the impact of US non-participation. The Marrakesh Accords pave the way for ratification of the Kyoto Protocol and implementation of emissions reductions. This would automatically lead the next round of negotiations to the second commitment period and efforts to re-engage the United States in this worldwide effort to tackle the problem of climate change.

On 23 October 2001, in the week leading up to the COP-7 negotiations at Marrakesh, the European Commission released a new phase of its climate change programme. This plan includes the implementation plans for the first phase, a proposed emissions trading directive, and plans for early ratification, which could lead to entry into force during the World Summit on Sustainable Development (WSSD) in Johannesburg in 2002. Unfortunately, I have not been able to take this new stage of European action on climate change fully into account, as it was agreed only after the text of this book had been finalized. However, my assumptions on the European emissions trading proposal are not inconsistent with the draft directive; moreover, it could easily be another two years before the final directive is agreed, and much can change in that time.

Having worked on the protocol since before Kyoto, I find it impossible not to be pleased at seeing this stage of the international negotiations completed. I have done my best, and I hope the work of the Sustainable Development Programme (SDP) has been useful in these negotiations and will continue to be so in the next stage.

Acknowledgments

I would like to thank all those involved in this project, my first book as lead author. First and foremost, my thanks go to the co-authors of the case studies; they have done an excellent job. As the final deadline approached, they were especially helpful in rapidly correcting any mistakes in my editorial changes and additions. Many improvements in the text have resulted from the work of the two study groups. I would like to thank in particular Gordon Edge, Tim Forsyth, Michael Jefferson, Jim Skea and Steve Drummond for their thoughtful comments and suggestions; they generated a lot of extra work, but it was certainly worth it. Any remaining errors are mine; all those who helped me would have known better!

I would also like to thank the supporters of this project, in particular the European Commission and Seeboard, along with all the general supporters of the SDP. I hope they find the book worth the wait.

My colleagues have been of great help to me during this project, contributing in the form of discussions and advice on content and organization, as well as through their involvement in the many other projects, of great importance in my development and of profound intellectual interest, that have been going on in parallel with the work on *Climate Change and Power*. I extend particular thanks to Duncan Brack, for offering me the opportunity to become a research fellow and providing a stimulating working environment; and to Michael Grubb, for leaving – and therefore leaving behind a vacancy for climate policy research – and for helping me get started with this project, as well as for his cooperation on so many other projects. John Mitchell, Malcolm Keay and Walt Patterson have been of great help with intellectually challenging discussions on this and other subjects. I would also like to thank Kate Kinsman and Ruth Tatton-Kelly, without whom nothing happens in SDP, Gillian Bromley for her work on my English, and Margaret May of the Publications Department for getting this book into print.

Finally, I would like to thank my friends and family, especially my parents, for their support despite the difficulties of distance and language; and above all I give my thanks and love to Kate, my partner, for her support and understanding in the small hours of the night when I was still writing.

February 2002   C.V.

About the authors

Coos Battjes *(The Netherlands)* formerly worked at the Policy Studies business unit of the Netherlands Energy Research Foundation (ECN), The Netherlands. His work included research on the (Dutch) electricity sector and national climate policy. Before joining ECN he received his PhD from Groningen University on the modelling of energy stocks and flows. He now works for NUON, one of the Dutch electricity distribution companies.

Michiel Beeldman *(The Netherlands)* is working at the Policy Studies business unit of the Netherlands Energy Research Foundation (ECN), The Netherlands.

Regina Betz *(Germany)* is scientist and doctoral candidate in the Department of Energy Technology and Energy Policy at the Fraunhofer Institute for Systems and Innovation Research in Karlsruhe, Germany, where she works on analysing transaction costs in various emissions trading systems. She is also a consultant to the German government on climate policies, especially the Kyoto mechanisms. She studied economics at the University of Trier (from which she gained her diploma) and in the UK.

Frank Gagelmann *(Germany)* is a scientist and doctoral candidate at the Centre for Environmental Research (UFZ) in Leipzig-Halle, Germany, analysing the innovation effects of emissions trading. Until autumn 2001 he was working as a researcher in the Department of Energy Technology and Energy Policy at the Fraunhofer Institute for Systems and Innovation Research in Karlsruhe, Germany. He studied economics at the University of Trier (gaining his diploma) and in the UK.

Christophe de Gouvello *(France)* is research fellow at the International Research Centre on Environment and Development at the French National Scientific Research Centre (CIRED-CNRS), France. He is a specialist in energy economics, focusing on regulation of energy systems in different contexts (in both industrialized and developing countries), and on the interfaces with development, technical change and climate change issues.

Poul Erik Grohnheit *(Denmark)* has been senior scientist at the Systems Analysis Department of the Risø National Laboratory, Denmark, since 1980.

At Risø he has built up expertise in national energy planning, international energy–environment–economic modelling and electricity market liberalization. Before arriving at Risø he had gained practical and research experience in town planning and local government.

Eberhard Jochem *(Germany)* is a senior scientist in the Department of Energy Technology and Energy Policy at the Fraunhofer Institute for Systems and Innovation Research in Karlsruhe, Germany. He is an internationally acknowledged expert in technical and socio-economic research in the field of energy and environment. He is vice-chair of Working Group III of the Intergovernmental Panel on Climate Change, a member of the Advisory Committee for Sustainable Development of the German government, and co-founder and head of the Centre for Energy Policy and Economies (CEPE) at the Swiss Federal Institute of Technology (ETH) Zürich, Switzerland, where he also teaches.

Dirk Koewener *(Germany)* works at the Fraunhofer Institute as a scientist and doctoral candidate. His work focuses on energy consumption in the commercial and public sector. In his doctoral dissertation he applies concepts from energy services to water supply and waste-water treatment. He holds a diploma in industrial engineering from the University of Karlsruhe.

Marcella Pavan *(Italy)* took her first degree in economic and social science at Bocconi University (Milan) and her MSc in environmental and natural resource economics at University College London. Formerly coordinator of international research projects and relations at Fondazione Eni Enrico Mattei in Milan, she is now head of the Environment and Fiscal Office at the Italian Regulatory Authority for Electricity and Gas.

Fieke Rijkers *(The Netherlands)* is working at the Policy Studies business unit of the Netherlands Energy Research Foundation (ECN), The Netherlands.

Gerrit Jan Schaeffer *(The Netherlands)* has been working as renewable energy expert in the Policy Studies business unit of the Netherlands Energy Research Foundation (ECN) since 1998. The main focus of his work has been on European renewable energy policy in general and green certificate systems in particular; he is project leader at ECN for several green certificate projects. He studied applied physics and business management, receiving his

PhD in philosophy of science, technology and society from the University of Twente for his work on the socio-technical dynamics of fuel cell development.

Joachim Schleich *(Germany)* is a scientist in the Department of Energy Technology and Energy Policy at the Fraunhofer Institute for Systems and Innovation Research in Karlsruhe, Germany. His work focuses on national and international environmental and energy policy. He holds degrees in economics from the universities of Mannheim and Florida, and a PhD in applied economics from Virginia Tech (Virginia Polytechnic Institute and State University). He also teaches energy economics and energy policy at the University of Kassel.

Nicola Steen *(United Kingdom)* was policy analyst at the Association of Electricity Producers (AEP) at the time of writing the case study on the United Kingdom. The AEP is the trade association in the UK that represents generators' interests; it has over 100 members, ranging from small, family-owned enterprises to multinationals, which among them use many technologies and a wide range of fuels, including fossil, nuclear and renewables. Nicola is now with CO2e.com, the global internet hub for carbon trading.

Christiaan Vrolijk is an Analyst at Natsource-Tullett (Europe) Ltd. He wrote this book while a research fellow at the Energy and Environment Programme (now Sustainable Development Programme) of the Royal Institute of International Affairs (RIIA) studying international climate change issues (1998–2002). Following almost two years as a research assistant, he took up the fellowship to develop a new project entitled initially 'Economic instruments in European electricity: levelling the carbon playing field'. He led the organization of several large research projects and workshops on energy and climate policy in Russia, and on 'quantifying' the Kyoto Protocol. He led the development of RIIA's own emissions trading model, has contributed to several briefing papers, and organized many meetings following the negotiations on climate change policy.

Acronyms and abbreviations

ACBE	Advisory Committee on Business and the Environment
ADEME	Agence de l'Environnement et pour la Maîtrise de l'Energie (France)
AEP	Association of Electricity Producers (UK)
AGBM	Ad-Hoc Group on the Berlin Mandate
AIJ	activities implemented jointly
Annex I	Annex I parties are the industrialized countries undertaking specific commitments under the UNFCCC and Article 4.2 of the Kyoto Protocol (almost synonymous with Annex B of the Kyoto Protocol, which includes minor adjustments)
Annex II	Annex II parties have taken on more financial commitments than Annex I parties
Annex B	Annex to the Kyoto Protocol listing initial national commitments
AOSIS	Association of Small Island States
BDI	Federal Association of German Industry
CBI	Confederation of British Industry
CCGT	combined cycle gas turbine
CCL	The climate change levy: the UK's tax on business use of energy. This tax forms the basis for both the UK's emissions trading scheme and negotiated agreements between government and industry
CCLA	climate change levy agreement
CDM	The clean development mechanism is defined in Article 12 of the Kyoto Protocol. It is similar in some ways to JI, but governs project investments in developing countries (non-Annex I parties) that generate CERs for Annex I parties
CEEC	Central and east European countries
CEGB	Central Electricity Generating Board (UK)
CER	certified emission reduction
CHP	Combined heat and power: a generation technology that is designed to produce both heat and power for industrial or district heating purposes

CH_4	methane: a gas emitted from wet rice production, livestock, decay (e.g. in landfill sites) and fossil fuel production. Methane has a global warming potential (over 100 years) 21 times that of carbon dioxide
CO_2	carbon dioxide: the main anthropogenic greenhouse gas, released by burning fossil fuels, deforestation, some land-use changes and cement production
COP	The Conference of the Parties to the UNFCCC: the supreme body of the convention, it meets each year. Meetings to date are: COP-1, Berlin (28 March–7 April 1995); COP-2, Geneva (8–19 July 1996); COP-3, Kyoto (1–10 December 1997); COP-4, Buenos Aires (2–13 November 1998); COP-5, Bonn (25 October–5 November 1999); COP-6, The Hague (13–24 November 2000); COP-6bis, Bonn (16–27 July 2001); COP-7, Marrakesh (29 October–10 November 2001)
CSS	commodity/service system (Netherlands)
DEFRA	Department for Environment, Food and Rural Affairs (UK)
DETR	Department of Environment, Transport and the Regions (UK)
DfID	Department for International Development (UK)
DSM	Demand-side management
DTI	Department of Trade and Industry (UK)
ECCP	European Climate Change Programme
ECN	Netherlands Energy Research Foundation
EEC	energy efficiency commitment (UK)
EEG	renewable energy sources act (Germany)
EESOPs	energy efficiency standards of performance (UK)
EITs	economies in transition: the CEEC and FSU countries whose economies are in transition to market systems
EPA	Environmental Protection Agency (US)
ERU	emissions reduction unit
ERUPT	emissions reduction unit procurement tenders: Dutch tenders for JI projects
ETG	Emissions Trading Group (UK)
ETH	Swiss Federal Institute of Technology
ETS	emissions trading system/scheme
EU	European Union

FCCC	UN Framework Convention on Climate Change; adopted in 1992, it entered into force in March 1994
FSU	Former Soviet Union
G77	The Group of 77; along with China, it forms the main negotiating group of developing countries, representing over 120 parties in many international negotiations. The group includes countries with very different objectives, including OPEC and AOSIS
GDP	gross domestic product
GEF	Global Environmental Facility
GHG	greenhouse gas(es)
GTPA	general tax on polluting activities (France)
HVDC	high voltage direct current
IEA	International Energy Agency
IPCC	Intergovernmental Panel on Climate Change: the institution, established in 1988 by governments through UNEP and the WMO, to provide an authoritative assessment of the state of knowledge concerning climate change. The IPCC enlists several hundred scientists and other researchers from around the world to write reports that are subject to peer review globally, and publishes 'Policymakers' Summaries' of the findings that are agreed line by line by the participating governments. The IPCC's *First Assessment Report* was completed in 1990, the *Second Assessment Report* in 1995. The *Third Assessment Report* was released in 2001. The IPCC also publishes reports on special issues
IPP	independent power producer
IPPC	integrated pollution prevention and control [directive]
IRP	integrated resource planning
ITFCC	Interministerial Task Force on Climate Change (France)
JI	joint implementation: a term used widely and in many different ways to reflect ways of implementing commitments jointly. In the Kyoto Protocol, the term has become identified with the generation and transfer of ERUs under Article 6, in which investment in a project located in one Annex I party may generate a

	credit for the investing party. Prior to Kyoto the term was also used in relation to possible projects in developing countries, now subsumed under the CDM
JUSSCANNZ	group of countries working together, tending to counterbalance the EU on the one hand and the G77 on the other. The group consists of Japan, the United States, Switzerland, Canada, Australia, Norway and New Zealand, though Norway and in particular Switzerland have frequently stood somewhat apart from JUSSCANNZ positions
KfW	Reconstruction Loan Corporation (Germany)
LCPD	large combustion plant directive
LULUCF	land use, land-use change and forestry: these are among the activities regulated under the Kyoto Protocol; emissions from these activities are treated separately from other emissions and are restricted to certain categories of human-induced changes
MOP	Meeting of the Parties (to the Kyoto Protocol, i.e. when the protocol has entered into force)
N_2O	nitrous oxide: emissions of this gas derive mainly from fertilizers, fossil fuel burning and land conversion for agriculture. N_2O has a global warming potential (over 100 years) 310 times that of carbon dioxide
NCP	national climate programme
NETA	New Electricity Trading Arrangements (UK)
NFFO	Non-Fossil Fuel Obligation (UK)
NGO	non-governmental organization
NO_x	nitrogen oxide
NPTCC	National Programme for Tackling Climate Change (France)
NRE	new and renewable energy
OECD	Organisation for Economic Cooperation and Development. In this book OECD is used to refer to those countries in Annexes I and II of the Convention, i.e. excluding Turkey and some EITs and newly industrialized countries that joined during the 1990s
Ofgem	Office of Gas and Electricity Markets (UK)
OPEC	Organization of Petroleum Exporting Countries
PCF	Prototype Carbon Fund of the World Bank

QELRCs	quantified emission limitation and reduction commitments
REC	renewable energy certificate
RECS	Renewable Energy Certificates System
RES	renewable energy sources
RES-E	electricity from renewable energy sources
RIIA	Royal Institute of International Affairs
ROC	renewable obligation certificate
SDP	Sustainable Development Programme
SO_x	sulphur oxide
SRO	Scottish Renewables Order
TPA	third party access; r-TPA = regulated third party access; n-TPA = negotiated third party access
TSO	transmission system operator
Umbrella Group	The Umbrella Group, which emerged at Kyoto and afterwards, brings together the JUSSCANNZ countries (except Switzerland) with the Russian Federation and Ukraine. After President Bush announced that the United States would not ratify the Kyoto Protocol in March 2001, the Umbrella Group continued for the most part without US participation
UNEP	United Nations Environment Programme
UNFCCC	*See* FCCC
VDEW	German Electricity Association
VIK	Association of Industrial Energy and Power Industry (Germany)
VKU	Association of local authority public utilities (Germany)
VOC	volatile organic compound
VV	*Verbändevereinbauung* (Germany)
VROM	Dutch environment ministry
WMO	World Meteorological Organization
WSSD	World Summit on Sustainable Development, to be held in Johannesburg, South Africa, 26 August–4 September 2002
WTO	World Trade Organization

Units

°C	degrees Celsius
amp	ampere
g	gram
GW	gigawatt
GWh	gigawatt hour (1 million kWh)
kg	kilogram
kWh	kilowatt hour
Mt	million tonnes
Mtoe	million tonnes of oil equivalent
MW	megawatt
MWp	megawatt peak
tC	tonne of carbon
tCe	tonne of carbon equivalent (for amounts of greenhouse gases, using global warming potentials)
tCO_2	tonne of carbon dioxide
tCO_2e	tonne of carbon dioxide equivalent (for amounts of greenhouse gases, using global warming potentials)
toe	tonne of oil equivalent
TW	terawatt
TWh	terawatt hour (1 billion kWh)

Currencies

€	euro; from 1 January 2002 the national currency of four of the case study countries, replacing the French franc, German mark, Italian lira and Dutch guilder
e	eurocent (100e = €1)
$	US dollar (= €1.11 Jan. 2002)
c	dollar cent (100c = $1)
£	pounds sterling (= €1.60 Jan. 2002)
p	pence (100p = £1)
DKK	Danish crown (= €0.13)
FF	(= €0.15)

Executive summary

The process of electricity liberalization and concerns about climate change clash. This book describes the conflict of policies and processes on these two themes. On the one hand, liberalization of the power market could lead to a reduced emphasis on environmental regulation, with detrimental effects on emissions of greenhouse gases. On the other hand, market forces reward efficiency of production, reducing waste, and could be used to great advantage in pursuing environmental goals.

After ten years of international negotiations leading to the Framework Convention on Climate Change, the Kyoto Protocol and now to the Marrakesh Accords, it is undeniable that the future is 'carbon-constrained'. Greenhouse gas (GHG) emissions, in every sector and in every country, will have to be reduced in the long term. In the shorter term only the industrialized countries are affected. The Kyoto Protocol has set out GHG emission targets for 2008–12 for the industrialized countries, including those with economies in transition. The protocol allows these targets to be met in the most economically efficient way, through the use of various flexibilities, including the Kyoto mechanisms.

The EU has taken on a joint target of –8% from 1990 levels, redistributed among the member states through the European 'bubble'. The European policy framework is very important for domestic climate policy in the member states. Four key policies areas are of interest and are explained in this book: electricity liberalization, the renewables directive, energy security and the European Climate Change Programme (ECCP).

The ECCP consists of a raft of proposed policies, particularly in the fields of energy efficiency, renewable energy and emissions trading. These policies are aimed at bringing about a radical change in Europe. To date, European emissions reductions have come to a large extent from 'lucky accidents', such as the UK's dash for gas and the German 'wall fall profits'. Without further policies, emissions in the EU could increase substantially, possibly even to 8% *above* 1990 levels.

Three classes of economic instruments are identified: regulatory, fiscal and flexible. These various instruments focus on five areas: improved energy efficiency, increased use of natural gas, increased share of renewables, introduction of energy or carbon taxes, and introduction of an emissions trading scheme (ETS). Many countries will put in place a combination of policies that will result in a mixture of responses by generators and end users.

Case studies

This book describes and analyses the climate policy regimes in the electricity sectors of six EU member states: Denmark, France, Germany, Italy, the Netherlands and the UK. The case studies were chosen to reflect a wider range of sectors and countries than these six alone, possibly even wider than just European countries. These six countries represent the four largest power sectors in Europe, as well as one medium sector (The Netherlands) and one small sector (Denmark). This selection of six also covers a range of very different fuel and technology bases, from nearly exclusively nuclear to largely coal or natural gas, and from large central power plants to small combined heat and power plant. The sectors also range from the completely liberalized to the still largely monopolistic.

The Danish power sector is heavily based on coal-fired power plants, many of which use CHP technology, making the sector heavily interwoven with heat demand. The Danish policy towards climate change has focused on a long-term effort to increase supply and demand efficiency and infrastructure.

In France, where carbon emissions in the power sector are low, the emphasis of climate policy is on other sectors. However, further liberalization could jeopardize the emissions target, because new merchant plant, almost certainly fossil-fuel-based, would increase emissions. Climate policies focus on some efficiency measures for the small percentage of fossil-fuel power plants, and increasing demand-side efficiency.

The German liberalization has prompted a dramatic cut in electricity prices, reducing the economic viability of both renewables and CHP plants. Despite the cut-throat competition in the Germany market, the long-established culture of long-term (voluntary) agreements prevails over market forces in the effort to reduce emissions.

The Italian power sector will change dramatically as a result of the liberalization process, most likely leading to emissions reductions. However, important measures have also been taken involving end-use tariffs conducive to demand-side management, renewable obligations and feed-in tariffs. The combination of progressive carbon taxes, increasing the price of coal-fired electricity by 40% and of oil and gas by 6% and 3%, and the further introduction of market forces is probably the most effective climate policy.

The Dutch power sector is already dominated by low-carbon natural gas, and has a relatively high share of combined heat and power (CHP), reducing the potential for easy emissions reductions. The government has chosen to pursue new long-term agreements with industry, including draconian measures on coal-fired plants. The Dutch government will enter the emissions trading market itself with the aim of achieving half of the Dutch commitment abroad.

The UK power industry has already achieved emissions reductions of about 20% below 1990 levels since liberalization and the opening of the gas market. The UK ETS excludes the direct emissions of the power sector; however, other measures have been taken in the power sector to reduce emissions, including the new renewables obligations and the climate change levy (CCL).

Interactions and implications

The six countries studied have all taken measures to reduce emissions. The national programmes, together with the European Commission's climate change programme, will lead to emissions declining further towards the Kyoto target of –8%. The domestic programmes have many elements in common, but also differ on substantial issues.

The member states have remained loyal to their traditional regulatory systems. In Germany and the Netherlands, for example, agreements define the role for industry up to the commitment period; in Denmark the longer-term perspective is continued with a focus on energy efficiency, infrastructure and emissions caps. Different national circumstances drive the choice of national climate policy instruments. The French rules, for example, have to take into account that most of the country's power is produced by non-carbon-emitting nuclear power plants. The Danish rules can build on the existence of many (small) district heating systems.

Action is being taken across the member states that will reduce emissions. Some countries already have measures in place or in progress that will reduce emissions to their burden-sharing target by 2010. These new or existing measures do not seriously threaten their competitiveness and do not require full harmonization in the EU. The current NCPs have been built in cooperation with industry, and much political capital (from government and industry) has been invested in these programmes. It would be unwise to discard this work and risk an unravelling of the national agreements by imposing new and sometimes opposite or incompatible harmonized rules. Full harmonization is unnecessary for the first commitment period.

However, further convergence and harmonization will be required when emissions reduction targets become more demanding in the second, third and further commitment periods. These targets will have to be more rational and less political in order to succeed, giving more scope for such convergence across EU member states or an even wider group of countries.

Conclusions

National power industries are responding to concerns about climate change, currently for the most part through actively engaging in the debate, co-operating in pilot studies and making investments in renewable energy. The differences among national policies have not negatively affected industrial competitiveness so far, for markets are still rather diverse, emissions targets are wide-ranging, and existing national legislation is disparate. Some policies are converging, in particular the market-based policies such as emissions trading and renewables obligations with trading of certificates. This is partly due to the involvement of internationally operating industry and learning from other countries.

The future of the electricity sector is 'carbon-constrained', and emissions will have to be reduced. Any long-term investment decision must take this reality into consideration, despite market pressures focusing on the near term. Even in the short term, to meet the Kyoto Protocol targets, it is most likely that the power sector will have to do more than its fair share.

Part I
Climate change and economic policy instruments

1 Climate change and the power industry

Two islands have recently disappeared under the waves of the South Pacific Ocean. Tebua Tarawa and Abanuea, of the tiny island state Kiribati, have been flooded by rising sea levels.[1] Neither of these two islands was inhabited, but many more are threatened, including the remaining thirty-three islands of Kiribati. Continuing sea-level rise could threaten the survival of thousands of islands whose highest points are often not more than a few metres above sea level, as well as other low-lying areas – among them many with substantial animal and human populations.

As a result of growing fears for the climate, negotiations for a global fight against climate change started in the late 1980s. The UN Framework Convention on Climate Change (FCCC) was negotiated at the 'Earth Summit' in Rio de Janeiro in 1992 and entered into force in 1994. However, the commitments made under the FCCC proved inadequate and negotiations began to strengthen them. These efforts resulted in the adoption, at the Third Conference of the Parties to the FCCC (COP-3) in Japan in December 1997, of the Kyoto Protocol. This protocol sets out legally binding quantified emission limitation and reduction commitments (QELRCs) for the industrialized countries. The overall target amounts to a 5.2% reduction in emissions from 1990 levels, for a basket of greenhouse gases, by the commitment period 2008–12. But agreement on the details of implementation proved elusive, and at COP-6, in November 2000, the international negotiations collapsed. The resumed COP-6, meeting again in the summer of 2001, finally achieved the desired outcome on the outstanding issues in the form known as the 'Bonn Agreement'. However, the process now has to move on without the participation of the United States, withdrawn from the protocol at the beginning of 2001 by the newly elected President George W. Bush.[2]

In the industrialized countries, the power sector emits roughly one-third of GHG emissions, mostly from burning fossil fuels in large-scale power stations. This makes the sector both large and relatively easy to regulate, and consequently the prime vehicle for industrialized countries' governments in their efforts to achieve the target set at Kyoto.

---

[1] Alex Kirby, 'Islands Disappear under Rising Seas', *BBC News Online*, 14 June 1999.
[2] Chapter 2 will discuss the history of the international negotiations in more detail.

However, the ongoing process of liberalization throughout the industrialized countries reduces the possibilities for 'easy' regulation of the power sector. Liberalization is pursued for many reasons, including increasing industrial competitiveness through lower energy prices. Cost reductions by the power sector and lower prices for consumers could lead to increased demand and emissions.

This book, *Climate Change and Power*, will focus on the interaction of these two highly dynamic fields: first, the international process to combat climate change, considered to be the greatest environmental challenge facing the world, which started only a decade ago but has already eclipsed many other environmental treaties; and second, the policies geared towards liberalizing the European electricity sector, started in 1989 in the UK and kick-started for the rest of Europe with the 1996 EU electricity directive. Developments in both these fields progress very quickly, and no doubt by the time of publication the international negotiations on the Kyoto Protocol will have moved on from the Bonn Agreement, and electricity markets will have opened up further than anticipated.

1.1 Climate change

A continuous stream of temperature records was set in the 1990s, making it by far the warmest decade on record. The El Niño year of 1998 was the warmest on record, each of the first eight months a record-breaker in its own right. The year after El Niño, La Niña, is supposed to be relatively cold; but in fact 1999 was the fifth *warmest* year on record. Looking at Figure 1.1, a warming trend seems hard to deny; and this trend was confirmed again with new temperature records in 2000 and 2001, the latter being recorded as the second warmest year in 140 years.

In 1995 the Intergovernmental Panel on Climate Change (IPCC) in its *Second Assessment Report* concluded that 'the balance of evidence suggests a discernible human influence on global climate',[3] and it predicted temperature increases of 1–3 degrees Celsius (°C) by 2100. The *Third Assessment Report*, finalized in 2001, was much more forceful in its language, stating

---

[3] IPCC, *Second Assessment Report. Climate Change 1995: The Science of Climate Change* (Cambridge: Cambridge University Press), pp. 4 (Summary for Policymakers), 439 (ch. 8). For a full discussion of the outcome of the *Second Assessment Report* see Duncan Brack and Michael Grubb, *Climate Change: A Summary of the Second Assessment Report of the IPCC*, RIIA briefing paper, no. 32, July 1996.

Figure 1.1: Variations of the earth's surface temperature over the last 140 years

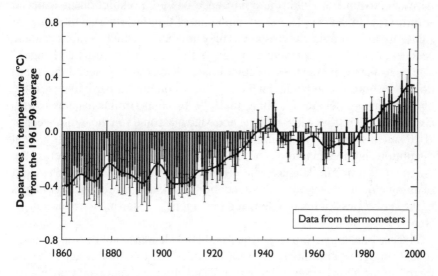

Source: IPCC, *Third Assessment Report. Climate Change 2001*, Working Group I: *The Scientific Basis*, Summary for Policymakers.

that 'there is new and stronger evidence that most of the warming observed over the last 50 years is attributable to human activities'.[4] This report also predicts a much stronger temperature increase of between 1.4 and 5.8°C, nearly double the 1995 forecast. Research by the National Center for Atmospheric Research in the United States also concluded that it is humans, and not natural events of some kind like volcano eruptions or sunspot activity, that are responsible for global warming. Sir John Houghton of the Hadley Centre, chairman of the IPCC, claimed that there was now 'virtual unanimity' among scientists that warming was taking place.

Floods in Bangladesh, floods around the Yangtze river in China, forest fires in Russia and hurricane Mitch, to name but a few of the worst climate disasters

---

[4] IPCC, *Third Assessment Report. Climate Change 2001* (Cambridge: Cambridge University Press), Working Group I: *The Scientific Basis* (Summary for Policymakers), p. 10; see www.ipcc.ch/pub/spm22-01.pdf.
[5] Reuters (Frankfurt), 29 Dec. 1998. These costs far exceed the estimates of the mitigation costs; see e.g. 'The Kyoto Protocol and the President's Policies to Address Climate Change', US administration, July 1998.

in 1998, caused record economic losses totalling \$138bn.[5] Hurricane Mitch brought disaster in Central America during the COP-4 negotiations in Buenos Aires in November 1998; the conference passed a resolution in which it 'expresse[d] to the people and governments of Central America its strongest solidarity in the tragic circumstances they are facing, which demonstrate the need to take action to prevent and mitigate the effects of climate change'.[6] The ever-increasing costs of weather related losses have grabbed the attention of insurance companies, which are now committed participants in the climate change debate. La Niña, in 1999, brought similar disasters, with Cyclone Eline hitting Mozambique and Madagascar. Even the 'quiet' year of 2000 saw a series of floods in the UK and mainland Europe, causing great disruption and financial loss. The floods in Britain took place just before the failed COP-6 in The Hague, where Deputy Prime Minister John Prescott, blaming climate change for the inundation, reminded his fellow negotiators of the seriousness of the problem and the urgency of starting to reduce emissions.

The use of energy from fossil fuels and land clearance are the main causes of anthropogenic emissions of carbon dioxide. These economic activities are therefore the main causes of human-induced climate change; they are also at the very basis of much of our economic life. Thus, to reduce emissions in order to mitigate climate change 'the world community is confronted with a radical challenge of a totally new kind';[7] meeting it will not necessarily reduce our wealth but will certainly change our ways.

Under the 1992 FCCC, parties to the convention committed themselves to stabilize GHG concentrations 'at a level that would prevent dangerous anthropogenic interference with the climate system'.[8] The headline commitment for the countries listed in Annex I of the convention, the industrialized countries,[9] was to return GHG emissions to 1990 levels, and to show a reversal in the trend (of growing emissions) before the year 2000. Against the odds, for

---

[6] Resolution 1/CP.4, 14 Nov. 1998.

[7] Royal Commission on Environmental Pollution, 22nd Report, *Energy: The Changing Climate* (London: Stationery Office, June 2000).

[8] FCCC, Art. 2.

[9] Annex I consists of the members of the OECD and former Comecon eastern bloc countries. South Korea and Mexico joined the OECD after the Rio Earth Summit of 1992 and are thus not included; the status of Turkey as an Annex I country is under debate. Of the former Soviet Union the Russian Federation, Ukraine, Belarus and the Baltic states are in Annex I, and Kazakhstan has submitted a request to join. Of the new republics emerging from the break-up of Yugoslavia only Croatia and Slovenia have been included in Annex I.

Annex I as a whole this objective was met, though mainly as a result of the economic transition in eastern Europe and the former Soviet Union rather than of measures taken by the Organisation for Economic Cooperation and Development (OECD) countries. Indeed, emissions from the OECD are nearly 9% above their 1990 levels in 1998, according to International Energy Agency (IEA) statistics.[10]

In 1995 the parties agreed that these commitments were inadequate and they began 'a process to enable it to take appropriate action for the period beyond 2000, including the strengthening of the commitments of Annex I Parties'.[11] Specifically, it was decided to 'set quantified emission limitation and reduction objectives within specified timeframes'. The negotiating process based upon this 'Berlin Mandate' culminated at COP-3 in Kyoto, Japan, in December 1997.

The Kyoto Protocol calls for actual reductions of emissions by the industrialized countries of Annex B.[12] These commitments add up to a 5.2% reduction from 1990 levels by 2008–12, calculated for a basket of GHGs, including carbon dioxide (CO_2), methane (CH_4), nitrous oxide (N_2O), some industrial gases (HFCs, PFCs, SF_6), and emissions and removals arising from land use, land-use change and forestry (LULUCF or 'sinks'). Table 1.1 sets out the specific targets for each country or group of countries for the first commitment period (2008–12); the Kyoto Protocol calls for rolling commitments, with stricter targets after 2012.

The Kyoto Protocol is a landmark in international environmental policy for its complexity and inclusiveness, having about 180 countries on board. However, Kyoto was the beginning of the process rather than the end point, and negotiations are still continuing to fill the gaps left in the original protocol. From 2 to 14 November 1998 the conference of the parties met again to follow up on Kyoto in its fourth session (COP-4) in Buenos Aires. COP-4 resulted in the Buenos Aires Plan of Action, setting up a whole new round of negotiations. Further details were discussed at COP-5, in Bonn in 1999; a conference that did not generate headline-grabbing news. The Buenos Aires Plan of Action aimed to resolve the outstanding issues of the Kyoto Protocol by the end of 2000, at the sixth conference of the parties. With time pressing on, an extra negotiating session in Lyon and weeks of informal negotiations

---

[10] International Energy Agency, *CO$_2$ Emissions from Fuel Combustion, 1971–1998* (Paris: IEA, 2000).
[11] Decision 1/CP.1, 7 April 1995, the 'Berlin Mandate'.
[12] The list of countries in Annex B of the Protocol is virtually the same as the list in the FCCC's Annex I; see note 9 opposite.

Table 1.1: The Kyoto Protocol targets

Party	Quantified emission limitation or reduction commitment (% of base year or period)
European Union	92[a]
United States	93
Japan, Canada	94
Australia	108
Other OECD countries	92–110
Russia, Ukraine	100
Other EITs	92–95

[a] The targets for the individual EU member states are differentiated within the EU Bubble; see Table 2.1.

Source: The Kyoto Protocol.

were added. However, COP-6, in November 2000, in The Hague, failed to reach agreement, even after extra days and nights of negotiations; and it fell to the resumed session of the conference, COP-6bis, in July 2001, to reach the 'Bonn Agreement', fulfilling the Buenos Aires agenda.

The main greenhouse gas, CO_2, is released during the use of fossil fuels, which supply most of the industrialized countries' energy needs. A protocol to limit these emissions, and thus the use of fossil fuels, would therefore also limit the potential for economic growth. Some early studies suggested substantial losses of gross domestic product (GDP) if limitations on GHG emissions were imposed. Most recent studies, by contrast, show only small costs, 'equivalent to forgoing a few months of GDP growth', losses which are 'hardly discernible compared with the projected overall growth and uncertainties [in GDP]'.[13] However, as a result of the high-cost perception the protocol includes various flexible mechanisms as the most cost-effective way of limiting emissions; these elements of Kyoto will discussed in more depth in Chapter 2.

Some studies and some recent experience show that large reductions in emissions can be achieved through efficiency measures that were simply overlooked previously. It is possible to look at emissions reduction obligations not as added costs, but as business opportunities. Emissions are waste, and waste means inefficiency and thus excess costs; measures to reduce emissions could reduce waste, and therefore costs. There are also great side-benefits from emissions reduction measures, such as reduced local air

---

[13] Michael Grubb with Christiaan Vrolijk and Duncan Brack, *The Kyoto Protocol: A Guide and Assessment* (London: RIIA/Earthscan, 1999), pp. 164–5.

pollution – which causes 24,000 premature deaths in the UK alone[14] – and reduced congestion.

1.2 The electricity sector

The electricity sector is one of the main sources of CO_2 emissions, accounting for around one-third of all such emissions in the OECD.[15] Figure 1.2 displays the sectoral breakdown of emissions, and shows that the energy sector's contribution is larger than that of any other sector, at 32%. The energy sector as a whole also causes substantial emissions of methane. In 1990 fuel methane emissions together accounted for about 5% of the total GHG emissions in Annex I parties.[16] Many of these countries, therefore, will turn to the power sector for measures to deliver a substantial part of their Kyoto commitments.

The share of electricity in final energy demand has been rising fast, and is projected to rise further in the future. The IEA projects faster increases in electricity use than in any other energy use, with an annual growth rate of 2.9% globally between 1997 and 2010.[17] This analysis shows a strong linear dependence of electricity demand on GDP, largely unaffected by external influences such as the oil crises. Some other energy uses are growing much more slowly, or have reached a stable level, partly as a result of users switching to more efficient electrical appliances. These trends make it hard to stop the growth of the power sector and its emissions.

According to the IEA,[18] new generating plants will be built with a capacity of over 1,300GW worldwide between 1997 and 2010 – that is, before the end of the Kyoto first commitment period. By 2010, 30% of all production capacity will have been built since the Kyoto Protocol was agreed. The total investment associated with this expansion could be a staggering $1,400bn – equal to the German GDP or a quarter of US GDP. In the OECD, close to 500GW of new capacity is projected to be built by 2010, at which point more than 20% of generating plants in these countries will have been built since Kyoto at a cost of nearly $440bn, far exceeding any estimate for the cost of climate change mitigation commitments.

[14] Royal Commission on Environmental Pollution, *Energy: The Changing Climate*.

[15] IEA, *CO₂ Emissions from Fuel Combustion*.

[16] *International Energy Outlook 2000* (Washington DC: Energy Information Agency, US DOE, 2000).

[17] *World Energy Outlook* (Paris: IEA, 2000).

[18] Ibid.

Figure 1.2: CO$_2$ emissions per sector in the EU-15, 1999

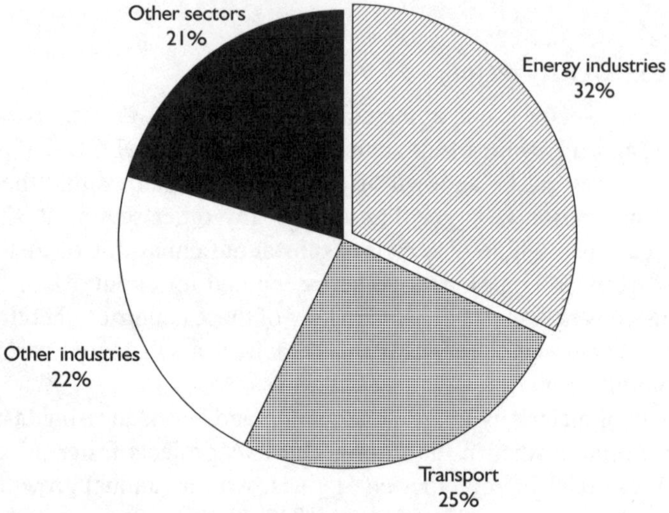

Source: European Environment Agency, Annual European Community Greenhouse Gas Inventory 1990–1999, submission to the secretariat of the UNFCCC, Technical Report No. 60, 11 April 2001; see http://reports.eea.eu.int/Technical_report_No_60/en/tech60.pdf.

Along with transport, the power sector is crucial both for meeting the Kyoto commitments and for the longer-term success of emissions reduction targets. The sector is growing fast in both industrialized and developing countries. If efficiency in minimizing emissions is taken into account from the start, emissions can be kept much lower than projected levels at a much lower price. With an incentive to reduce emissions, the more fuel-efficient plants and those using renewable energy sources will be chosen at no or little extra cost, with marked results in terms of reduced emissions. Increased investment in the new technologies will reduce costs further and make these technologies even more competitive, leading to further reductions compared with the business-as-usual projections. It is also argued that an increased share of smaller, fuel-efficient cogeneration and renewable generating capacity will make the large, heavily polluting plants more uneconomic, eventually making them redundant.

The IEA analysis quoted above forecasts that by 2010 emissions from the power sector will have risen by 50% globally and by about 30% in the OECD from their 1990 levels. In Europe this increase would be somewhat less, because of the special circumstances in Germany and the UK. In Germany emissions have declined slightly since 1990 due to the reunification with the eastern *Länder*, where several inefficient, heavily polluting plants using local lignite were closed. In the UK the 1989 electricity law introduced competition in power supply, and a change in regulation in the gas market led to a massive switch to cleaner natural gas – the 'dash for gas'. As a result emissions in the UK power sector have fallen by over 20% from 1990, while profits have increased many times over.

There is a further reason why parties will seek a large role for the electricity industry in the mitigation of GHG emissions: namely, the relative ease of regulating the sector. The power sector consists of a limited number of sources, all relatively large. Most national electricity sectors are (still) heavily regulated, and many governments have strong interests (through ownership or otherwise) in the sector.

However, there is also an opposing policy trend in the OECD countries and elsewhere: liberalization of the electricity sector. The market liberalization process was started to reduce prices and reduce government expenditure in the massive investments needed. Liberalization should lead to lower prices, increased international trade in electricity and increased consumption. Market liberalization is sometimes also called 'deregulation', indicating a retreat by government from intervention in the market. Additional environmental regulations, such as emissions targets, could therefore be seen as contrary to the object of liberalization – a process that often, though not necessarily, goes hand-in-hand with privatization of the electricity companies, which also reduces government influence on the sector.

There are numerous ways for the electricity sector to reduce emissions. However, a competitive market might not allow companies to make the necessary investments, unless government regulations attach a price tag to emissions. Carbon taxes, emissions trading or other such policies will make emissions reduction investment opportunities more valuable for the industry. Some of the trends of liberalization will be amplified: fuel-switching from coal to gas, for example, where natural gas it is available, and building industrial cogeneration plants. Some other options are more contrary to liberalization, such as district heating systems and demand-side management (DSM). A non-exhaustive list of emissions reduction opportunities in the power sector would include:

* fuel-switching;
* industrial cogeneration;

- district heating;
- renewable energy technologies;
- other non-fossil fuel technologies (nuclear);
- other supply-side efficiency measures;
- demand-side efficiency (energy services);
- CO_2 capture (greenhouse fertilizer, improved oil/gas recovery).

This book studies the interaction of the trends of liberalization and environmental protection in some European countries. All are members of the EU, which in 1996 adopted the electricity liberalization directive in 1996; this sets the baseline for these countries' electricity policy. The book analyses the environmental policies available to the governments within the European internal market for electricity. The analysis is done through case studies, spanning the entire range of EU electricity systems, from France's centralist approach to the UK's fully privatized sector and the German federal system. Three other countries – Denmark, Italy and the Netherlands – are included to cover an even greater range of systems and widen the usefulness of the conclusions from this study. The book also considers the levels on which some of the policies operate: local, national or supranational.

1.3   The need for European action

The EU has followed a very 'green' strategy in the climate negotiations. Now it is important that it will be able to deliver on its claim with act as 'honest broker'. Currently, its emissions are relatively low, compared with those in the 'new world' countries; growth in emissions of some individual EU member states has been slow, and overall emissions have even declined since 1990, thanks to trends in some key countries, such as the UK and Germany.

However, the EU has scrutinized the situation it is facing and recognized that tough measures are required. According to the ECCP, launched in March 2000,[19] European GHG emissions are set to rise to 6–8% above 1990 levels under business-as-usual conditions by 2010; this opens up a substantial gap for the EU, committed at Kyoto to reducing emissions by 8%. Moreover, in Kyoto the EU pushed for as little flexibility as possible, proposing emissions reductions of 15% without the use of flexible mechanisms. Now the EU countries will have to take the lead in ratifying the protocol and in implementing domestic measures to ensure the targets are met.

---

[19]   See http://europa.eu.int/comm/environment/climat/eccp.htm.

Figure 1.3: Actual greenhouse gas emissions compared with the interim target, 1999

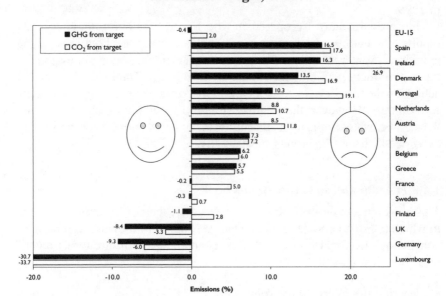

Source: Presented as Annex I of COM(2000)88, 8 March 2000. Data from Annual European Community Greenhouse Gas Inventory 1990–1999, submission to the secretariat of the UNFCCC, Technical Report No. 60, European Environment Agency, 11 April 2001; see http:// reports.eea.eu.int/Technical_report_No_60/en/.

Note: The 1999 interim target is calculated assuming a linear reduction between 1990 and 2010 for the EU burden-sharing target of the member states.

In 1999 emissions in the EU as a whole were 4% below their 1990 level, just under the interim target. The decline is due to the massive reductions that took place after the UK's electricity liberalization in 1990 and the re-unification of Germany. Both the UK and Germany are currently on course to meet their agreed target under the EU bubble,[20] with emissions having declined to substantially below their 'interim' target. However, both countries still have to bring about further reductions of a few percentage points if they are to meet their bubble target, and these further reductions have to be achieved without a 'dash for gas' or reunification. Apart from Germany,

---

[20] The EU-15 countries agreed to redistribute their targets such that some countries took on more demanding goals and others were given more lenient ones. For more on the EU bubble, see Chapter 3.

the UK and Luxembourg, all other EU countries have CO_2 emissions above their 1990 levels. Figure 1.3 graphically depicts the situation facing the EU in 1999.

The latest inventory prepared by the European Environment Agency reports that a continuation of present policies would cancel out most of the emissions growth under a business-as-usual scenario, leaving emissions in the commitment period about 1% above 1990 levels. The ECCP is aimed at achieving the further reduction of emissions, so that the EU complies with its Kyoto target. However, the trends visible in Figure 1.3 are alarming; even the member states with targets that allow for growing emissions have already exceeded their interim targets substantially.

1.4   The aim and structure of this book

This book aims to describe the circumstances of the European power sector in which policy to combat climate change is being formulated, and to draw conclusions from several case studies concerning the future directions of these policies. The book will:

- describe the international framework for climate change policy, in particular the Kyoto Protocol and the Framework Convention;
- describe the policy framework for the electricity sector in Europe, including the liberalization directive, the renewables directive and the European bubble;
- describe the various economic instruments available for climate change policy and explore the use of these instruments in European power sectors;
- describe the interaction of climate change policies and liberalization trends in the EU countries, in particular the potential incompatibility between the aims of liberalization and those of climate protection;
- explore the need for harmonization of policies throughout the European Union, in the context of the existing burden-sharing;
- draw some conclusions about the different economic instruments, their interactions and their application at domestic or EU-wide level.

The book is divided into three parts. Part I introduces the climate change debate and the role of the electricity sector in this debate. Part II describes six case studies of European national electricity sectors. Finally, Part III draws some conclusions about the possibilities for electricity sector policy and emissions reduction measures.

Chapter 2 introduces the outcome of recent negotiations on climate change. These negotiations have focused to a great extent on the flexibility mechanisms of the Kyoto Protocol, including emissions trading, joint implementation (JI) and the clean development mechanism (CDM). Some experience with these mechanisms – sulphur emissions trading in the United States, both JI and CDM under the activities implemented jointly (AIJ) programme, and other cross-border investment projects – will be discussed.

Chapter 3 discusses various European policies (both already implemented and under consideration) for the electricity sector. First the 1996 European directive on electricity liberalization will be discussed. Later directives and green papers, dealing with energy security, renewable energy and emissions trading, are also discussed.

The final chapter of Part I, Chapter 4, explains the economic instruments available for use in climate policy in the European electricity sector. Among others, carbon taxes and emissions trading will be highlighted.

Part II describes the case studies of six different European electricity sectors. The main issues here are the different market structures of the sectors across Europe, the different technologies and fuels currently used and the options available for change or new investment, and divergent policy cultures. An important feature is the continuing liberalization in the European electricity markets as a result of the electricity directive. Six countries with divergent market structures have been chosen for case studies: Denmark, France, Germany, Italy, the Netherlands and the United Kingdom. These countries both make up the largest share of European electricity and include most basic market models. The case studies were prepared by national specialists, with some light editing by the lead author. The case studies are preceded by a short chapter on the differences among the case studies and reasons for the choice of these particular countries for study.

Part III analyses the interactions, implications and conclusions to be gleaned from these case studies. The forms of instruments likely to be developed, at both the national and the European level, are described, with a discussion of the appropriate level of harmonization. The potential impact and the potential interactions of different instruments, within and between countries, including issues relating to international trading in electricity and emissions, are discussed. Chapter 12 briefly summarizes the case studies and lessons learned. Chapter 13 considers the interaction of liberalization and climate protection, market instruments and European cooperation. Even though deregulation potentially reduces the policy options available, it also has some inherent positive impact on emissions from the sector. Chapter 14, finally, draws some conclusions.

2 The Kyoto Protocol mechanisms

When fossil fuels are used CO_2, the main GHG regulated by the Kyoto Protocol, is released into the atmosphere. Most of the energy that drives the economies of the industrialized countries is based on these carbon-emitting fossil fuels. Without any alternative, therefore, the Kyoto Protocol could be a very expensive agreement by limiting economic growth. Some studies do indeed indicate that emissions targets could lead to substantial reductions in the growth of GDP. There are, however, also great costs associated with the current polluting way of production.

Cost efficiency in reducing emissions was one of the key aims in the climate negotiations. While the EU was initially of the opinion that this could be achieved through common policies and measures, others favoured a more market-based approach and an extension of approach to include a wider range of GHG sources, such as the non-CO_2 gases, and factors such as emissions and sinks from land-use change. In the late 1980s tradable permits were proposed as an efficient solution that was both practical and equitable.[1] Increased flexibility through emissions trading would substantially lower the costs of emissions reduction and make it more likely that governments would agree to greater emissions control. International emissions trading was seen as the most efficient and direct route to international flexibility. The United States and some other countries of the OECD were enthusiastic proponents of this policy's incorporation into the climate regime.

The principal idea behind emissions trading is simple. An entity is given an emissions target which it is not allowed to exceed. Then it can decide how to meet this target: either though reduction measures at home, or by buying 'credits' from another entity with an emissions target that it finds easier to meet. Thus two countries or companies will exchange emissions quota if that is in their economic interest. In principle, emissions trading separates who has the reduction commitment – and therefore bears the costs – from where and by whom the emission abatement actually take place.

Where emissions have a direct regional impact, as is the case with acid rain and smog, the split between the reductions and the location is not trivial and free trading of emissions is impossible, because it could lead to local

---

[1] See e.g. Michael Grubb, *The Greenhouse Effect: Negotiating Targets* (London: RIIA, 1989).

pollution 'hot spots'. However, although there will be large regional differences in the effects of climate change – some regions will get warmer, others colder, wetter or drier – this does not depend on regional differences in the concentrations of the gases; the problem is global. From a climate point of view, GHG emissions are homogenous: a tonne emitted in New York is the same as a tonne emitted in New Delhi. GHGs, therefore, are ideally suited for emissions trading.

This chapter describes the international framework of the Kyoto Protocol and the Bonn Agreement on the flexible mechanisms and emissions targets.

2.1　The rationale

By the late 1980s and early 1990s interest in emissions trading as a means of controlling GHGs had grown, especially in the United States. There were various reasons for this:

- The US experience with its tradable permit system to control sulphur dioxide (and ozone-depleting substances) was widely seen to have been a success: emissions were reduced at much lower cost than originally predicted, because of the flexibility of the permit system and the incentives it gave for innovation.
- The great US reliance on cheap energy called for the most cost-effective approach to limiting CO_2 emissions. Emissions trading promised to deliver the lowest-cost option.
- Emissions trading is more attractive to industry than other economic instruments (such as carbon taxes), because the system creates a tradable asset. Even if a company has to buy permits to cover all its emissions, it still acquires the value of those permits as an asset which can in principle be sold in the future if emissions can be reduced. This contrasts with a tax, which extracts revenue from the firm without adding any compensating value. In addition, governments may give out some or all of the permits initially, reducing the cost to industry. In many countries (including the United States) taxes have proved extremely controversial and difficult to implement, primarily because of industrial opposition, so that other market-based approaches have attracted growing interest.

In the context of climate change there were additional reasons for the increased interest.

- Proponents argued that emissions trading increases the flexibility and efficiency of commitments, making it more plausible for governments to agree to greater emissions control, at lower cost.
- Emissions trading could also be an efficient solution to difficulties in target-setting. It could reduce the call for special consideration of different national circumstances, because it would greatly reduce cost differences between countries. This could make it possible to agree on one flat-rate reduction target.
- In the longer term, with reduction targets set for more countries, including developing countries, emissions trading could be the easiest way to move towards equal global emission allowances, without putting an unbearable burden on the high-emitting industrialized countries.

Emissions trading turned into the 'crux on which, from some perspectives, Kyoto stood – and nearly fell'.[2] Article 17 of the Kyoto Protocol enables (intergovernmental) emissions trading; other articles set up additional forms of flexibility.

In 1992, in the negotiations in Rio, the parties to the FCCC had already agreed that parties could act on their commitments jointly with other parties. In 1995, at the first conference of the parties, the Berlin Mandate established the pilot phase of AIJ, which was the first real step towards a mechanism for international cooperation in emissions reductions, but at the same time retarded the introduction of a real trading mechanism.

The Kyoto Protocol includes three dimensions of *international* flexibility: international emissions trading (Article 17), joint implementation (JI, Article 6) and the clean development mechanism (CDM, Article 12), which will all be explained in section 2.3. All these forms of flexibility, by reducing the overall costs of the Kyoto agreement, reduce the inequalities between the commitments of the various parties to the protocol. Thus the most important prospect for a market for GHG emissions was established with the Kyoto Protocol. The protocol also opened the way for domestic industrial emissions trading schemes.

---

[2] Michael Grubb with Christiaan Vrolijk and Duncan Brack, *The Kyoto Protocol: A Guide and Assessment* (London: RIIA/Earthscan, 1999).

2.2   The European Union 'bubble'

In the international negotiations the EU proposed a flat-rate emissions reduction target for all parties, even though internally its members had already agreed on a burden-sharing formula. The initial pre-Kyoto agreement ranged from increases of up to 30% for the poorer 'cohesion countries'[3] to cuts of 25% by some more advanced countries, while all non-EU countries would be bound by the 15% reduction (covering three GHGs only). This proved unacceptable to other countries, and differentiated targets were negotiated. However, for political reasons the EU insisted on one target for the whole of the EU, with the possibility of sharing the commitment within this 'bubble'. Article 4 of the Kyoto Protocol gives the EU this flexibility (which it is potentially available for other country groupings as well). After Kyoto the EU member states reached a new agreement among themselves, reflecting the final target set (−8%) and the additional gases and sinks taken into account. This new internal distribution has reduced the spread of targets within the EU, but it is still large. Table 2.1 gives the individual targets for the member states; Figure 2.1 displays the spread of these targets compared with the overall spread of the Annex B Kyoto targets.

Table 2.1: Differentiated targets of the EU member states

Member state	Target (% change from 1990 level)
Austria	−13
Belgium	−7.5
Denmark	−21
Finland	0
France	0
Germany	−21
Greece	+25
Ireland	+15
Italy	−6
Luxembourg	−28
Netherlands	−6
Portugal	+27
Spain	+15
Sweden	+4
UK	−12.5
EU total	−8

[3] The EU economic and social cohesion policy aims to reduce development disparities and focuses its support programmes in particular on Greece, Portugal, Spain and Ireland.

EU member states vary according to certain economic and institutional factors; indeed, some of the problems faced by the EU reflect those that could arise, on a larger scale, at the global level in the negotiation of a co-ordinated climate change strategy. There is a 'North–South' dimension, with four countries in a markedly less advanced stage of development than the others; these poorer 'cohesion' countries do not want to bear the responsibility for past emissions of other EU countries, and they fear any constraint on energy consumption as an obstacle to their main aim of economic growth. EU climate policy declarations have recognized this disparity and acknowledged that emissions from these countries are likely to grow in the context of overall reductions, requiring bigger reductions from some other member states if the overall EU target is to be achieved.

Figure 1.3 in the previous chapter showed the actual GHG emissions in 1999, compared with the interim targets. Notwithstanding the differentiation in targets within the European bubble, the performance and additional action required from members differs greatly across the Union. Only Luxembourg, Germany and the UK are below their targets; France, Finland and Sweden are close to their target for all GHGs, but their CO_2 emissions are too high; and most of the other countries have growing emissions, and are a long way off their targets.

Figure 2.1 displays the targets for the fifteen EU countries in the 'bubble' in comparison with the other Annex B countries. In Kyoto, the EU, along with some of the accession countries (those that are in negotiations to join) had taken on the highest reduction target of 8% – more than the United States (7%) and Japan (6%). The highest allowed increases were negotiated by Australia at 8% and Iceland at 10%. However, within the EU bubble, the targets are spread much more widely, from reductions of 28% for Luxembourg and 21% for Austria, Denmark and Germany, to increases of 25% for Greece and 27% for Portugal. The emissions reduction commitment undertaken by some of the EU countries is therefore very large compared with their international competitors, even with the German 'wall fall profits' or the UK's 'dash for gas'.

2.3   The Kyoto mechanisms

Emissions trading is in principle a simple idea. Each participant in the system is subject to an allowed level of emissions, such as total allowable GHG emissions over a given period. However, they are also allowed to trade these allowances: one may emit more, if another agrees to emit less and sells the

Figure 2.1 The EU bubble targets compared with Annex B targets

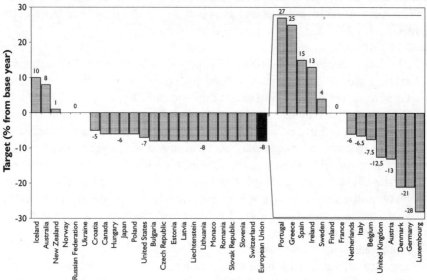

balance of its allowance to the first. Economically, emitters with low abatement costs will choose to reduce emissions and sell their excess allowances, whereas polluters with high abatement costs will prefer to buy emissions 'credits'. If necessary, the overall allowable emissions total can be reduced over successive time periods. Such a system has economic benefits, because it creates an incentive for participants to reduce emissions in ways that are most cost-effective. A given level of emissions reduction is therefore achieved at least cost. The administrative requirements may be modest: as with any binding constraint, emissions need to be monitored effectively for each participant, and trades need to be registered and tracked, but this is not an onerous task. As long as penalties for not achieving the target emissions level were high enough, each participant would comply with its cap.

This administrative task is, however, complicated under the Kyoto Protocol. The protocol established three different mechanisms for international transfers: (intergovernmental) emissions trading, JI and the CDM. These mechanisms suffer from inconsistencies and are hampered by additional objectives that are not necessarily leading to emissions reductions. The parties ultimately responsible under the Kyoto mechanisms are the countries that signed up to the protocol. It is difficult to set up a compliance system that would work without countries having to give up some degree of sovereignty, which they are almost invariably reluctant to do.

There are some inconsistencies between the mechanisms and the Kyoto targets, and others among the mechanisms themselves:

- The commitments are defined for the period 2008–12 (the 'first commitment period'). This time is needed for countries to turn around their emissions trends and bring levels down to their Kyoto targets; however, for the most part it will be industry that has to achieve the reductions, and companies need incentives *now* if they are to find it profitable to take the actions that will be required to meet the targets in ten years' time.
- In order to provide an incentive, early and cumulated crediting is allowed for the CDM, the most complex and novel of the mechanisms, which will involve investment in regions where typically projects may take many years to get going. Early and cumulated crediting is not specified for JI among Annex I countries, where governments and companies are already more geared up for action.
- Sinks of all categories are allowed under JI, but only afforestation and reforestation are allowed in the CDM. Sink activities in JI are capped together with domestic savings by the amount specified in Appendix Z of the Bonn Agreement, while CDM LULUCF activities should not exceed 1% of a party's base-year emissions for each of the five years in the commitment period.
- The Bonn Agreement strongly discourages the use of nuclear power to generate emission reduction units (ERUs) through JI,[4] or certified emission reductions (CERs) under the CDM. However, reductions due to the increased or extended use of nuclear power in Annex B countries can be used to meet the Kyoto targets or be traded under Article 17.
- Monitoring and certification procedures are different between the two project-level mechanisms (the CDM and JI); emissions trading, in theory the simplest mechanism but one on which a great deal hangs politically, remains wholly undefined.

The unfinished business of Kyoto's mechanisms for international transfer of emissions reductions was immense, as the subsequent Buenos Aires conference illustrated starkly. COP-6 also showed the deep differences of opinion

---

[4] 'Parties included in Annex I are to refrain from using emission reduction units generated from nuclear facilities.'

between the negotiating factions in Annex B. Yet agreement – finally reached at COP-6bis – was badly needed, because action to reduce emissions needs to start soon and will get harder every year. To date there is some, but still too little, experience with the trading mechanisms; the Bonn Agreement has at least made further 'learning by doing' possible.

In environmental terms the Kyoto targets for the first commitment period are modest, making only a minute change in CO_2 concentrations. However, Kyoto is only the first step of a rolling programme of targets that could ultimately deliver huge emissions cuts; and even the first commitment period targets are a break from the trend in many OECD countries. Emissions are still rising, and without Kyoto emissions levels for the industrialized countries are expected to be nearly 30% above those in 1990. Thus for the OECD the Kyoto commitments mean a steep change from 'business as usual', and are seen as difficult and costly.

It was politically very important to reduce the overall costs of the emissions reductions required by the protocol. An agreement binding parties to very high costs is unlikely to be ratified; lower overall costs increase the likelihood of success. Classic economic theory shows in essence that costs are lower with a wider choice of responses. And even though recent studies all show moderate economic losses, 'hardly discernible compared with the projected overall growth and uncertainties therein', it was imperative that the Kyoto agreement included flexible commitments so that it was seen to be economically efficient, with minimal waste of resources spent.

All three of the international transfer mechanisms of the Kyoto Protocol are variations on the simple emissions trading model. Article 17 on emissions trading allows transfers between parties (governments) of Annex B. JI (Article 6) involves investments in specific projects that will enable participating countries to reap the emissions reduction credits. The CDM (Article 12) is similar to JI, because it is based on investments in specific projects, but for political reasons it caries tougher conditions on sustainable development and developing country adaptation to climatic changes. Both project-based mechanisms seem to be more credible, steering investment towards climate-friendly technology, whereas emissions trading leaves open the possibility of large trades in assigned amounts being conducted without any action being taken. The three mechanisms are discussed briefly in the next three subsections and in Appendix 1.

The Kyoto mechanisms will still have to compare favourably with other measures – such as carbon taxes or technology standards, for example – if these novel, still relatively unknown instruments are to be implemented. The

UK, for example, introduced its new CCL in April 2001, despite protests from industry and other stakeholders. Some other countries have also introduced carbon taxes; but the lessons that can be learned from these initiatives are limited because the taxes are at low levels and the main emitters are excluded. In the UK, the plans for the CCL sparked discussions within industry on emissions trading. A proposal was developed jointly by industry and government, and the ETS will commence in January 2002, relieving participants from the obligation to pay the tax (for more details see Chapter 11, the UK case study).

The Kyoto mechanisms are now seen as an integral part of the deal of the Kyoto Protocol. It is recognized that without this flexibility many parties would not have been able to agree. The environmental NGOs, initially so opposed to flexibility, now focus on ensuring that the mechanisms do not diminish the environmental gains enshrined in the protocol. The merits that the Kyoto mechanisms can bring are recognized by all stakeholders.

2.3.1   International emissions trading

Emissions trading is defined in Article 17 of the Kyoto Protocol: 'The Parties included in Annex B may participate in emissions trading for the purposes of fulfilling their commitments under Article 3 [i.e. the emissions reduction targets]. Any such trading shall be supplemental to domestic actions for the purpose of meeting quantified emission limitation and reduction commitments under that Article.'

Article 17 states that *parties* – i.e. countries, represented by their governments – may trade. It is therefore questionable whether a domestic ETS or an international *industrial* ETS will be governed by Article 17. It is possible that a domestic trading scheme would fall under Article 2: 'Each Party ... shall implement and/or further elaborate policies and measures in accordance with its national circumstances.' Intergovernmental transfers must be conducted in units of assigned amounts, that is, measured in the basket of gases and sinks during the commitment period. Private-sector trading, however, may be denominated in any subset of these gases and periods, and will probably begin with CO_2 emissions from power generation and industrial processes.

Emissions trading is the ultimate flexible instrument for reaching a specific reduction target. Voluntary agreements usually give the freedom to reach a target *how* and *when* you want. Joint implementation gives the opportunity to invest *where* you want to reduce emissions. But emissions trading gives all these options by allowing the purchase and sale of emissions allowances, which means that emissions reductions will take place where they cost least, anywhere in the world. Experience with ETSs and modelling work show possible financial savings of over 75% compared with a situation without emissions trading.

However, some problems might also arise from international transfers, and these were often brought to the table by NGOs during the negotiations. Emissions trading and the other Kyoto mechanisms are very innovative and their effectiveness is still uncertain. Before Kyoto, it was also argued that negotiating these mechanisms would take up more time than was available, time that could better be spent on other issues. In particular, the monitoring and compliance systems of the protocol are now substantially more complicated and need yet more time to be negotiated and put in place. Trading in 'hot air', the excess emissions allowances granted to economies in transition, was also a particular concern of the NGOs and some countries, since these trades would not lead to actual emissions reductions from the baseline. Apart from this, the large financial resource flows from international transfers, resulting from trades in allowances necessary to gain substantially from the mechanisms, will also be politically difficult to implement.

2.3.2 Joint implementation

Article 6 of the Kyoto Protocol says that 'any Party included in Annex I may transfer to, or acquire from, any other such Party emission reduction units resulting from projects'. Again, the details are lacking in the protocol, and additional rules should be defined later by the conference of the parties. COP-4 set the timetable for the key issues on JI, leaving the ultimate decisions to be taken by COP-6. The agreement reached in Bonn at COP-5 specified only a minimum number of issues.

Joint implementation is a concept that has been around for much longer than emissions trading. Other international protocols have used the concept of this project-based mechanism for meeting their targets with success. Under the Berlin Mandate, the conference of the parties decided to allow a particular form of JI, the AIJ pilot phase, emissions reductions from which would not be eligible to count towards reduction targets; this phase would provide a means of learning by doing and finding out the relevance and possibilities of international flexibility without the complicated rules and structures needed if crediting was to be granted.

Under JI a donor can invest in a project that will reduce emissions and receive credits for it. This mechanism is directly in line with established industry practice: invest and reap credits from the investment. Therefore, the protocol allows parties to authorize 'legal entities' (for example, companies) to participate in JI.

JI is a less contentious issue than emissions trading, because under JI money will be invested in *real* projects that will achieve *real* emissions reductions: for example, to improve the energy efficiency of existing industrial plants, build highly efficient new plants, produce energy from renewables or generate carbon sinks (forests). Virtually all JI projects are expected to be in the economies in transition (EITs), although some might take place in the south of Europe. These countries badly need investment, and the additional benefit of emissions credits could steer investment towards cleaner projects.

One of the problems that arises with JI projects is the definition of the baseline used to calculate the credits earned. However, this issue is much more urgent for projects under the CDM, where the host country does not itself have an emissions reduction target under the Kyoto Protocol. JI does not raise the problem of 'hot air', which is stressed by the EU and environmental NGOs – the danger that emissions reduction credits will be traded internationally without resulting in any actual net global reduction in emissions – because it invests in real emissions reduction projects. Interestingly, a proposal on the negotiating table in The Hague, and officially submitted by the Russian Federation in Bonn, turns emissions trading with Russia – and possibly other EIT countries – after the event into JI, by reinvesting all revenues arising in emissions reduction projects. This proposal was tabled to deal both with the environmentalists' opposition to the use of Russian 'hot air' and with the longer-term emissions trajectory of Russia; for if these revenues were not reinvested, emissions would rise again while the allowances were sold, leaving Russia in great 'climate debt' in the second or third commitment period. This 'Green Investment Scheme' is supposed to be part of the documentation laid before the Duma, the Russian parliament, for ratification of the Kyoto Protocol.[5]

An early beginning to JI projects is the key to meeting the targets of the Kyoto Protocol. Annex I emissions are projected to rise from their current

[5] For more information on the Russian position and this proposal, see Anna Korppoo, Christiaan Vrolijk and Jonathan Stern, *Energy and Climate: Russian–European Partnership*, report of a workshop organized by the Royal Institute of International Affairs (UK), the Centre for Energy Policy (Russia) and the Ministry of Energy (Russia), in association with the Ecological Committee of the State Duma (Russia), Moscow, 14–15 May 2001.

level (at 5% below 1990 levels) and can be curbed only by real investments in mitigation. An early start will ensure that there is time to implement the many hundreds or thousands of projects needed. It also sets the EITs on a cleaner growth path early, improving energy efficiency while allowing their economies to grow without returning to pre-1990 polluting technologies. For the countries on the 'Western' side, these early JI projects will show the practicality and huge opportunities of such projects, and the combination of low cost and high gains they can yield. Early JI could, therefore, lay the foundation for the actual implementation of the Kyoto Protocol targets, with the Russian Federation in a pivotal role.

2.3.3 The clean development mechanism

The CDM will have a similar role to joint implementation, giving credits to the investor companies or countries, while curbing the emissions of the host country and directing it on to a cleaner and more sustainable path of economic development. It could also bring about a large volume of early emissions reductions cheaply, negating the fears of the Annex B countries that meeting the Kyoto targets would be prohibitively expensive.

The clean development mechanism is defined in Article 12 of the Kyoto Protocol. It has three main purposes: '[1] to assist Parties not included in Annex I in achieving sustainable development and [2] in contributing to the ultimate objective of the Convention, and [3] to assist Parties included in Annex I in achieving compliance with their quantified emission limitation and reduction commitments under Article 3'.

Even though the CDM was the 'Kyoto surprise', a completely new article that appeared in the last hours of COP-3, the text of Article 12 is more elaborate than that of the articles providing for JI and international emissions trading. Even so, many details were left undecided. The Buenos Aires Plan of Action set a negotiating track for deciding on the issues of all three of the Kyoto mechanisms by COP-6 at the end of 2000; however, it was only at the resumed session of COP-6, in July 2001, that agreement was reached on the key outstanding issues.

A few details *were* given in the Kyoto Protocol's Article 12 itself:

• Emission reductions achieved with CDM projects have to be approved by an 'operational entity', a certifier, before they can be offset against emissions targets. The CDM credits are called certified emission reductions (CERs).

- Legal entities, i.e. organizations other than the parties themselves, are allowed to operate under the CDM, as they are under JI. This means that an Annex I company could invest in an emissions reduction project in a developing country and claim the credits. Of course, the reductions would still have to be certified and approved by both the company's executive board and the (host and donor) parties involved.
- Article 12 para. 10 explicitly states, in contrast to the provisions for emissions trading or JI, that credits can be obtained from 2000 onwards. The desire for an early start of this mechanism is thus embedded in the very text of the protocol. This has been one of the reasons why the COP has put discussions on the CDM right at the top of the agenda. Of course, as mentioned earlier, it is also expected to bring huge benefits relatively quickly and cheaply. Accordingly, in Bonn parties agreed to establish the CDM board by COP-7, to stimulate early action.

Further decisions were needed to clarify a few key ambiguities in the CDM:

- It was unclear whether the credits of the CDM were to be fungible; that is, whether they are to be denominated in the same *currency* as the other mechanisms. A lack of fungibility was seen by some as protection for the developing countries from possible stiff competition among themselves to host the projects; such competition could lead to a 'Dutch auction' with deteriorating standards and diminishing benefits for the hosts. It is in the interest of donor countries that there be a market for CDM projects, with the cheapest winning the investment; they have therefore sought the additional flexibility of fungibility for the CDM to reduce costs. The Bonn Agreement clearly defines the CERs as fungible.
- While sinks are mentioned under JI, the protocol did not make it clear whether sinks were to be included in the CDM. Sinks are not mentioned in Article 12, but nor are they explicitly excluded from the CDM. Arguments about the potential size of the CDM when land-use change activities are included, the sustainable development benefits of forestry activities, baselines, the permanency of sinks and the interpretation of legal text are all advanced on both sides. In Bonn parties agreed to include only two sources of sinks: afforestation and reforestation. However, eligible credits from sink projects are limited to only 1% of the donor country's base year emissions, which in practice limits the CDM sinks to just under 50MtCe annually.

- As mentioned on page 22, parties are virtually prohibited from using CERs generated from nuclear projects in the CDM and ERUs generated likewise in JI. However, lifetime extensions, upgrades or new plants in Annex I countries count directly towards meeting the Kyoto targets domestically, and reductions could therefore be traded as assigned amounts under international emissions trading.
- The Kyoto Protocol stated that an adaptation tax would be levied on activities under the CDM, but did not specify the level of this tax. It was argued that the levy should be extended to all three mechanisms, to create a more level playing field and not make the CDM uncompetitive by imposing additional burdens on it. As President of COP-6, Minister Pronk's proposal in The Hague included a 2% tax on the CDM alone, payable in credits to be sold on the market, with a minimum market value of US$1bn; if this minimum was not achieved, the tax would be extended to all three mechanisms. In Bonn, parties agreed on the 2% levy without a minimum amount.

There remain uncertainties of various kinds that are preventing industry from investing in clean development projects:

- *Political uncertainty:* It is still uncertain whether the Kyoto Protocol will ever enter into force. However, many governments are likely to offer offsets against tax or domestic regulation in the event of the international framework failing.
- *Allocation uncertainty:* Most national governments have not allocated emission caps to industry, or imposed any other GHG emissions restraint on them. This means that industry is uncertain about whether it needs to invest abroad to gain credits or will be able to reduce 'at home'. With fungible credits, any excess reductions could be sold on the market.
- *Baseline uncertainty:* The COP has not decided on the rules for setting baselines; consequently, investors cannot calculate the amount of CERs to be gained from a project.
- *Value uncertainty:* Because there is still no market for emissions credits, the value of the CERs is uncertain, increasing the risk of the project.
- *Timing uncertainty:* Although the protocol states that CDM projects can generate credits from the year 2000 onwards, it is uncertain whether projects carried out before the details are set by the COP, and before the protocol is ratified, can be counted as 'additional' to the baseline. However, many countries seem to want credits even for the current AIJ projects.

For some countries, the CDM may be primarily a bridge towards adopting commitments and joining the international trading system. The mechanism could therefore serve as a way out of the impasse between, on the one hand, the call for 'developing country participation' by the United States and some other Umbrella Group countries, and, on the other, the position of the developing countries and the EU that there will be no binding emissions commitments for non-Annex I countries in the first commitment period.

2.4 Early experience with emissions trading

After a few decades in the realms of academic theory, the idea of emissions trading entered the policy debate in the late 1980s. In 1990 US President George Bush Sr signed the Clean Air Act Amendments, setting up the US Acid Rain Program, which included trading of sulphur emissions allowances, the first real ETS. At the same time this policy was proposed for regulation of GHG emissions. The Kyoto Protocol established the basis for a GHG emissions market with the three Kyoto mechanisms. However, there is still little experience of emissions trading outside the United States. In the climate negotiations, the conference of parties has called repeatedly since its establishment in 1995 for a statement of the lessons drawn from the pilot phase of AIJ. Again, in 2000 parties called for an extension of the pilot phase for further learning and evaluation. This section will investigate what useful experience has been gained to date.

2.4.1 Small schemes

The Montreal Protocol[6]   In 1987 the Montreal Protocol on Ozone Depleting Substances (such as CFCs) was agreed, with over 180 countries having ratified it to date. This protocol introduced production and consumption quota that were in principle tradable. A rapidly declining number of allowances was redistributed with quota trading to an also declining number of factories that continued production. The most active – but still very small – market was in the United States and Canada, where it helped to rationalize production. A total phase-out was achieved in 1995 in the industrialized

---

[6] This section draws from Dean Anderson and Michael Grubb (eds), *Controlling Carbon and Sulphur: Joint Implementation and Trading Initiatives* (London: RIIA, 1997) and Dean Anderson, Duncan Brack and Michael Grubb, *Emissions Trading and the Control of Greenhouse Gases*, RIIA briefing paper no. 37, May 1997.

countries. Russia, after initial problems, has now closed its last production facility. Initially, developing countries had no obligations, but since the new replacement technology proved cheaper, production has stopped growing and they are also en route to total phase-out, scheduled for 2010.

Three key contributory factors in the success of the Montreal Protocol can be identified:

1 the high visibility of the problem caused by the regulated gases, namely the hole in the ozone layer;
2 the invention of a cost-saving alternative – albeit *after* the ratification of the protocol;
3 trade measures for non-signatories of the protocol: parties to the Montreal Protocol were prohibited from selling the ozone-depleting substances or the related technology to non-members; this created a strong incentive to sign the Protocol, which virtually the whole world has now done.

EU quota systems   In EU legislation some problems were tackled with a quota system. Two examples are the quotas for milk and fish.[7] In both cases, the quota was initially distributed among all member states. Without further regulation, markets sprung up and quotas were traded across companies and across borders. This spontaneous emergence of a market, as a form of self-regulation within the set limits of a quota, is possibly the most important lesson from this experience for GHGs: even without setting up emissions markets, trades will take place.

In the special case of electricity, there is one more interesting note to make. In both the milk and the fish quota systems, you can buy the related assets with and without attached quota. For example, it is possible for a farmer to buy quota alone, cows with or without quota, and land with or without quota. Similarly, in the electricity sector it will be possible to buy or sell a power plant with or without credits, and to buy or sell power with or without the resulting carbon emissions.

US markets other than sulphur[8]   Apart from the Acid Rain Program there is also other experience in the United States, such as the very small systems for

---

[7] For a detailed analysis of the EU fish quota, see Gregory Valatin, 'Quota Trading Systems in EU Fisheries', *Review of European Community and International Environmental Law* (*RECIEL*), vol. 9, no. 3 (2000).
[8] This section draws on Anderson and Grubb (eds), *Controlling Carbon and Sulphur*, and Anderson et al., *Emissions Trading and the Control of Greenhouse Gases*.

production allowances for lead in petrol and smog-causing ozone. The regional programme RECLAIM in Southern California set up a trading system for sulphur oxides and nitrogen oxides (SO_x and NO_x), which was a success, but the system failed for volatile organic compounds (VOCs) because it proved impossible to produce reliable measurements. Because these emissions have a very regional effect, unlike GHGs, which cause *global* warming, the trades had to be confined to the region affected.

Two key lessons can be drawn from this experience. First, a good monitoring system is imperative. In the case of the Kyoto markets this could become a problem in some countries, for some sectors or (smaller) companies, and for some non-CO_2 emissions that are more difficult to monitor. Second, the market was left to be developed by brokers, who treat these environmental markets like any other market and started trading in options and futures. Using the possibility of banking allowances much of the trade now involves futures, taking advantage of current low prices and perceived long-term needs.

Failed UK sulphur market   In the late 1980s the UK government attempted to set up a market for sulphur emissions. However, contrary to the great success of the US experience, the British system died a premature death. The main cause of this failure was bad target-setting: the regulated industries had undershot the emissions targets long before the system came into being, possibly helped by the 'dash for gas' resulting from the electricity liberalization. Thus this was not a failure of the market, but a failure of the political process.

2.4.2   The US Acid Rain Program[9]

The main experience with market mechanisms in environmental regulation is undoubtedly the US Acid Rain Program, which introduced trading in sulphur emissions allowances under the Clean Air Act Amendments of 1990. The objective of the programme was ambitious: to attain an emissions reduction of around 60% from 1980 levels. In the first phase the largest emitters had to reduce from 10Mt in 1990 to about 5.7Mt in 1995–9; from 2000 smaller emitters will be capped as well, with total annual emissions allowances around 9Mt (down from 25.9Mt in 1980). The market for sulphur is strictly regulated and all trades have to be reported to the Environmental

---

[9] Much of the information for this section is available on www.epa.gov/airmarkets. Some of this section draws on Anderson and Grubb (eds), *Controlling Carbon and Sulphur*, and Anderson et al., *Emissions Trading and the Control of Greenhouse Gases*.

Figure 2.2: Allowance prices and emissions in the US sulphur market

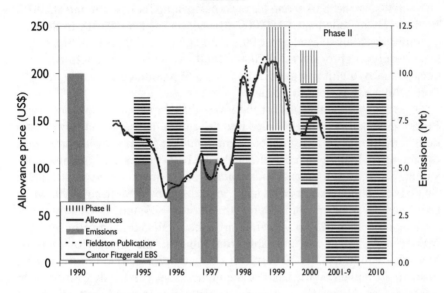

Source: US Environmental Protection Agency; see www.epa.gov/airmarkets.

Protection Agency (EPA). The emitters have to install certified measuring equipment and are subject to very high penalties when emitting in excess of the allowances. The penalties are around ten times the market price per tonne and possible prison sentences for the managers.

The cost estimates made before the start of the programme were nearly $5bn per year, but annual compliance costs are now less than $2bn. Consequently, market prices have been far below the initial estimates. The allowance prices have been rather volatile since the early trades in 1994. With the market getting tighter (see Figure 2.2), and the prospect of the scheme moving into the second phase of smaller units in 2000, market prices rose in 1998 and 1999 to double the lows of 1996.

The estimated marginal costs of abatement for these second-phase units is above US$200/t. In the first few years of the programme, however, many allowances were banked because of over-compliance. These banked allowances leave room for emissions growing to above the target level, and indeed 2000 emissions (which included the phase II units) exceeded for the first time the amount of allowances. However, phase I emissions declined again rapidly in

2000 and banked allowances far exceeds current needs, causing market prices to drop again to much lower levels.

To kick-start the market and leave some opening for new entrants the EPA holds an annual auction of 150,000 allowances (of 1 ton each). In the first year this was a substantial part of the market, but in 2000 the auction represented only slightly over 1% of the total. Allowance transfers between economically distinct organizations in 2000 amounted to nearly 13 million, with a value close to $2bn.

There are various reasons for the lower-than-expected compliance costs. First, the banking option designed into the emissions market has given freedom in the timing of investments. Second, market forces show the true costs of mitigation, helping managers to make the best choices and inspiring innovation. Third, developments independent of the market have contributed: flue gas desulphurization costs have gone down by 40% from 1990, while efficiency has gone up from around 90% to over 95%; mine productivity has risen by more than 6% per year; rail tariffs have fallen dramatically, by 40%, making low-sulphur coal available from mines further away. However, the low price could also be the result of over-compliance due to investments made in abatement on the basis of the higher costs previously estimated. In this case, the sulphur allowance prices would not represent the total cost of sulphur reduction, or indeed the long-term marginal costs. At best, the allowance prices could fall as low as the operating costs. This bottom price has been estimated at $65 per ton of SO_2,[10] which coincides with the lowest cost seen on the market.

Several lessons can be learned from the Acid Rain Program experience:

- Huge cost savings can be made. Independently of the prices of the sulphur allowances, Ellerman et al. conclude that the cost reduction from emissions trading as compared with estimated costs of command and control measures has been around 50%.[11]
- Transaction costs can be very high, as we also see in the present JI projects. If transaction costs prove to be high for GHGs the market would, in practice, be restricted to the very large emitters (such as the power sector) and only when the targets are tough enough (and thus compliance costs are high).

---

[10] A. Denny Ellerman et al., *Markets for Clean Air: The US Acid Rain Program* (Cambridge: Cambridge University Press, 2000), p. 225.
[11] Ibid.

- Reliable reporting and monitoring is essential. Reliability of measurement can vary between pollutants, and also between the different GHGs. The EPA used certified monitors and regular reporting, which costs $200–300m per year – around 10% of the total compliance costs, and only a small share of the savings.
- Compliance with seller liability works well and keeps the transaction costs relatively low. A good enforcement mechanism is needed for seller liability.
- The EPA's enforcement mechanism, with very high financial penalties plus a reduction in the following year's allowances, along with possible prison sentences, seems to work: the sanctions have never been needed.

2.4.3   The AIJ pilot phase and early trading

The AIJ pilot phase was set up by the first conference of the parties in Berlin in 1995. It was to serve as a learning-by-doing mechanism for climate-friendly investments. However, experience for developing countries (CDM-type projects) has been limited: of the ninety-five projects listed in the second synthesis report,[12] only twenty-seven took place in developing countries; the other sixty-eight were situated in the Annex I EITs. COP-4 in Buenos Aires therefore decided to extend the pilot phase of AIJ to continue capacity-building for the (project-based) Kyoto mechanisms. It decided that the AIJ projects should focus especially on the Annex B parties with economies in transition and the developing countries that lacked experience so far.[13] The COP's decision also included a deadline for final conclusions at the 'end of the decade', at or before COP-6 in 2000. This would mean that the final conclusions of the pilot phase experience would be drawn up before crediting of CDM projects began.

The fourth synthesis report on AIJ, presented to the COP in 2000, reports on 140 projects,[14] of which nearly 60 were in developing countries, including several projects in Africa, where only one project had taken place by 1998.

---

[12] FCCC/CP/1998/2.
[13] Decision 6/CP.4, 14 Nov. 1998.
[14] FCCC/SB/2000/6, 3 Aug. 2000. The July 2001 *Joint Implementation Quarterly* (published by the Foundation JIN, Paterswolde, the Netherlands), reported 176 projects, not all of which are official AIJ projects.

However, the total reduction in emissions achieved through these projects is still modest, at around 5.5MtCe annually (120MtCe over their average lifetime of twenty-two years), only a tiny fraction of the forecast demand for reductions under the protocol.[15]

To date, most AIJ projects have been in the energy efficiency and renewable energy sectors. However, the small scale of these projects has meant that the emissions savings they generate are limited. The three-quarters of all projects that fall into these two categories generated only one-quarter of the total savings made. Fugitive gas capture projects – mainly fixing leaking methane pipelines – though only few in number, account for 30% of the savings. Forest preservation, restoration and reforestation projects, mainly taking place in the tropics, even though their inclusion in the CDM was still under debate, accounted for 38% of emissions reductions from just 10% of all projects.

So far, only thirty-seven host countries have gained experience with international flexibility through the AIJ pilot phase. Also on the donor side, only a few countries have started investing. In Europe the Nordic countries and the Netherlands in particular have built up substantial experience in JI, while the United States has also been a large investor. Most of the investment projects (59%) have taken place in the EITs, with the Baltic countries being the most favoured locations.

The Dutch government, host to the (collapsed) COP-6 Part I, has recently opened up JI projects to tender through its ERUPT programme. This takes their AIJ experience a step further. The government had a budget available of just over €20m, aiming for credits at a price of around €5/tCO$_2$ (just under €20/tC). Companies can bid in with a project, which has to comply with the government's rules. The projects offering best value for money (taking into account both price and the security of the project) are selected, and payments will be made on delivery of the ERUs.

The ERUPT 2000 tender has resulted in reductions of 4.2MtCO$_2$e (1.14MtCe) at an average price of €8.46 per tonne (just under $8/tCO$_2$e, or $30/tCe). As a result, the Dutch government concluded that JI works, and is now looking for a second tender, including CDM-type projects, in the autumn of 2001 (for more information on this see Chapter 10, the case study of the Netherlands). At

---

[15] Emissions reduction estimates were adjusted in the fourth synthesis report to account for the IPCC methodology, resulting in substantially lower estimates for reductions than those mentioned in the previous synthesis reports. The actual amounts of emissions reductions are taken from the list of AIJ projects: www.unfccc.int/program/aij/aijproj.html, 18 July 2001.

the same time a commission has been set up to report to the government on a domestic emissions trading system.[16]

A recent study for the World Bank reported that early carbon trading has already exceeded $100m since the first trades took place in 1996/7. The study, prepared by Natsource, an emissions brokerage, said that more than 55MtCO$_2$e had been traded at prices between $0.60 and $3.00 per tonne.[17]

Run by the World Bank, the Prototype Carbon Fund will implement emissions reduction projects that will be compatible with the Kyoto Protocol. The funds available are restricted to $180m, to emphasize the temporary nature of this learning-by-doing approach. Over twenty companies (many of them electricity companies) and countries have signed up as participants, including (among the countries studied in this book) the Netherlands, the German company RWE, Gaz de France, and two financial institutions, Deutsche Bank and the Dutch Rabobank. Projects have started, and the target carbon price has been set at $10/tCe ($3/tCO$_2$e) or below.

2.4.4 Emissions trading simulations

There has been no lack of theoretical studies on emissions trading. However, its feasibility on a more practical level was not tested for some time after Kyoto. Only the four Nordic countries had experimented, just before COP-3, with emissions trading, based on the FCCC stabilization target and the perceived countrywide marginal costs curves for domestic emissions reductions. Since then, various emissions trading simulations have been established to test the theory, gain experience and find possible solutions to likely problems.

Three key experiments have taken place so far. In September 1998 BP started an internal emissions trading market among its business units, including company-wide units in the oil and chemicals sectors. In 1999 the European electricity utilities started a simulation of a parallel power and emissions trading market, GETS-1. With various improvements and a slightly wider constituency, a second round of GETS took place in 2000. The third experiment, including countries and companies from various sectors, was run by the IEA, also in 2000.

Some trades have taken place between US and Canadian companies. For example, 10,000tCO$_2$e was sold by Californian generator PG&E, via emissions

---

[16] A. Denny Ellerman, *Tradable Permits for Greenhouse Gas Emissions: A Primer with Particular Reference to Europe*, MIT Joint Program on the Science and Policy of Global Change (JPSPGC), report no. 69, Nov. 2000; see http://mit.edu/globalchange/.

[17] Reuters (UK), *Global Trade in CO$_2$ Emissions Reaches $100mn – Study*, 3 Aug. 2001.

broker Natsource, to an environmental non-profit organization that will
retire the quota; and $3.5MtCO_2e$ from the US oil and gas producer
Petrosource was sold to various parties in the Canadian market, brokered by
CO2e.com. Most of these trades have taken place in order to meet shorter-
term internal emissions reduction commitments by the companies involved.
Other trades were only a small part of larger trades, e.g. for the use of electricity production capacity or for newly built plants. The sellers sometimes
sold reductions they had already achieved through unrelated changes to their
operations, such as fuel-switching or closure of inefficient plant.

BP's internal emissions trading[18]   BP decided that 'it is important to make
a start and learn from practical experimentation with emissions trading'. Sir
(now Lord) John Browne, chief executive of BP, announced a voluntary
emissions reduction target of 10% below 1990 levels by 2010. He established an internal emissions trading system, which initially (September 1998
to December 1999) included twelve business units. Since 1 January 2000
this system has been expanded globally to all business units of BP, and it is
now actually operational.

The GHG targets, on the basis of which emissions trading takes place, are
allocated on a 'grandfathering' – taking into account historical emissions
levels – and efficiency basis. The targets can be met through direct emissions
reductions or through purchase of permits. The GHG targets are part of the
performance contracts binding the business unit leaders. This means that the
business unit leaders are personally responsible for meeting the targets. Costs
and revenues from emissions trading are identified separately, but do affect
the bottom line of the business units.

One of the new features of the BP scheme is the inclusion of 'credit-based
trading', essentially the facility to include JI or CDM projects in the company scheme, when the rules are sufficiently clear. Although BP has started
its internal emissions trading before the international rules have been set by
the conference of the parties, it does not foresee much investment in the
project-based mechanisms until a mature emissions trading market is in
place and the rules are clarified.

Already the experiment, by putting a value on GHG emissions, has created innovative business strategies in the search for cost-effective solutions.
'Understanding the cost of abatement on a project-by-project level is vital
for Business Units to engage in emissions trading,' says the BP's May 2001

---

[18] BP, *Greenhouse Gas Emissions Trading in BP*, May 2001.

report on its ETS; a database of ideas and cost curves has been constructed to share experience throughout the business. In the early stages of this experiment only a small number of trades took place at prices of $17–22/tCO$_2$. The too-perfect allocation of permits among the participating business units, accurately taking into account the effects of expected growth and future investments, substantially reduced the number and size of the emissions trades. In 2000 around 2.7MtCO$_2$ (just over 0.7MtC) changed hands, at an average price of $7.60/tCO$_2$e (nearly $28/tCe).

GETS-2[19]   In 1999 Unipede/Eurelectric, with the Paris Bourse and the IEA, brought together European electricity companies to simulate simultaneous electricity and GHG allowance trading. One year later the experiment was repeated, now with Euronext and PricewaterhouseCoopers, on a larger scale and with more refinements. Various allocation methods were analysed, as well as a UK-style 'unit sector'[20] and project-based trading mechanisms. The objective of the simulation was to learn by doing and to evaluate various implementation options.

Both emissions trading and the additional project-based trading contributed to the economic efficiency of meeting the GHG targets. The dual market of electricity and carbon was quickly established and helped in clarifying the trade-off between the two for the power industry. The result was a clear shift in fuel choice for electricity generation away from high-carbon coal and oil to gas and non-fossil fuels. The carbon market, however, was not enough to stimulate additional renewables production appreciably.

Even though emissions trading lowers the cost of meeting the Kyoto targets, it does not take the place of actual investments. Emissions reductions happen only through fuel-switching, use of more efficient technology, etc.; the possible use of surplus allowances by some parties under the Kyoto agreement will not lead to lower emissions. Emissions trading, on the other hand, allows the participating companies/countries to optimize the timing of their investment or other policy. The carbon price established in the market also helps emissions reductions to be integrated in investment decisions.

Interestingly, the method of allocating emissions allowances did not change the overall cost of the reductions. It did significantly influence the financial transfers between companies, which is only to be expected among a group of

---

[19] *GETS-2 Report* (main report and appendices), Eurelectric, Euronext and PriceWaterhouseCoopers, 6 Nov. 2000.
[20] See Chapter 11 for a further explanation of the 'unit sector'.

companies using diverse generation technologies. However, the fact that the cost of emissions reductions was stable shows that the market worked close to the ideal.

IEA emissions trading simulation[21]   The IEA's simulation, presented to the COP-6 in The Hague, covered the widest range of industrial sectors and countries. Again, many European countries were represented, but other Annex B participants were also included, among them the United States, Japan, Australia and Russia. This wide range of participants, and therefore of targets and marginal costs, led to substantial cost savings through trading. However, trading did not deliver the reductions at the lowest price.

Countries needed to take, and did take, domestic action, even without any certainty about the future allowance prices. Some of these domestic measures could be adjusted in response to the price that does emerge; however, policy stability might be deemed more desirable. This price uncertainty also led to differences in domestic marginal costs between countries. The resulting domestic reductions achieved between 25% and 75% of the 'emissions gap' for most (buying) countries.

A perfect market would result in the lowest possible costs, with equalized marginal costs across countries. Even though a 60% cost reduction was achieved through emissions trading compared with domestic measures only, the reduction could have been even greater. It was not the substantial market power of some parties, such as Russia, that caused this imperfection. Two reasons were found: first, parties did not know each others' marginal abatement costs and had to start taking domestic action; second, future emission trends were uncertain, forcing parties to be cautious.

Four key lessons can be drawn from this simulation. First, domestic measures have to be taken which cannot necessarily be adjusted to international carbon prices, or cannot even easily be expressed in monetary terms. Second, the timely availability of inventory data is a prerequisite for the emissions market. Third, the targets post-Kyoto will affect current investment decisions. Fourth, each participant pursued its own emissions reduction strategy, ranging from risky trading positions to conservative domestic measures; the real-world market will also combine all these various strategies.

---

[21] Richard Baron, International Energy Agency, 'Emissions Trading: A Real Time Simulation', paper presented to COP-6 at The Hague, 13–24 Nov. 2000.

2.5 The impact of flexibility

The Kyoto Protocol limits emissions of GHGs for the industrialized countries. The primary GHG, making up about 80% of the basket of gases regulated under the protocol,[22] is CO_2, released when burning the fossil fuels that drive the industrialized countries' economies. Limiting these emissions was therefore seen as potentially limiting economic growth and as very expensive. It was therefore of the highest importance that any protocol attempting to regulate GHG emissions was seen as cost-effective.

This target of cost-effectiveness was pursued by negotiators on all fronts, particularly by the non-EU OECD countries. Many forms of flexibility were included in the targets:

- differentiated targets;
- an absence of prescribed policies and measures;
- regulation of a basket of gases, including CO_2, CH_4, N_2O and various industrial gases;
- provision for emissions and sinks deriving from land-use change and forestry activities;
- international transfers of emissions allowances between Annex B countries (with targets) through emissions trading and JI;
- creation of emissions allowances through projects in developing countries that have no emission targets under the CDM.

Classic economic theory predicts that all these dimensions of flexibility would reduce the costs of the agreement. As long as the emissions reductions, and therefore the benefits for the climate, are real, this is not a problem. However, there is potentially a tension between minimizing the cost of meeting the Kyoto targets and the longer-term goal of stabilization of GHG concentrations in the atmosphere. As mentioned above, some of the flexibilities could hinder innovation in new emissions reduction technologies. The resulting cost reduction could also reduce pressure to curb the longer-term trends.

The EU proposed a text for quantitative ceilings in the Kyoto Protocol including the specific term 'supplemental to domestic action'. This proposal would limit the extent to which the richer parties could buy their way out of emissions reductions, and could create some additional pressure to innovate and curb trends. However, only a few restrictions on any of the flexibilities

---

[22] Weighted according to the global warming potentials.

listed previously survived the Bonn Agreement: there are some caps on LULUCF activities within Annex I countries and for the use in the CDM, and there is also a *qualitative* cap on the use of the Kyoto mechanisms, saying that 'domestic action shall thus constitute a significant element of the effort' by Annex I parties. There was disagreement about the level of flexibility granted in some provisions, such as sinks and the CDM. Again, the Umbrella Group countries argued for full flexibility, while the EU and most developing countries urged for limitations. All the flexibilities of the Kyoto Protocol are now seen as a crucial part of the Kyoto agreement.

Various studies, summarized by Grubb et al.,[23] estimate the total cost of the Kyoto agreement at 0.2–2.0% of GDP (0.3–1.4% ignoring the outlying studies), compared with economic growth in the period until 2010 of around 30%. These estimates for the global cost of domestic implementation of the targets, mostly for CO_2 only, average around US$115bn annually. Some of these studies include an analysis of the impact of the Kyoto mechanisms, reducing costs by about 75%. The inclusion of the whole basket of GHGs reduces costs even further. No economic study has yet thoroughly analysed the cost impact of the inclusion of sinks, but large emissions uptakes are available at low cost, again potentially reducing the costs substantially.

These studies show the massive cost saving potential of international flexibility. This potential is especially large because of the targets for (some of) the EITs. Because emissions since the late 1980s have dropped sharply, by 10–50% below base-year levels, the targets for some countries are not very challenging. Their emissions reductions have more than compensated for the growth in emissions from the OECD countries since 1990, leaving Annex B emissions in 1998 at around the Kyoto targets, about 5% below 1990 levels.[24] The Russian Federation and all of the republics of the former Soviet Union (FSU) in Annex B, for example, will have emissions staying below their target, even if nothing is done, and consequently have large amounts of allowances to sell.

The Kyoto commitments represent a big reduction from current levels of emissions for nearly all the OECD countries, and a big increase for all the central and east European countries, especially the ones less advanced in their economic transition that are not currently on track for EU membership.

---

[23] Grubb et al., *The Kyoto Protocol*; also in the IPCC's *Third Assessment Report*.
[24] Emissions reported to the UNFCCC; see FCCC/SBI/2000/11, 5 Sept. 2000. However, estimates of emissions in 1999 and 2000, not officially reported to the UNFCCC, show an increase from these levels to 3.3% below 1990 (Michael Jefferson, personal communications).

Figure 2.3: Gap between Kyoto commitments and projected emissions levels in principal Annex B groups

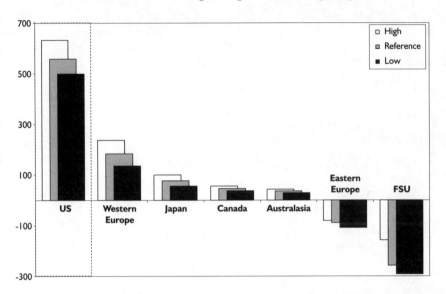

Source: Author, derived from emissions projections in *International Energy Outlook 2001* (Washington DC: Energy Information Administration, US DOE, 2001).

This unbalanced distribution will result in huge quantities of allowances being transferred from 'East' to 'West'.

Taken at face value, the predictions of global cost for mitigation at the level of the Kyoto commitments are not very high, even without any international flexibility from other GHGs (for some) and sinks. Compared with the economic growth predicted for the coming decade and the uncertainties therein, the impact of Kyoto might not even be discernible. The emissions restrictions of the Kyoto Protocol are not trivial politically, but are clearly inadequate on their own to lead towards atmospheric stabilization of CO_2 levels, or to induce the necessary technological changes.

All the flexibility involving emissions trading, other gases and sinks will have profound effects on the distribution of emissions among parties. Imported permits and mitigation efforts focused on the other gases and enhancement of sinks could leave emissions of CO_2 much higher than the initial targets set in the protocol. For the United States (if it ratifies the Kyoto Protocol) and Japan, emissions could end up at 10% above 1990 levels without breaching

Figure 2.4: Assigned amounts and possible greenhouse gas emissions under the Kyoto Protocol

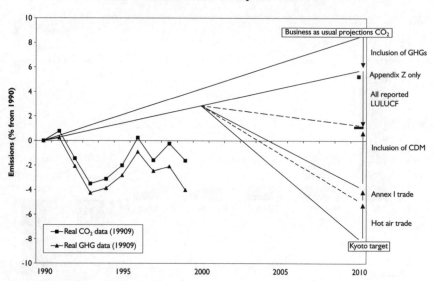

Source: Author, using the CERT model developed for the World Bank NSS and the 'Quantifying Kyoto' Workshop. Emissions data from European Environment Agency inventory 1999.

Note: This particular scenario was run with ABARE-GTEM projections and cost functions, including the US as party to the Kyoto Protocol (if the US were excluded, more cheap 'hot air' trade could be expected). The author included possible impacts of the inclusion of LULUCF according to Appendix Z of the Bonn Agreement. However, the impact of LULUCF projects under the CDM (which would add up to a maximum 1% of 1990 emissions) is not included. The quantity of all LULUCF emissions reported to the UNFCCC by the EU member states is also indicated by an arrow.

their Kyoto targets (7% and 6% below 1990 levels, respectively); and the difference could be even greater for some smaller countries. Figure 2.4 displays the results of a study by the author for the EU. Even though the EU is not expected to be very dependent on emissions trading outside the Union, the figure shows that emissions trading models predict substantial transfers. In 2010 GHG emissions would be 1% above 1990 levels, only 5% lower than business as usual, and 9% above its –8% Kyoto target.

Significant use of the CDM or sinks would violate the collective aim of the protocol to reduce industrialized countries' emissions to at least 5% below 1990 levels. This could potentially undermine the industrial country leadership which is needed to start the next round of commitments including some developing countries.

Even if costs are low, the influence of the Kyoto Protocol will be noticeable throughout the economy. Energy users will rationalize their behaviour, and cost savings from this source could substantially offset the abatement costs. In the energy market the influence will be relatively large, but even here it is mostly limited to a substantial reduction in consumption of coal and a concomitant shift to natural gas. This shift to gas will be very noticeable in some European electricity sectors, and will bring about significant emissions reductions, as can be seen from the UK experience. However, these reductions might not be enough, in particular in view of fast-rising demand.

Fears on the part of the Organization of Petroleum Exporting Countries (OPEC) that its market will disappear because of the Kyoto targets are an understandable overreaction: oil consumption will hardly be affected. Most oil in Annex B is used in the 'captive' transport market, much of the demand

Figure 2.5: Influence of climate change measures on European energy demand

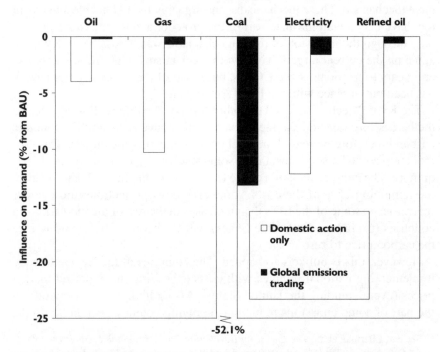

Source: A. Denny Ellerman, Henry D. Jacoby and Annelène Decaux, *The Effects on Developing Countries of the Kyoto Protocol and CO₂ Emissions Trading*, MIT JPSPGC report 41, Nov. 1998.

for Middle East oil is from parties outside Annex B, and demand for gas will increase. Nevertheless, any reduction of demand could lead to an oil price collapse, according to various studies,[25] and many concessions were made to oil-producing countries in the Bonn Agreement. Figure 2.5 shows the projected impact of Kyoto on energy use in Europe (assuming US participation, without the other GHGs and sinks). With pure domestic action the impact can be large, especially for coal consumption; emissions trading, however, reduces the impact substantially. Climate change and the mitigation policies of the Kyoto Protocol will have substantial impacts on the energy sector, of both a restricting and a stimulating kind: for example, it will restrict the activity of fossil-fuel-based companies, but will open up opportunities for renewables and cogeneration.

2.6　Conclusion

The Kyoto Protocol includes three mechanisms for international flexibility: international emissions trading, joint implementation and the clean development mechanism. These mechanisms, and arguably the EU bubble agreement too, have become an intrinsic part of the protocol and its emissions targets; only through the inclusion of these mechanisms was it possible in Kyoto to agree on the current targets. The Kyoto mechanisms might have taken several years to negotiate since COP-3, but much of the necessary framework has been put in place with the Bonn Agreement.

The Kyoto mechanisms and the other form of flexibility allowed, such as the basket of gases and the inclusion of sinks, have reduced the economic cost and therefore increased the likelihood of meeting the targets. This cost reduction could be very substantial; some studies suggest reductions of 75% or more. The non-participation of the United States might have reduced even the remaining 25% of the costs; some emissions projections show larger reductions in some of the EITs than increases in the rest of the industrialized countries (excluding the United States), which theoretically would reduce the carbon price to zero.

However, this is unlikely to happen. The countries of the EU are already implementing national policies with costs exceeding the expected market prices (even including the United States). Also, oligopolistic behaviour on the part of some emissions reduction supplying countries can drive up the

---

[25] See e.g. Ellerman et al., *The Effects on Developing Countries of the Kyoto Protocol and CO_2 Emissions Trading*; Ulrich Bartsch and Benito Müller, *Fossil Fuels in a Changing Climate* (Oxford: Oxford University Press, 2000).

price. Indeed, the Russian Green Investment Scheme, welcomed by the EU, would regulate the price to gain funds for real investments in Russia.

Despite continuing political negotiations, real emissions (and derivatives) are already being traded, building experience and building on experience from other regimes such as the US Acid Rain Program, the AIJ pilot phase and company-based ETSs. Emissions trading and the other mechanisms have become an intrinsic and necessary part of the protocol while also reducing costs.

3 The policy framework in Europe

Industry in the EU member states does not have to deal only with national regulations; a vast stream of European policies and regulations also impact on the national markets. A mêlée of directives, policies and proposals attempt to influence the markets in the Union, both centrally from Brussels and nationally in the member states. This chapter aims to explain the most important European rules and regulations for the power sector.

The UK Climate Change Programme published by the government in 2000 shows the importance of the energy sector in reducing emissions. While only 35% of the country's GHG emissions in 1990 came from the energy sector, it delivers 62% of the projected savings (as compared with business as usual) in the year 2000. The electricity liberalization programme in England and Wales accounts for more of the emissions reductions than the climate change programme. Two key conclusions can be drawn from this experience. First, that the electricity sector is of crucial importance in meeting the Kyoto targets; second, that there is a strong link between the sector's liberalization on the one hand and its ability to reduce emissions on the other. Conversely, however, the liberalization process can also make environmental regulation more difficult, moving environmental protection down the priorities list for the market players.

The energy sector is very important to the industrialized countries' economies. Energy consumption and economic growth have been linked since the industrial revolution, as witnessed by the strong correlation between wealth and energy consumption across the world. Access to abundant and cheap energy for industrial production is one of the key components of economic competitiveness. This is no less the case for the 'new economy' with its service providers draining power from the grids. The EU has therefore also targeted the energy sector in pursuit of its goals of economic integration. A single European energy market is one of the key stages for the EU on the road to integration.

Various directives have been agreed in Brussels aimed at delivering this single energy market. The most important is the electricity liberalization directive (96/92/EC) of 1996, explained in section 3.1. Although liberalization is progressing at a faster pace than anticipated, with full liberalization to be achieved by 2003 in most member states, the directive still allows the best part of a decade for it to be finalized in all countries. However, a new Commission proposal wants to speeds up the process, with full liberalization in all member states by 2005.

There are other important parts of the European energy policy framework; two of these, which aim to guide the market in particular directions, are the renewables directive and the green paper on energy supply security; these are described in sections 3.2 and 3.3 respectively.

The EU also has established the ECCP, which has produced several papers on climate change, including *EU Policies and Measures to Reduce Greenhouse Gas Emissions* and *Greenhouse Gas Emissions Trading within the European Union*. Section 3.4 discusses the ECCP.

3.1 The EU electricity liberalization directive[1]

The European Council adopted the electricity liberalization directive, directive 96/92/EC concerning common rules of the internal market in electricity, on 19 December 1996. The directive entered into force two months later. Member states were given two years to comply, opening up a part of the market for competition. However, the UK market had already introduced competition, and the Danish sector was driven by the Nordic market opening, rather than the European directive. Three countries in special circumstances, Belgium, Ireland and Greece, were given exceptions.

The market structure for power generation is an important component in the choice of technologies and fuels used, dictating the price and influencing the ability to reduce emissions. The case studies will show different market structures and their impacts on responsiveness to environmental policy.

The directive sets the minimum pace for the liberalization process of the electricity market. This process will take place in stages. The largest electricity consumers, large energy-intensive industrial entities, became eligible to choose their supplier freely two years after the entry into force of the directive, on 19 February 1999. These industries, defined as consuming more than 40GWh annually, have a market share of 26.5%. One year later, smaller – but still very large – consumers, with a minimum consumption of 20GWh per year, became eligible to choose their supplier. In 2003 yet another tranche of industry, those firms with electricity use exceeding 9GWh, will become eligible in all EU member states. The total minimum market share of eligible customers

---

[1] Much of the information is derived from the Commission's 'Guide to the Electricity Directive'; see http://europa.eu.int/comm/energy/en/elec_single_market/index_en.html.

will be 33% in 2003. However, many countries have opened their markets much faster than this.

In response to the demand for rapid completion of the internal market for energy made by the European Council of Lisbon on 23–24 March 2000, a new European Commission proposal aimed to speed up the liberalization process of both the electricity and gas directives.[2] Among other points, the Commission proposes to amend the directive's timetable so that all non-domestic customers are free to choose their supplier by 2003,[3] and domestic customers become free to do so in 2005 at the latest.

The directive covers generation, transmission and distribution. The opening of the power market establishes the basis for a more competitive sector. Old monopolies are broken down and new entrants are given a chance to compete. Eligible customers can 'shop around' for better suppliers of their power; they can choose a company other than the one that used to hold the monopoly franchise. The resulting competition among the electricity companies for their customers was expected to push down prices, making the whole of the European economy more competitive. This expected cost reduction was always a key reason for governments to press forward with the new legislation, frequently despite reservations from both the industry and the public.

However, the main intention of the directive is to achieve one common European electricity market and to increase competitiveness of the European economy as a whole, not just to lower prices. This is an important and fundamental part of the single, frontierless European market. In the move towards a single European market, a more level playing field is required. Regulations, taxes, the labour force, supply industries are all moving towards convergence; the power sector is just one of the many industries becoming subject to new rules Europe-wide, albeit one that affects all others.

Despite the goal of one single European electricity market, the implementation of the directive gave rise to 'the development of 15 competitive but fragmented markets'.[4] The 'Florence process' was set up to deal with the problem of diverging market developments. After reaching agreement on harmonization of cross-border tariffs, the process initially stalled on the issues of congestion management (how to deal with overcrowding on the electricity

---

[2] COM(2001)125 final, 13 March 2001.
[3] Opening of the gas market for non-domestic customers would follow one year later; full market opening, however, is also proposed for 2005.
[4] *Power Economics*, Jan. 2001, p. 23.

network) and cross-border connections, but agreement was reached on dealing with the diverging markets in November 2000.

The liberalization process disallows a monopoly in the generation of electricity. Two procedures for building new-generation plant are prescribed in the directive, both of which must be implemented according to objective, transparent and non-discriminatory criteria.[5] Virtually all countries have opted for the authorization procedure, under which anyone wanting to build and operate a new power plant is allowed to do so, providing the set criteria are met. The other option available to member states was that of tendering, which might be used in France alongside the authorization procedure. Under this approach, a central authority decides what capacity is needed and calls for bids which are then impartially assessed.

The member states' preference for authorization is a clear victory for the market. Under tendering, some central authority has to analyse the need for more capacity; under authorization, market forces will determine whether it is profitable to build new plant. The authorization procedure means that no one wanting to build capacity in the EU will be prohibited from doing so (subject to the criteria being met), even in the present circumstances of over-capacity. This opens up the generation market for new entrants and stimulates competition.

The more recent Commission proposal to open up the market more rapidly also included other measures to stimulate increased competition in the market.[6] Tendering for new generation capacity is now 'generally accepted to be less likely to lead to the development of competitive markets', and the Commission therefore proposes to delete this provision from the directive. However, for reasons of energy security, member states would still be allowed to use the tender provision under exceptional circumstances.

Key to the market for electricity is the access to the grid. Without access, customers cannot be served and competition is worthless. Three grid-access options are given in the directive: single-buyer, negotiated and regulated access. Under regulated third party access (r-TPA), prices for grid access are published and non-negotiable. Negotiated third party access (n-TPA), chosen only in Germany and in some cases for international grid access,

---

[5] These criteria can relate to the equipment used, siting, environmental protection, safety, energy efficiency and other factors; they can also set rules for the companies on such aspects as their technical and financial capacities.

[6] COM(2001)125, 13 March 2001.

allows negotiations over the cost of access to the grid, although there is a dispute settlement procedure and average prices have to be published regularly to help new entrants. Both r-TPA and n-TPA allow generators and consumers of electricity to close competitive supply contracts without intermediaries.

The single-buyer system is different. Generation might be competitive, but the grid can be accessed only in order to sell the electricity to a single monopolistic buyer. The feed-in price is regulated, which leaves some – albeit little – room for competitive contracts with eligible customers. The Commission now proposes to delete the single-buyer option for TPA from the directive.

An independent transmission system operator (TSO) will be responsible for operating, maintaining and developing the grid system. The independence must ensure a non-discriminatory dispatch of generators, allowing them to export their production on to the network. Without effective unbundling and fair and non-discriminatory conditions for access the development of real competition is unlikely, says the Commission. The most recent Commission proposal proposes to require as a minimum that transmission be carried out though a subsidiary company, legally and functionally separate from day-to-day generation and sales activities. The further opening of the market will require similar measures for the distribution network: here legal separation of component parts is proposed for 2003.

Grid access for indigenous fuels or renewables may be prioritized by the TSO. However, there is an upper limit of 15% market share, over which no priorities are allowed. This clause is part of a wider public service obligation which covers the protection of final customers' basic rights, the protection of vulnerable customers, social and economic cohesion, security of supply, regularity, quality and price of supplies, and environmental protection. For example, all consumers could be required to buy a certain percentage of renewable electricity. However, this obligation cannot be used to favour domestic generators.

A reciprocity clause has been added to the directive. This clause offers a means of avoiding imbalance in the market when member states open their markets to different extents. Thus, when a customer is eligible in one electricity market but not in another, grid access may be refused under the reciprocity clause. This clause cannot be used when there is a qualitative difference in eligibility, or different environmental standards. With full market opening now proposed for 2005, this provision would cease to exist by that date. Cross-border transmission tariffs, which could stop effective competition in some cases, are now proposed, to be set according to transparent, cost-reflective

Table 3.1: European electricity market reform

Country	Separation of transmission	Entry into generation	Market opening (%) 2000	Market opening (%) 2003	Generation ownership
Austria	Legal	Authorization	30	50	Mixed
Belgium	Legal	Authorization	35	100	Privatized
Denmark	Legal	Authorization	90	100	Municipal/coop
Finland	Ownership	Authorization	100	100	Mixed
France	Management	Authorization	30	35	Public
Germany	Management	Authorization	100	100	Private/*Länder*/municipal
Greece	Management	Authorization	30	35	Public
Ireland	Legal	Authorization	30	35	Public
Italy	Operational	Authorization	30	40	Public/divest
Netherlands	Legal	Authorization	35	100	Municipal/privatized
Portugal	Legal	Tendering	30	35	Mixed
Spain	Ownership	Authorization	54	54	Privatized
Sweden	Ownership	Authorization	100	100	Mixed
UK	Ownership	Authorization	100	100	Privatized

Source: International Energy Agency, *Competition in Electricity Markets* (Paris: IEA, Feb. 2001).

rules improving prospects for a Europe-wide market. Additional physical interconnections have been built to cope with increased trade.

As a result of the directive, most of the EU member states have opened their markets quickly beyond the minimum requirements. Electricity prices (for the eligible customers) have fallen in virtually all countries by 10–20%.

In its 2001 proposal for completing the internal market,[7] the Commission describes the positive and negative environmental consequences of the electricity liberalization. On the positive side, improvements in power plants, increases in efficiency and a switch to gas (which is cleaner than coal) all reduce the pressures on the environment generated by the power sector. On the negative side, declining prices could stimulate demand and reduce efforts to save energy and invest in new renewable energy sources. However, the Commission argues that certain provisions already in the directive could compensate for such negative impacts by requiring environmental protection to be prioritized as part of the public service obligation and by the TSO giving priority to renewables. Further measures have been taken by the member states (for examples, see the case studies in Part III), and the Commission proposes additional initiatives:

---

[7] Ibid.

- a directive on the promotion of renewable energy sources;
- a strategy to double the share of CHP;
- more stringent emissions levels for power plants;
- new measures to increase energy efficiency.

Liberalization of the power market always includes demonopolization, with more generators, suppliers and traders entering the competitive market. As a result, government loses the control it had before through the often government-owned former incumbents. Technological development also changes the market and reduces government control over power production. After growing bigger and bigger since the beginning of the twentieth century, in the 1990s plant sizes started to get smaller. This trend was driven particularly by the development of highly efficient gas turbines, and in particular the loss of economy of scale with these turbines. Industrial-scale gas turbines, able to compete with the large, dedicated power plants, have reduced in size from hundreds of megawatts, to tens and now even just a few megawatts. Micro-CHP, which could bring a revolution to the power sector, brings heat and power to small consumers even to the level of single households. This technology is now close to meeting market prices.

However, despite all the benefits of embedded generation (generation of electricity in the lower voltage networks closer to the customer), such as increased stability and reduced need for high-voltage transmission capacity, the current electricity networks are not well prepared to deal with this possible change. The shift from very large to very small power generation plants would also reduce government influence on the sector and on emissions. With dispersed emissions sources, small industrial units and micro-CHP, the power sector would become more like the transport sector, with its individually emitting cars and trucks, whose emissions are considered near-impossible to cap.

3.2   The European renewables directive

The EU has identified three key objectives of its energy policy: improved competitiveness, security of supply and the protection of the environment.[8] The electricity liberalization directive aimed at creating one single European electricity market, and therefore focused on the objective of improved competitiveness. However, the directive was also designed in such a way as to

---

[8] *An Energy Policy for the European Union*, white paper, COM(95)682, 13 Dec. 1995.

promote the other two objectives. The security of supply objective was the subject of a new green paper from the European Commission that was called for by the directive; this is discussed further in the next section. The protection of the environment was integrated in the provisions of the directive, through the priority treatment of renewable electricity by the TSO and the public service obligation.

However, different support schemes for renewable energy exist in the member states; and this, according to the Commission, distorts the internal market for electricity. It therefore examined possible ways to reduce the distortions in the market while still effectively promoting renewable energy sources. The renewables directive is designed to do this by harmonizing some of the support systems, without full harmonization in the short term; in the long term an equal price for renewables should arise in the internal market.

After earlier proposals to promote electricity from renewable sources of energy, the European Commission launched the current debate in 1997.[9] Initially, a Europe-wide system of green certificates which would replace any existing support mechanism was envisaged. However, German industry in particular lobbied hard to retain their existing generous support mechanism. The 1997 white paper, allowing existing feed-in systems to continue, was endorsed by the Council of energy ministers in May 1998, leading to a proposal for the renewables directive in May 2000.[10] At the second reading of the new directive, on 4 July 2001, the European Parliament adopted some amendments; these were accepted by the Commission,[11] and the directive was finally adopted by the European Council on 7 September 2001.[12]

The EU has set itself a target of sourcing 12% of the total energy consumption from renewables by 2010, a doubling of the current level of only 6%. Because of the relative ease of use of renewables in the production of electricity compared with, for example, automotive energy, the target share of renewables in the electricity mix is set much higher, at 22.1%. It is believed that such a substantial penetration of electricity sources that do not emit GHGs, if reached, will contribute substantially to meeting the Kyoto target for the EU of emissions 8% below the 1990 level (see Table 3.2).

---

[9] *Energy for the Future: Renewable Sources of Energy*, white paper for a Community strategy and action plan, COM(97)599 final, 26 Nov. 1997.

[10] COM(2000)279 final, 10 May 2000.

[11] See COM(2000)884 final, 28 Dec. 2000; COM(2001)445, 24 July 2001.

[12] European Commission press release, 'Accord définitif sur la promotion des sources d'énergie renouvables dans le marché de l'électricité', IP/01/1255 (Brussels, 7 Sept. 2001).

The EU understands that support systems are needed to promote renewable energy sources, since they are still more expensive than others, and will remain so in the short and medium term. Various schemes have been developed to include the environmental benefits of renewable technologies. In a situation with only captive customers, these schemes will not cause distortions. However, in the current partially liberalized European electricity market, support systems will influence the market. First, trade in renewable energy itself will be affected. If support systems differ substantially, the lack of a level playing field across member states could trigger inefficient cross-border trade in renewables. Second, if eligible consumers do not have the same obligation to pay for the support of renewables, they will choose a supplier not subject to the 'renewables levy'.

Various support systems exist at present. Renewable energy generators receive aid through support for their research and development, help in their capital investments, tax exemptions, and fixed buyback prices. These aid systems are financed through a complementary support system financed by consumers or distribution companies. The fixed price support system sets an indirect target for the renewables share through the price level; this system is used in several countries, including Germany and Spain. Another system requires a quota of renewables to be met with 'green certificates', introducing market forces in meeting the targets. This system, where the exact target amount of renewables can be set, is now used in the UK, the Netherlands and Ireland, and is soon to be introduced in Denmark and Flanders.

The Commission recognizes that these support systems are temporary mechanisms and will therefore not pursue them as unjustified. In 2000 the European Parliament adopted new guidelines for state aid, allowing an extended period of ten years for renewables.[13] The Commission also looks at the proportionality of the support measures and the level of any levy. At the moment a comparison among the various support schemes used and under consideration in Europe is hard to make, since all of them are in their infancy; in years to come, such comparisons will become easier to make, and some systems might be prohibited. The Commission has voiced its support for levies imposed on actual consumption rather than on transmission because of the transparency of the former.

In March 2001 the European Court of Justice ruled that the German feed-in law (*Stromeinspeisunggesetz*) cannot be considered state aid. Not only does the German legislation not violate illegal state aid rules, the court found

---

[13] *FT EU Energy Policy*, no. 140, Aug. 2000.

that the environmental protection aim of reducing GHG emissions justifies rules that could potentially hinder intra-Community trade. Purchase obligations with guaranteed feed-in prices have been the most successful mechanism in promoting the development of renewable energy sources in Europe. The court's decision states that 'provisions which require private electricity [companies] to purchase electricity from renewable energy sources at minimum prices ... and distribute the financial burden resulting from that obligation ... do not constitute State aid ... In the current state of Community law concerning the electricity market, such provisions are not incompatible with Article 30 of the EC Treaty.'[14]

Some support schemes introduce competition between renewables suppliers. These schemes are likely to minimize the level of support needed and push costs of renewables down. The system of 'green certificates' automatically creates a market price for renewables. Low-cost suppliers will enter this market for green certificates.

The renewables directive therefore obliges member states to set specific targets for electricity produced with renewable energy technologies. The directive calls for priority for renewables in grid access, accelerated planning procedures for new renewables schemes, and non-discriminatory grid connection costs. National support systems are allowed to continue; the directive does not call for a complete harmonization of aid. However, the Commission can make a proposal for harmonization once the directive is in force, four years after the implementation of the directive.

On 1 January 2001 six countries, including Denmark, the Netherlands and Italy, started a test phase of trading 'green certificates' in Europe under the direction of the Renewable Energy Certificates System (RECS) secretariat;[15] interestingly, Norway, not in the EU, also joined this initiative. The number of countries will most likely increase over time, in particular because of the EU's chosen approach in the directive. This 'flexible mechanism' for stimulation of renewable energy sources is very similar to emissions trading under the Kyoto Protocol. The protocol has set the maximum amounts of emissions allowed; it is then up to industry to limit its emissions, buy allowances or invest in projects that offset emissions, such as JI and the CDM. With green certificates a minimum percentage target is set for electricity produced with renewables; the electricity companies can meet the target through increasing

---

[14] 'European Court Backs Renewable Energy' (Brussels: SolarAccess.com, 20 March 2001).
[15] Reuters (UK), 14 Dec. 2000.

Table 3.2: Renewables in EU member states: 2010 targets and 1997 shares, including large hydro (%)

Member state	Share 1997	Target 2010	Increase	1997 share of large hydro
Austria	72.1	78.1	6.0	61.4
Belgium	1.1	6.0	4.9	0.2
Denmark	8.7	29.0	20.3	–
Finland	24.7	31.5[a]	6.8	14.3
France	15.0	21.0	6.0	12.8
Germany	4.5	12.5	8.0	2.1
Greece	8.6	20.1	11.5	8.2
Ireland	3.6	13.2	9.6	2.5
Italy	16.0	25.0	9.0	11.5
Luxembourg	2.1	5.7	3.6	–
Netherlands	3.5	9.0[a]	5.5	–
Portugal	38.5	39.0[a]	0.5	33.7
Spain	19.9	29.4	9.5	16.3
Sweden	49.1	60.0	10.9	44.0
United Kingdom	1.7	10.0	8.3	0.8
European Union	13.9	22.1	8.2	10.7

[a] These targets were changed from the indicative targets set in the Commission proposal. The Energy Council agreed to cut Portugal's target (including large hydro) from 45.6% to 39%, Finland's from 35% to 31.3% and the Netherlands' from 12% to 9% (*ENDS Daily*, 7 Dec. 2000).

Source: European Commission press release, 'Accord définitif sur la promotion des sources d'énergie renouvelables dans le marché de l'électricité', IP/01/1255 (Brussels, 7 Sept. 2001), annex; the proposed directive, COM(2000)884.

their share of green power or buying certificates from other renewables projects.

In May 2001 the Commission also proposed a directive on the energy performance of (and use of renewable energy sources in) buildings.[16] Given the very large share of energy consumption in buildings (40%) and the longevity of buildings, the impact of this directive could be substantial.

3.3   The green paper on energy supply security

The EU imports about 50% of its energy needs. Energy consumption is growing, and consequently dependence on foreign energy supplies could become higher still if no action is taken. In particular, the dependence of the Union on

---

[16] COM(2001)226 final, 11 May 2001.

Box 3.1: Green certificates and emissions trading

The interaction between green certificates and emissions reductions is not yet clear. Under joint implementation, the avoided emissions from a plant generating power from renewable sources would be expressed in emission reduction units (ERUs), or certified emission reductions (CERs) under the clean development mechanism. However, could the output from these renewables plants be regarded as 'green' as well; and consequently, could green certificates be claimed at the same time as emission credits for the same project?

The (EU) renewables target has been set with the dual purpose of stimulating new, clean technologies and lowering GHG and other emissions. It is therefore most likely that a 'green certificate' has to include the 'emissions avoided', which would also avoid double counting. On the other hand, it an be argued that green certificates are designed to stimulate new, renewable energy technologies, as a mode of diversification away from the fossil-fuel economy. This reasoning would allow emissions avoided to be claimed separately, which could create additional value for these projects.

The expected carbon price would stimulate some renewables generation, but not as much as the requirements set in the renewables directive. Of course, the higher share of renewables leads to lower emissions than under business as usual. This will have its effects on the market price for emissions reductions. Denny Ellerman remarks that 'the lower domestic carbon price resulting from a [renewables] requirement . . . will lead either to more export or less import of carbon permits with consequent effects on the world market price'.[a] However small the impact of the renewables requirement on emissions may be, Ellerman also comments that the 'carbon markets are unlikely to be large initially'.

Appealing as it may be to separate the stimulation of a new and preferred technology from the emissions reduction target, this would create additional problems. First, 'green electricity' sold to consumers in some countries can be marketed only as electricity without any emissions – the consumer is not interested in the technology. Indeed, the UK emissions trading market rules specifies this linkage: renewable obligation certificates can be *converted* into emissions credits at a fixed rate. One of the first projects to be rewarded emissions credits under an ERUPT contract is a renewable energy generation plant. Second, when green certificates can be imported from outside the EU, the 12% target would be worthless unless other countries also take on targets. There is more than enough renewable energy production already to satisfy 12% of the EU's energy needs across the world. However, assuming – as most negotiators of the Kyoto Protocol do – that all renewable projects are 'additional', there is virtually no devaluation of the GHG target.

[a] A. Denny Ellerman, *Tradable Permits for Greenhouse Gas Emissions: A Primer with Particular Reference to Europe*, MIT JPSPGC Report No. 69, Nov. 2000, p. 25.

---

imports of fuels with highly volatile prices, oil and gas, is a heavy economic burden; in 1999 – when oil prices were low – energy imports accounted for 6% of total imports, or €240bn. After two decades of decreasing interest in energy security issues, the high point of which was reached with the liberalization directive, leaving security issues to the market, the 2000 green paper on energy supply security set out to look for solutions to this structural weakness of the

Union.[17] It seeks to minimize the risks of the dependence on imports of energy – not necessarily to maximise self-sufficiency.

The launch of the green paper was very timely, coming directly after the fuel protests of the autumn of 2000 that were sparked by the high oil prices of that time.[18] The paper emphasized the links between energy security and energy prices, renewables and environmental regulation, in particular the reduction of emissions.

The new challenges facing the EU have to shape the decisions taken about new investments and the direction of energy policy. New investments in the energy sector will determine the direction of policy for the next thirty years or so, and therefore have to be made very carefully and taking these new challenges fully into account. First, environmental concerns shape the debate about the future use of nuclear energy; and the Kyoto Protocol targets limit the possibilities for extended dependence on fossil fuels. Second, the liberalized internal energy market has changed the role of the actors in the energy sector. Third, the common market and common targets have made the member states much more interdependent, so that national energy policy influences the markets in other countries in Europe.

The Commission proposes to refocus energy policy on the demand side; energy taxation and other policies could bring about both substantial savings in energy use through efficiency measures and a shift towards more environmentally friendly uses and sources. On the supply side, the priority should be given to climate change considerations. This calls for an emphasis on the further development of renewables, including the target of doubling the current renewables share in energy supply, through continued and increased financial support. Also on the supply side, the Commission proposes to extend the oil stock provisions to natural gas, as well as widening the source countries of imported fuels.

In the medium term, the paper argues, the nuclear option has to be reassessed. At present, a phase-out of nuclear power is under consideration, or effectively happening, in many member states. With increasing competition and decreasing public confidence, the nuclear industry has seemed to be dying a slow death in Europe; but the green paper emphasized the importance of a continued high market share for nuclear in the power industry. However, there is little evidence that the investments required for nuclear power, and

---

[17] *Towards a European Strategy for the Security of Energy Supply*, green paper, COM(2000)769 final, adopted by the European Commission 29 Nov. 2000.
[18] See e.g. John V. Mitchell and Müge Dolun, *The Fuel Tax Protests in Europe, 2000–2001* (London: RIIA, Sept. 2001).

the risks associated with it, are popular in the market; Finland has ordered a fifth reactor, and the industry is stable in France, but it is declining everywhere else.

Of highest priority in the electricity sector is the political imperative of security of energy supply. As noted earlier, the green paper was published at the height of the oil price spike of 2000, when protests against the petrol price briefly crippled life in west European countries and when the 'Californian energy crisis' brought rolling black-outs and rocketing electricity prices. But the electricity sector, in its first few years of liberalization, is still feeling its way into contracts that deliver security in a liberalized market. The market, in principle, can take care of security risks, including oil and gas price spikes and supply problems.

The green paper's emphasis on demand-side efficiency and renewables offers new scope for electricity companies. A renewables target applied to the final consumers will not impact greatly on the utilities, apart from offering yet another market niche. That is also the case with demand-side efficiency measures. Electricity suppliers have some experience and are in the best position to offer services in this area. With a competitive market for electricity, prices decline and margins contract. Energy services offer the opportunity for extra value added and higher returns on investment.

The green paper calls for a long-term strategy, focusing on five main fields;[19]

1 stopping waste of energy by increasing energy savings, especially through demand-side tax measures;
2 an alternative transport policy to prevent a 40% growth in emissions;
3 a doubling of the share of new and renewable energy sources;
4 maintaining a relative autonomy, mainly through the nuclear option; and
5 finding common solutions for common problems, such as a coherent energy taxation system steering consumption to environmentally friendly sources, a strategic oil *and gas* reserve, etc.

The impact on the electricity sector of the future directive on energy security is still unclear. Harmonized energy taxation, increased energy efficiency measures, and general support for all non-fossil energy sources, including both renewables and nuclear, could be on the table.

---

[19] European Commission press release, 'The Commission Launches an Overall Debate on a Future European Energy Strategy with a Green Paper on Energy Supply Security', IP/00/1368 (Brussels: 29 Nov. 2000).

3.4   The European Climate Change Programme

Since the start of the climate change negotiations, the EU has negotiated as one block. Of course, the EU as a union needs to speak with one voice. However, this has been difficult at times. The differences among the various member states are often as large as those between any other two developed countries in the negotiations. Political thinking has been converging in the EU, but in some cases the national backgrounds are still very different and agreements are difficult to reach. Economic circumstances in the EU member states are also very diverse, with the cohesion countries at a level of development already achieved by other member states many years ago, and therefore with very different priorities.

Whereas the EU is competent to negotiate economic agreements, in the environmental negotiations, including those on climate change, national governments are the negotiating parties. Still, the EU speaks with one voice, thanks to many hours of internal negotiations; but this has proved difficult, both in the Kyoto negotiations and at the other conferences of the parties since then.[20]

In Kyoto the EU negotiated for one emissions reduction target, as a 'bubble' for the whole of the Union, within which individual targets could be distributed among the member states. Before COP-3, the levels of reductions for each of the 15 states had been agreed; but the new bubble agreement and the additional gases taken into account sparked off another round of internal negotiations to redistribute the overall target. (The bubble arrangement was described in section 2.2.)

In order to have an effective EU negotiating position and a feasible internal redistribution of the target, it is necessary to have a common EU strategy. In 1998, the EU published a paper on moving towards a common 'post-Kyoto strategy'.[21] On 8 March 2000, the Commission released the blueprint for an ECCP, including policies and measures to reduce emissions and introduce emissions trading. This strategy is aimed at achieving entry into force of the Kyoto Protocol by 'Rio+10' in 2002. The ECCP is set up to bring together stakeholders to cooperate in the preparation of common policies and measures to reduce emissions.

---

[20] For an analysis of the internal European policy debates before and during negotiating sessions, see Joyeeta Gupta and Michael Grubb (eds), *Climate Change and European Leadership: A Sustainable Role for Europe?* (Dordrecht: Kluwer Academic, 2000).

[21] 'Climate Change: Towards an EU Post-Kyoto Strategy', COM(98)353, 1998.

The EU planned to start ratification procedures for the protocol directly after COP-6 in The Hague. However, the failure of this summit and the subsequent suspension of COP-6 made this impossible. The Bonn Agreement of July 2001, settling the major outstanding issues of the Kyoto Protocol, has again opened a window for ratification and implementation of the protocol by the WSSD, 'Rio+10'.

In the debate over ratification in the EU two key issues require consideration. First, the burden-sharing arrangement asks for a joint ratification by the EU and its member states. Second, a plausible implementation plan has to be agreed before the protocol can be ratified. While some member states face high abatement costs, because they have taken the 'low-hanging fruit' – easy emissions reduction opportunities – in previous years, even the countries with growth targets under the European bubble need to implement measures to limit the projected growth in emissions. The implementation plan consists of at least two parts: policies and measures; and the use of the Kyoto mechanisms.

3.4.1 Policies and measures

Emissions in the EU are projected to rise substantially in the coming decade, to about 8% *above* 1990 levels by 2010, against a target of an 8% *reduction*. Transport is the main cause for concern, with emissions from this sector set to rise by 40%. The demand for power and heat is rising, and consequently, so will emissions. The service and domestic sectors also have the potential for rapid rise in energy consumption. Only the industrial sector is projected to produce lower overall GHG emissions.

The ECCP is set up to identify and develop the elements necessary in the EU strategy.[22] The 'low hanging fruit', mentioned above, has been used in the past; now further reductions will have to come from more costly measures. The programme's emphasis is initially on the supply and demand side of the energy sector, transport, the Kyoto mechanisms and industry. A second wave of policies could be initiated later, focusing on the agricultural sector, sinks (forestry), waste, research and other international cooperative measures such as capacity-building and technology transfer.

The overall strategy of the EU includes:

---

[22] 'EU Policies and Measures to Reduce Greenhouse Gas Emissions: Towards a European Climate Change Programme', COM(2000)88, 8 March 2000.

- a long-term strategy for sustainable development (see box 3.2);
- the green paper on energy security, including the action plan for energy efficiency and renewable energy sources (see section 3.2);
- a fuel efficiency agreement with passenger car manufacturers, a directive on complementary fuel specifications (scheduled for 2005), a common transport policy and as green paper on urban transport;
- new guidelines for state aid in the area of environmental protection.

The Commission is also proposing a more harmonized energy tax, even though previous attempts were unsuccessful because of lack of will on the part of the Council.

Specific common and coordinated policies and measures that are being reviewed in the ECCP include, among others:

- incorporating environmental considerations in the further development of the liberalized electricity and gas markets;
- increasing the share of renewable energy and decentralized electricity generation plant (see section 3.2);
- increasing the use of combined heat and power;
- promoting efficiency in energy supply and industrial processes, including more efficient and cleaner technologies, and reducing losses;
- capturing and storing CO_2;
- increasing efficiency standards for electrical equipment (energy efficiency measures in the domestic and tertiary sector could bring emissions down by 140MtCO$_2$ at a cost of €50 per tonne – around $45–50/tCO$_2$e, or $160–170/tCe – according to the ECCP);
- increasing energy services for smaller users;
- improving energy efficiency of buildings and infrastructure.

3.4.2   Emissions trading

The green paper   The European Commission's green paper on trading in GHG emissions within the EU was 'intended to launch a discussion on greenhouse gas emissions trading within the European Union, and on the relationship between emissions trading and other policies and measures to address climate change'.[23] It was launched in tandem with the ECCP.

---

[23] *Greenhouse Gas Emissions Trading within the European Union*, green paper, COM(2000)87, 8 March 2000.

Box 3.2: A sustainable Europe for a better world

At the Gothenburg European Council of 15–16 June 2001 the Commission submitted its proposal for an overall policy on sustainable development.[a] This policy would cut across many of the EU's policy areas. The four key priority areas highlighted in the proposal are:

- limiting climate change and increasing the use of clean energy;
- addressing threats to public health;
- managing natural resources more responsibly; and
- improving the transport system and land-use management.

Many of these issues incorporate, have influence on, and are influenced by climate policy. Decisions and actions on the Common Agricultural Policy, waste policy, biodiversity and integrated transport policies will have a strong influence on GHG emissions.

[a] *A Sustainable Europe for a Better World: A European Union Strategy for Sustainable Development* (Commission's proposal to the Gothenburg Council), COM(2001)264 final, 15 May 2001.

The green paper identifies emissions trading as an 'integral and major part of the Community's implementation strategy'. However, emissions trading will have to coexist with policies and measures – still the focal point of most of the Union's environmental legislation – because the Commission recognizes that the EU will have to use all the policies possible to meet its commitments.

The green paper sets out the intention, already voiced by the Commission in June 1998,[24] to start a trading scheme in 2005, a few years before the first commitment period, in order to gain experience with this relatively new instrument for environmental protection. This date of the intended start of the emissions trading scheme is also the date that 'demonstrable progress' is demanded by the Kyoto Protocol, Article 3.2. However, the publication of the proposal for the directive was postponed in the summer of 2001, leaving little margin for error if the scheme is to start in 2005.

The paper recalls some of the Union's experience with tradable allowances (some of which were mentioned in section 2.4), the quotas for ozone-depleting substances under the Montreal Protocol, the fish catch quotas under the Common Fisheries Policy and the milk quotas under the Common Agricultural Policy. Some degree of flexibility was allowed under all of these three schemes. Under the EU implementation rules for the Montreal Protocol international

---

[24] *Climate Change – Towards an EU Post-Kyoto Strategy*, COM(1998)353, 3 June 1998.

transfers were initially limited, but full flexibility was allowed in later stages. Again, fishing quota trading is allowed, but restricted. Milk quotas are fixed for member states, but individual producers are allowed to trade in the quotas within national borders.

The green paper argues that the establishment of different national emissions trading systems would create different prices and raise problems on the internal market. The Commission therefore finds an EU-wide approach necessary, to ensure a level playing field and avoid barriers for the internal market. There is a trade-off between this wish of the Commission and the autonomy of the member states; but national trading schemes would be less transparent and more complicated for the participating industries. One of the green paper's key arguments in favour of full EU-wide integration is the additional savings made compared with national schemes without intra-EU trading, which could add up to one-third of the total costs.

This European emissions trading market in which companies are involved is seen by the Commission as a domestic policy, and not as the implementation of Article 17 of the Kyoto Protocol. However, any system should be flexible so as to be able to adapt and expand, for example in order to include accession countries. Also, when international emissions trading starts from 2008 onwards, the European scheme is aimed to be compatible with all three Kyoto mechanisms.

To limit problems in the internal market, emissions trading would be designed to form part of a coherent framework of common and coordinated policies and measures for reducing GHG emissions and implementing the Kyoto commitments. It will be a major task to ensure that it is compatible with other policies and measures, such as energy taxes, regulatory or technical standards, and environmental agreements. Energy taxes and emissions trading, for example, should be designed in such a way that they act as complementary instruments for covering the totality of emissions.

The rules for emissions trading should be simple and transparent. However, the paper acknowledges the trade-off between simplicity and fairness. Existing legislation provides the classification for entities involved in the trading scheme. Plants covered in the large combustion plant directive and the integrated pollution prevention and control directive together emit about 45% of the EU's carbon emissions. These sectors consist of a relatively small number of large plants that can be easily monitored. The key to limiting risks of distortion between large point sources and small, and between 'trading' sources and 'non-trading' sources, is the application of strict policies and measures to non-trading sources, with the option for these firms of voluntarily opting in to the trading system.

It is interesting to note that the EU proposal includes the electricity sector. The Danish act on CO_2 quotas for electricity production (see Chapter 6) entered into force on 1 January 2001, but it is unknown when the trading system will start in practice. In the UK, despite strong interest from the companies, the government initially excluded the electricity sector from the climate change levy, and therefore from the sector agreements and emissions trading (see Chapter 11). The August 2001 framework for the UK emissions trading scheme allows electricity generators to enter into the scheme with emissions reduction projects – much like internal JI projects. The UK government states that 'an EU scheme should complement the national trading schemes', and aims for the schemes to be 'as compatible as possible'.[25]

The proposed directive[26]   Responses to the green paper, in general, argued in favour of some element of Community-level regulation, but with scope left for adaptation to national circumstances.[27] Denmark stressed the need for setting minimum financial penalties at the EU level. The Netherlands argued that the Commission should establish a framework to stop member states' systems diverging further. In contrast, the UK stated that coordinated national schemes could achieve a similar coverage, but targets should not be set at the Community level.

After EU-wide consultation with industry and NGOs, the proposed directive on emissions trading has moved on from the more idealistic green paper to a realistic proposal. The scheme would now cover 46% of the EU's CO_2 emissions (38% of all GHG in the EU), through 4,000–5,000 installations. Some concessions were made by the EU, such as the exclusion of the chemicals sector and the inclusion of an opt-out clause. The latter is particularly important for the UK, which has its own emissions trading scheme, and for Germany, which prefers the continuation of its own policy based on long-term voluntary targets. The decision to exclude the chemicals sector is explained by the sector's small direct CO_2 emissions and large number of installations.[28]

---

[25] *Framework for the UK Emissions Trading Scheme* (London: Department for Environment, Food and Rural Affairs, Aug. 2001; see www.defra.gov.uk/environment/climatechange/trading/index.htm.

[26] (Confidential) draft proposals for an emissions trading directive were circulated in the summer of 2001. The Commission was scheduled to discuss the proposal in mid-October 2001, but these discussions were postponed because of constraints on time.

[27] *Green Paper on Greenhouse Gas Emissions Trading within the European Union: Summary of Submissions*, prepared by Peter Vis, 14 May 2001.

[28] The chemical sector, which generates less than 1% of CO_2 emissions, constitutes about 34,000 installations, compared with 4,000–5,000 in the total scheme excluding chemicals.

The proposal differentiates between permits to emit and allowances. Permits must be held by all participants in the scheme and are not tradable. The permits set the obligation to hold allowances equal to the emissions. The allowances are allocated by the member states to the participants in the scheme, who can trade the allowances but must surrender allowances equal to their emissions by the end of the year. Additional allowances can be allocated for newly included sectors or 'because this is considered to be necessary in the light of market conditions'.

Whereas from 2008 the countries' emissions are capped under the Kyoto Protocol, the European scheme is proposed to start from 2005. The early years of its operation are designed to be a learning experience, with freely allocated allowances, lower penalties, more excluded sectors, etc. Before 2008, for example, the penalty for non-compliance is set a minimum of €50 per tCO_2 or twice the market price, whichever is the higher; after 2008 the minimum level is doubled.

The allocation of allowances to installations participating in the trading scheme is left to the member states. The rules proposed stipulate that the allocations must be made in a transparent manner and be based on the country's burden-sharing agreement and the technical potential of the installations, to 'ensure that allowances are not granted in respect of emissions that can be reduced or eliminated at very low or zero cost'. The normal state aid provisions, prohibiting discriminatory aid to domestic companies, also apply for allowance allocations, and it is specified that it is illegal to give incompatible state aid in the form of allowances that exceed the likely needs.

The EU points out two advantages of emissions trading over other measures to reduce emissions in relation to electricity liberalization:

1   if a power producer increases its exports, it can cover its additional emissions without burdening the host country; and
2   once the system is working, emitting a tonne of carbon dioxide will have the same price throughout the Union.

Chapter 4 will give a few more details concerning the interaction of emissions trading and electricity liberalization.

3.5   Conclusions

This chapter has explained the main regulations relating to the power sector in Europe in the area of climate change mitigation. The key elements are the electricity liberalization directive, the renewables directive and the ECCP. The green paper on energy security will take up many of the elements of these regulations and draw them within one framework.

The liberalization directive has set up a competitive market for power production. Large industrial users of power are already free to choose their suppliers everywhere in Europe, and other consumers will gain that right as well. Trade in electricity is increasing, cross-border trades are becoming more important and the increased interconnections make the European markets more interdependent. Despite success in the UK, where emissions declined substantially after liberalization of the electricity market, climate protection and emissions reduction are not high on the list of priorities in the liberalized market. Levels of imports and exports in general will have a larger effect on domestic emissions than regulation with a view to climate change mitigation. Denmark, for example, acts as the swing producer in the Nordic market, and emissions arising from exported electricity can amount to 10–20% of the national total. This is the main reason for the current price cap in the Danish trading system. Additional regulations are therefore necessary.

The liberalization directive has already set out some rules for preferential treatment of certain technologies or fuels for environmental or social reasons. The renewables directive has introduced further rules for renewable energy technologies, aiming to harmonize the national support schemes in the long run. However, because of differences among member states during the negotiations, current support systems are not yet harmonized, and renewed support is allowed to be granted as long as it is not incompatible with state aid provisions. On this issue, the European Court of Justice ruling concerning the German feed-in law is an important breakthrough, establishing that purchase obligations are not state aid.

There are within the EU constant battles among different competing agendas. In the case of climate change policies, the three key policy agendas are environment, energy (liberalization) and harmonization. The EU's environmental agenda includes the need to meet the Kyoto targets and the need to deliver on its image as honest broker in the international negotiations. The energy agenda covers both the liberalization of the energy markets and the increased concern about security of supply. Harmonization is another important objective of the European Commission: despite the clear differences among the member states in the burden-sharing agreement, there is the wish that any new regulation or new market, such as the emissions trading market, be harmonized.

The grand-scale harmonization of renewables support programmes in the Union envisaged with the proposed renewables directive ended in a messy compromise, including the European Court of Justice ruling, which allows differences among member states to persist for another ten years. The proposed directive on emissions trading has come at a time when few member states have yet invested political capital into (differing) domestic emissions trading systems. However, this does not mean the battle for a harmonized system is won.

4 Economic instruments for European electricity

This book analyses the responses to climate change in the power sector in a relatively homogeneous set of countries, all members of the EU. However, the countries use a wide spread of economic instruments for a variety of reasons. This chapter first outlines the economic instruments available for use in national policy and industry responses to them. These economic instruments can be classified under three headings: regulatory, fiscal and flexible instruments. However, many instruments have characteristics of more than one category. The often-used renewables portfolio requirement combines a regulatory approach, demanding a minimum percentage of renewables, with a flexible approach, by allowing trade in green certificates, and sometimes fiscal elements too, for example, subsidies or special tariffs.

Having examined the instruments and possible industry responses to them, the chapter describes in more detail five likely policy outcomes of the use of the different economic instruments:

1 improved energy efficiency;
2 an increased share of natural gas in the power sector;
3 the introduction of energy or carbon taxes;
4 the establishment of a renewables portfolio or obligation; and
5 the introduction of an emissions trading scheme.

These five sections outline the debate on climate change policies in the electricity sector in Europe. The interaction between market liberalization and climate protection is discussed, as is the other European agenda of harmonization. Emissions trading, and its derivatives such as renewables certificates and trading in efficiency targets, feature heavily in the liberalized markets. Indeed, these economic instruments can be viewed as embodying the liberalization of environmental protection: government sets the target, but the market delivers.

4.1 Economic instruments

In many countries in the EU some form of emissions control in the electricity sector already exists. This can take many different forms, but a few key control policies are used most frequently. These include voluntary agreements with the power sector, hard emissions caps, minimum standards and taxes.

Most of the current control on the power sector applies to emissions of substances other than CO_2. Sulphur emissions, causing acidification which led to dying forests and acid lakes, most noticeably in the Black Forest in Germany and in Scandinavia, have been capped in many countries since the 1980s. Eutrofying nitrous oxide is often regulated with prescribed technology. Emissions of particles and soot, which cause smog and breathing difficulties, have been reduced dramatically over the last few decades.

4.1.1   Regulatory instruments

Various forms of regulatory instruments are used in the electricity sector. The liberalization of the market, described in detail in Chapter 3, can also be seen as a regulatory instrument. However, many instruments are not easily classified under one heading.

Prescribed technology   In some cases emission regulation takes the form of prescribed technology, or a minimum standard of technology. Use of filters for capturing particles, low NO_x burners and flue gas desulphurization filters is standard practice in many countries.

Planning restrictions   Government also has the facility to use planning restrictions for (environmental) regulatory purposes. Plants that yield high emissions, are inefficient or are too intrusive in the landscape are denied planning permission. This approach has also frequently caused difficulty for renewable energy projects, such as wind farms, often located on high ground in remote areas.

Minimum requirements   Minimum requirements for technology, energy efficiency and share of renewables have been used throughout Europe. Some of these requirements are part of voluntary agreements, or are enforced through planning restrictions. Currently, the German government is considering setting a minimum share of cogeneration in power production. Germany and many other countries are also considering – in some cases, indeed, have already implemented, a minimum portfolio requirement for renewable energy. Often these minimum requirements will be defined so that parts of them can be traded; green certificates, for example, are already traded Europe-wide.

4.1.2 Fiscal instruments

In some countries, taxes and subsidies have been prominent regulatory instruments. Subsidies are granted for technologies that are 'good', such as renewable energy sources and energy-efficient technology. Taxes are levied on the use of technologies that are considered 'bad', such as emissions, waste and fossil-fuel use. However, industry is often exempted from these environmental taxes for competitiveness reasons.

To date most taxes are levied on fuel use or base materials rather than emissions. Taxes have also often been used for considerations contrary to environmental goals, such as the promotion of the use of domestic coal or fuel diversification. However, the Swedish example of a charge on emissions of NO_x has worked very well, reducing emissions of these gases by about half since 1992.[1]

In the field of environmental regulation subsidies are possibly used more than taxes. Targeted subsidies for renewables, cogeneration and other environmental technologies improve the competitiveness of these technologies. The subsidies can be dismantled once a sufficient market share or cost reduction (through economies of scale) has been reached, so as to reduce the distortions on the market.

A clear example of the use of subsidies is the current support system for renewables in most countries. Renewable energy suppliers receive a minimum feed-in tariff or premium on the market price, and have fixed long-term contracts. The new European renewables directive aims to move support systems towards being a more flexible instrument by allowing trade in certificates.

4.1.3 Flexible instruments

Flexible instruments, such as voluntary agreements, have been used in some countries for many years, but market mechanisms are becoming more popular with increasing liberalization of the electricity market.

Voluntary agreements Voluntary agreements with the power sector were often used to regulate, while giving as much flexibility to the sector as possible in how to reach the standards agreed. In some case, voluntary agreements gained more legal status by the targets being made compulsory; often, too, these 'voluntary' agreements have been backed up by the threat of taxes or legislation. Voluntary agreements have been used for reducing emissions,

---

[1] See e.g. *Acid News*, no. 2, June 2000.

increasing the share of renewables and promoting diversification. Germany and the Netherlands, in particular, have a strong tradition of these agreements between government and industry. The German electricity industry recently agreed to increase the use of cogeneration, while the government increased financial support and shelved plans to introduce a CHP quota system. The Dutch power producers using coal agreed to reduce emissions substantially, while the government agreed to scrap the fuel input tax. The UK has also moved towards using negotiated agreements as part of its climate change levy policy.

Emissions caps Emissions caps, which could also feature prominently in climate change policies and which are needed as a basis for emissions trading, have been part of the regulatory system for decades. For sulphur, these caps led to investment in filters or the switch to gas or lower-sulphur coal. Caps on the use of cooling water led to the investment in cooling towers and location of new plants near the sea.

Most recently, the Danish government has imposed emissions caps on the power generators, allowing them to trade the allowances or use an escape valve at a certain price. In practice the Danish system is a combination of emissions trading and an emissions tax, whichever generates the lower cost.

It is unlikely that emissions caps will now be implemented anywhere without the flexibility to trade emissions under this cap. This sort of flexibility – the trading of obligations – is indeed being allowed under many more systems, such as renewable standards and energy efficiency improvements.

4.1.4 Possible industry responses

There are many ways in which national governments can regulate the emission of GHGs from the electricity sector. The most prominent options used so far are mentioned earlier. Under the Kyoto Protocol all these options will be used in parallel to achieve the targets at the lowest cost. Emissions trading under a cap, carbon taxes and minimum renewable portfolios will feature most prominently in the EU. In Chapters 6–11 of this book these options are discussed in the context of six different EU member states' responses to the climate challenge.

There are numerous ways for the electricity sector to respond to these government measures and reduce emissions. However, the market does not allow the industry to take measures without an appropriate return. Many OECD countries have liberalized their power sectors, which complicates measures further. Because of emission restrictions, climate policy could interfere with, for example, power exports from the coal-dominated Danish sector with emissions caps to other countries in the Nordic market where no caps are in place: export prices of electricity would need to be adjusted to take into account the price of emissions allowances or reductions.

Government regulations attaching a price tag to carbon emissions, whether by carbon taxes, emissions trading or any other mechanism, will make more options valuable for the industry. Some of the trends of liberalization will only be amplified, such as fuel-switching from coal to gas where natural gas is available. Some other options are more contrary to liberalization, such as building industrial cogeneration plants, which are already in great difficulty in some price-competitive markets. A non-exhaustive list of emissions reduction opportunities in the power sector includes the following elements:

- fuel-switching;
- industrial cogeneration;
- district heating;
- renewable energy technologies;
- non-fossil-fuel technologies, such as nuclear;
- supply-side efficiency measures;
- demand-side efficiency measures, for example, through energy services;
- capture of CO_2, for use as greenhouse fertilizer, or to improve recovery from oil or gas fields.

Many of these options are to be used in the countries under analysis in this study, and will be further elaborated in the specific case studies in Chapters 6–11. They are discussed in general terms below.

Fuel-switching   The carbon content of fossil fuels is diverse. Switching from a high-carbon fuel to a lower-carbon fuel would reduce emissions of CO_2 and could deliver (part of) the Kyoto commitment. The most carbon-intensive fuel used in the European power sector is peat.[2] However, this is used only on a relatively small scale in a few countries, such as Ireland and Finland. More widespread is the use of lignite (brown coal), a cheap fuel much used in the new German *Länder*. Coal is the next most carbon-intensive fossil fuel. Oil has about 30% less carbon content than coal; gas is much cleaner again, with only about half coal's carbon.

---

[2] The use of peat in power generation requires technology similar to that used for biomass. Some people argue that peat is therefore a renewable source of energy. However, it is normally considered to be a young (few thousand years old) fossil fuel.

Many European power plants have a 'dual-fuel' function. This ability to fire two different fuels came into fashion directly following the 1970s energy crises. In these plants, fuel-switching is available without major investment or time constraints. The costs of switching can be relatively low, depending on the prices and heating efficiencies of the fuels in question. Even without efficiency gains, a switch from oil or coal to natural gas would achieve emissions reductions of a quarter and nearly half, respectively.

It is also possible to change the fuel for plants already planned but not yet constructed. This would change the investment costs, but could reap the benefits of, for example, cleaner fuel such as natural gas and more efficient technology. In the liberalized electricity market of England and Wales in the early 1990s, many of the existing coal-fired power plants were dismantled to be replaced by high-efficiency natural-gas-fired plants that were quick to build and had the rapid response times needed. Most new plant is designed for natural gas with combined cycle technology.

Of course, it is possible to switch to renewable energy sources. Without much investment, biomass can be cofired in coal-fired power plants, and biogas could take the place of natural gas. These options have been used in countries such as Denmark and the Netherlands. Indeed, one of the ways under consideration to comply with the new emissions standards under the Dutch climate programme is the cofiring of substantial amounts of biomass or waste. However, just as they may switch to more climate-friendly fuels, power companies can just as easily decide to switch back to coal or oil, for example, if the price of gas were too high.

Cogeneration and district heating   Cogeneration of heat and power delivers greater energy efficiency and often lower cost. Power from fossil fuels (and nuclear) is generated by creating steam which goes through a steam turbine to generate the electricity. However, there is still much heat in the steam when it comes out of the turbine; ordinarily, this is cooled to be fed back into the boiler, but in cogeneration this excess heat is used.

Industrial cogeneration was highly popular in the 1990s. Process industry needs high-temperature heat, which can be tapped from the steam in the cogeneration plant. Apart from the heat, the plant also cogenerates electricity which is used in the industrial processes or sold to the electricity grid. These cogeneration plants, often small-scale, are quick to build and cheap to run, making financial savings for the industry.

District heating uses the excess heat for different purposes: namely, for heating homes and offices. The heat required for these uses is of a much lower temperature, but still heat and power are generated simultaneously. A disadvantage of district heating is the need for an extensive heating distribution network, which is costly to build and operate. A large plant would often be far away from the heating demands of houses or offices in a city and would not be economical. Smaller plants can be located much closer to the demand, with consequently much smaller distribution networks. These smaller plants are more economical, but the heating network is often too large a capital investment in a liberalized electricity system.

The key to using CHP is the pre-existence of a heat market and infrastructure – which takes decades to build from scratch – or the availability of concentrated heat demand by industry. Competition from expanding natural gas networks throughout Europe could seriously harm the prospects for using CHP. Cut-throat price competition on the power market could also dent the prospects for cogeneration plants, reducing the returns for electricity exported to the grid.

Renewable energy technologies   Many renewable energy options are available for the power sector. However, these are nearly always more expensive than the traditional fossil fuel, nuclear and large hydropower schemes per kilowatt hour. Nevertheless, capacity in the new renewables is growing rapidly, in particular in the cheapest of the technologies, wind power. There are various reasons for this market expansion that apparently flies in the face of economic rationality, among them diversification, experience-building (for when the prices have dropped), the cultivation of an environmentally friendly image.

An additional reason that is not often mentioned is their 'distributed quality'. These renewable energy sources are small-scale and can often be close to the customers. Where customers are far away from the existing electricity network (not very relevant in much of Europe), renewables could fill the need for power without having to extend the network. Where customers are close to the edges of the network, with only a weak power supply, renewables could support the network and alleviate some of the constraints. But even in situations with a strong network, small-scale renewables support the lower-voltage network without back-up from the higher-voltage networks. In contrast, the large-scale deployment of wind power offshore would require substantial network reinforcements.

The current market in Europe supports renewables in yet another way. Renewables generate so-called 'green electricity'. This green electricity is sold separately to the end users with a mark-up of 1–2 eurocents. Some governments have also set minimum renewables obligations for the power companies, in order to meet the EU targets for renewable energy penetration and emissions. Electricity companies, therefore, trade 'green certificates' – just like emissions – to meet their requirements. A trading scheme for green certificates across six countries began at the end of 2000,[3] and more brokers are entering this market.

Non-fossil-fuel technologies   Large hydro schemes and nuclear power plants, both conventional technologies, do not emit CO_2 and could be expanded to meet the emissions targets. However, both technologies are under attack, endangering their role in the energy sector.

Large hydro schemes have long been controversial. Their effects on the local environment and river ecosystems are profound. Often located in areas of natural beauty, a large dam and lake change the environment. The recent *Dams and Development* report by the World Commission on Dams – an independent think-tank set up and financed by aid agencies, industry, governments and NGOs in 1998 to look at all the impacts of dams around the world – questioned the validity of large dam projects.[4] This report also questioned the real carbon savings to be made from large dams and lakes. Submerged biomass in particular in the shallow area of the lakes would emit large amounts of methane, which is much more powerful in global warming terms than CO_2. It concluded that the GHG emissions from reservoirs could be small compared with those from fossil-fuel plants, but could also be greater than those from alternatives in some cases.

The use of nuclear energy is controversial in many countries,[5] in particular in the EU, despite the positive stance taken in the green paper on energy security published in November 2000. Not only are environmental pressure campaigning strongly to have existing nuclear power plants closed, but the public in general is against the building of any new nuclear stations since the accident at Chernobyl in April 1986. Some recent problems with

---

[3] The six countries are The Netherlands, Norway, Sweden, Denmark, Belgium and Italy; the UK joined later.

[4] The World Commission on Dams, *Dams and Development: A New Framework for Decision-Making* (London: Earthscan: Nov. 2000); see www.dams.org.

[5] For a full and thoughtful discussion on the use of nuclear power, see Malcolm C. Grimston and Peter Beck, *Civil Nuclear Energy: Fuel of the Future or Relic of the Past?* (London: RIIA, Nov. 2000); and Malcolm C. Grimston and Peter Beck, *Double or Quits? The Global Future of Civil Nuclear Energy* (London: RIIA/Earthscan, forthcoming 2002).

fuel-processing safety and yet another major accident, this time with Western technology, in Tokamura, Japan, in September 1999, have further encouraged opposition to the use of nuclear power.[6] Nevertheless, Finland has recently ordered the building of a new plant using Russian technology, and France retains a positive attitude towards nuclear power – though it is the only other European country to do so. In the UK, though the nuclear industry has a large share in power generation, it seems unlikely to have opportunities to expand or even to replace existing plant in the domestic market; the government energy review initially offered the nuclear industry hope, but is likely to come out with a more neutral conclusion that the nuclear option should be kept open[7]. The coalition government in Germany, which includes the Greens, has ordered the closure of all nuclear plants – albeit only after an effective lifetime of about forty years. One of the two nuclear reactors in the Netherlands has already been shut down, because as a small research reactor it was not economically viable, and spatial planning restrictions make new plants impossible. Italy voted in 1987 against the use of nuclear power in a referendum. The Danish government ended its flirtation with nuclear two years earlier; the debate is now about the fate of the existing nuclear plants around Denmark, such as one of the Swedish plants only 20km from Copenhagen.

However, the nuclear power industry is not dead. Some developing countries would like to have nuclear technology, unfortunately often for the wrong reasons; and the new Russian energy strategy foresees a growth in nuclear power use. If both the risk of proliferation and problems with safety and radioactive waste could be resolved, the nuclear power industry could have a second life as a solution to intractable problems such as climate change.

Energy efficiency   Energy efficiency measures can be taken at various levels in the chain of energy production up to the point of to final use. Many options exist for improving the efficiency of both the production of electricity and its use. Most of the efficiency improvements should be made for economic reasons, but market forces might prevent the necessary investments or changes from taking place.

---

[6] For much more on this subject, see Hiroshi Matsumura, *Japan and the Kyoto Protocol: Conditions for Ratification* (London: RIIA, Oct. 2000).

[7] For information on the government energy review, see the Cabinet Office's Performance and Innovation Unit website, www.cabinet-office.gov.uk/innovation/2001/energy/ energyscope.shtml.

On the production side, some options have already been mentioned, such as cogeneration and combined cycle gas turbines (CCGTs). New production technologies offer greater efficiency, for example, through the use of higher temperatures that are possible with new materials. Other major improvements can be achieved through integrating production and use of energy; production closer to the end user (distributed energy production) reduces transportation losses and enables waste heat to be used effectively. New production technologies at the end-use side, such as fuel cells and micro CHP, therefore improve the efficiency of the energy system.

Demand-side management has been on the agenda for more than two decades, but current liberalization processes focus on selling more kilowatt hours at lower prices, encouraging more demand instead of efficiency. A shift away from this market-orientated approach to an 'energy services' approach could bring about major savings. An energy company selling the service of 'a warm house' will install the most efficient heating systems, double glazing and insulated walls, providing a warm environment at the lowest energy costs. Nevertheless, DSM, difficult enough in former times with monopolistic utilities, has become even more difficult under deregulation.

CO_2 capture   Apart from the fact that fossil fuels are limited – there are enough proven reserves for just the coming century – there would be little problems with their use if the emissions could easily be captured and stored. Technologies exist for CO_2 capture, as for other gases in power plant emissions, but they are expensive and reduce the efficiency of the plant. Nevertheless, further development of this option continues, and some technologies offer good potential. The technology of coal gasification, for example, could relatively easily be extended to capture CO_2. Also, the production of hydrogen from fossil fuels could be integrated with carbon capture.

CO_2 capture will be a solution to GHG emissions only if the captured gas can be stored permanently. So far, CO_2 has been used for fertilization in greenhouses (in which the plants grow faster with greater CO_2 concentration in the atmosphere) and to increase recovery from oil and gas fields. In greenhouses, natural gas is burned in gas turbines; the electricity output is used for lighting and the waste heat and CO_2 emissions are used to improve the growing conditions. In one experiment in the Netherlands, CO_2 is captured from a large natural-gas-fired power plant and distributed to greenhouse customers in the vicinity, who also use the low-grade heat from the plant. Even so, only part of the CO_2 is actually captured by the plants in the greenhouses. Producers of some oil and gas fields reinject CO_2 to increase production and extend the lifetime of the field – an economic practice where emissions taxes are high, as they are on the Norwegian North Sea fields.

Other storage options are being studied. Oil and gas companies are looking at the feasilibility of storing CO_2 in empty fields. Others are exploring the capacity of water-carrying layers in the ground or under the ocean, or indeed injecting the gas in the deep ocean to dissolve or in liquid form. Some options seem promising, but further research is needed, in particular concerning the permanence of the storage.

Aside from the use of forestry 'sinks', CO_2 capture and storage seems very expensive and an unlikely strategy in a liberalized power market in the foreseeable future.

4.2 Accelerated improvement of energy efficiency

Most of the country case studies in Chapters 6–11 identify scope for energy efficiency improvements. For the most part, government policy plans tend to concentrate on the supply side, where governments traditionally had greatest influence under centralized power production. The supply side is also easier to target, because of the relatively small number of actors. However, the key technology used for improving energy supply efficiency, CHP, might be losing the battle for market share; and without an increase in CHP capacity, many policy goals will become unattainable. Indeed, the German climate programme now recognizes this, and has introduced a new 'immediate aid programme' for CHP which is aimed at stemming the decline of cogeneration and maintaining its market share at the baseline level. Initially it planned the introduction of a CHP quota system (as did other countries), but this plan has now been shelved after reaching a 'voluntary' agreement with the industry.

Energy efficiency improvements are also sought in energy-intensive sectors of industry, and among final customers and small energy users. The key technology for energy efficiency improvements by large energy users is again CHP. However, other energy-efficient technologies are available. Governments are trying to design policies conducive to efficiency improvements; these mainly take the form of grants or tax deductions given to those who invest in energy efficiency technologies.

Small energy users, for whom energy bills are perceived as insignificant and unavoidable, are targeted by DSM. DSM was very popular in the period following the oil crises in the 1970s and early 1980s, but proved impractical when energy prices were low. In the current liberalizing market, DSM is an unlikely policy, for three key reasons:

* the liberalized market is bringing lower energy prices, reducing the price incentive to use energy efficiently and indeed stimulating increased consumption;
* DSM is an expensive policy instrument, and in the liberalized market it is not easy to see who will pay for it;
* reducing demand is a counterintuitive policy for power companies that want to expand market share.

Counter-arguments can also be put forward.[8] In a liberalized market, cut-throat competition in electricity as a commodity will lead to vanishing profits for the power companies. The current market looks like this, and will most likely result in mergers and further concentration until only a few global companies are left. However, when electricity is approached as an energy service, niche markets with high margins emerge. Most households are not interested in kilowatt hours; they want lighting, television and the kettle to make tea. Many companies are interested primarily in running their computer systems and air-conditioning. Power companies that offered these services instead of just kilowatt hours *would* be interested in reducing energy use for these particular services, because that would cut the costs of providing them and thereby increase profits. So far, the energy services market has not developed. However, there are encouraging signs. The Italian review of end-user tariffs has led to their application in a way that makes DSM a real possibility: tariffs are capped per customer, rather than per kilowatt hour. And in the UK, a new programme has been launched that obliges supply companies to deliver certain amounts of efficiency improvements, measured either in reduced consumption or in increased comfort; these 'efficiency obligations' are tradable.

Often, energy efficiency improvements have a payback period of only a few years at most; but the up-front costs make them seem economically ill-advised. A promising area of energy efficiency improvements is the buildings sector. About 40% of energy use is connected to the use of energy in buildings, for heating, lighting or other purposes. New efficiency standards being considered by several governments could deliver huge energy savings. Here the additional up-front costs of the efficiency measures are disguised in the

---

[8] See e.g. Walt Patterson, *Transforming Electricity: The Coming Generation of Change* (London: RIIA/Earthscan, 1999).

overall costs of the building or mortgage; but lower energy bills reduce the net costs to be paid monthly. However, housing standards in many European countries are rather low, so that standards will have to be raised substantially before results can be delivered; building standards are part of the climate or energy efficiency programmes in many European countries. Also, the energy bill of a domestic consumer or small enterprise is simply not high enough to focus attention on the possibilities for lowering this cost. Larger energy users, in particular the energy producers, however, have a clear incentive to implement efficiency measures.

As noted earlier, the CHP power market in the EU is in trouble. Fierce competition has led to very low electricity prices. On some markets the price for electricity produced by a CHP plant is too low to warrant the additional production at all. High-cost natural gas in CHP plants is unable to compete with electricity from long-written-off coal-fired power plants. The German government target of doubling the CHP share in power production, including the introduction of a novel tradable CHP quota system, has been heavily criticized by industry, especially the energy industry, which has come up with a competing proposal delivering similar or larger emissions reductions. The CHP quota system is now being used by the government as a big stick in case industry does not deliver on its own promised reductions. One concern about a quota system for power from CHP plants is that in order to meet the target, installations could be optimized for power production, rather than – more efficiently – for heat production.

The liberalized market for electricity encourages energy efficiency improvements by power generators for competitiveness reasons. However, much of the effort in this field will be in response to government regulation and support programmes, including for cogeneration. Efficiency measures on the demand side could get a real boost from the market penetration of energy services, but this potential has not materialized yet, and therefore is again dependent on government regulation.

4.4   The dash for gas

Liberalization of the electricity sector in the UK has served as a learning example for all other countries in the EU. Working arrangements are often copied, but problem areas call for different solutions. On the whole, the continental European countries have learned from the first liberalized electricity market in the EU, but have added their own interpretations, suited to the particular national circumstances.

One of the key results of the UK's liberalization was the dash for gas, due to the simultaneous opening of the gas market for power generation. Although most European countries already generate substantial proportions of their power from gas-fired plants, liberalization will bring about a further shift towards the use of natural gas. In continental European electricity liberalization, as in the UK, the gas market is opened up simultaneously, creating the additional push for power companies by the gas suppliers.

There are a few key reasons why a dash for gas will take place in any liberalized electricity system with access to natural gas resources:

- The gas-fired power plants are more flexible in operation than those using other fuels. This means that the output can be adjusted to demand, adding value to the capacity for load-following, even though most new plants are used for base load.
- The latest combined cycle gas turbine plants are of a very high quality, being advertised at 60% fuel efficiency. This is much higher than the best available technology for any other fuel. Their reliability is also unrivalled.
- The up-front investment costs are many times lower than for other fuels – including renewables. Present-day investment laws in the competitive electricity market are strongly biased against any large up-front cost. However, operating costs, especially fuel costs, are higher, despite the high efficiency.
- The planning of these new gas-fired stations is flexible. First, the environmental impact is low, with only few polluting emissions (such as NO_x and SO_2). This means that the plants are easier to site, and can be located closer to demand – on the edge of, or even in, a city, for example. Second, the system of the plants is modular, so that the total capacity of the plant can easily be adjusted by changing the number of gas turbines. The largest gas-fired combined cycle plant in Europe, for example, the Eemscentrale in the north of the Netherlands, consists of five separate large gas turbine modules, each with an output of just over 300MW. Turbine sizes are now becoming smaller without losses of fuel efficiency.
- The total building time of a new gas-fired power station is relatively short. Two or three years can be enough to take a plant from the minds of the company planners to full operation. Some CHP stations, built in cooperation with industry, can be even more quickly constructed. Coal-fired or nuclear plants take many years longer, up to ten years or more for the nuclear option.

As mentioned, the gas market is also being opened up for competition by the EU. Although this process started slightly later than that for electricity, the completion schedule of the internal market in gas is now pushed forward to coincide with that of the electricity market. As a result, natural gas is becoming available in the whole of the Union. Traditional supplies from Groningen (the Netherlands) and the North Sea are now in competition with gas from Russia, Norway and Libya. Increased competition in the gas market has also reduced prices. The traditional oil-price-plus approach is losing ground, and newer pricing methods, such as the coal price index, are also losing popularity; in their place, a real market price for natural gas has come into being.

The dash for gas in the UK caused a very large switch in fuel use by the generators. Before liberalization, gas was not used for electricity production at all. After liberalization, many new plants were built, all fired by natural gas, replacing outdated technology for firing domestically mined coal. As a result, just six years after the start of the liberalization process, in 1996, CO_2 emissions from the power sector were down an astonishing 26%. This lucky 'accident' has proved to be the most successful, if unwittingly introduced, climate policy to date.

Other economic changes in the UK caused the closure of heavy industry in favour of a new service-based economy. This has led to further reductions in emissions. Current emissions of CO_2 are nearly 10% below their 1990 levels, only a few percentage points above the UK's bubble target. Projections from the environment department show that this target will be met even without new policies.

The recent lifting of the gas moratorium that had been put in place by government in 1998, because it considered further investment in gas-fired power stations in contradiction to other elements of energy policy, will spark a few new investments, but nothing like the major shift in the early 1990s. The new market arrangements (NETA; see Chapter 11 on the UK) also do not favour gas as a fuel, but instead prioritize low-cost fuels, such as coal and nuclear, for base-load production. Thus the UK is unlikely to experience another dash for gas; however, comparable switches are expected to occur in many continental European countries. Even in the Netherlands, where over 50% of generation is already gas-fired, further gains in market share for gas are expected before the Kyoto commitment period. Even though the impact from the dash for gas in the UK, with its low-efficiency coal-fired plants, was particularly large, the emission reductions in many other countries will still be substantial, even in those that already have gas-fired power and higher efficiency standards.

The most prominent example of the expectations of mainland European countries is again the Netherlands, where the government and industry have now agreed that emissions from the country's coal-fired power plants will not be allowed to exceed the level of emissions they would have had if fired with natural gas.

Large reductions in emissions from a 'dash for gas' are also expected in the Italian power sector, where old oil-fired power plants are being replaced or getting badly needed investment as part of the sell-off of much of the generation plant of ENEL, the former monopoly generator, to reduce its market share to below 50%. The divested plants had to be representative (in age, fuel and location) for ENEL and the Italian power sector. However, obligatory investment plants were attached to these sales, which included new investment in the plants or early decommissioning and replacement by gas-fired power stations. If ENEL were also required to make similar investments in its old, inefficient generating stock – and if it is not, the new market entrants will be at a serious disadvantage compared with ENEL – the impact on emissions could be substantial. New companies that are not buying old capital stock from ENEL are also entering the market with new highly efficient CCGTs.

The increase in share of natural gas in the power sector will be attributable mainly to market liberalization. As noted earlier, gas-fired power plants are efficient, cheap, quick to build and flexible in operation, and therefore well suited to the free market. However, carbon taxes or further government regulation will also be contributory factors, for example, in Italy where existing capital stock has to be replaced, mostly by gas-fired CCGT power plants. However, coal-fired power plants are easy to adapt for biomass and waste cofiring, and might therefore remain important in the future market.

4.5 Energy or carbon taxes

Within the newly liberalized framework of the electricity liberalization directive, most EU countries will be redefining the role of taxes in this sector. Most governments are reviewing the existing structure of energy taxes, which generally neither yields the level playing field needed in a competitive market nor reflects the relative environmental impact of the various fuels – rather the opposite, indeed, with higher taxes on natural gas. Italy, with its progressive taxes, is the notable exception.

A carbon tax, in theory, should be able to deliver reductions of GHG emissions efficiently. In practice, the tax is rarely levied at the appropriate level, exemptions distort its operation, and/or the elasticity of demand simply does not generate the desired result. Setting the theoretically appropriate level of the tax is extremely difficult; many of the necessary economic data are lacking. As a consequence, economists tend to prefer hard caps, with trading of the allowances under this cap. Most economic models, simulating emissions trading, use a carbon tax with perfect market information and rational economic players as the best approximation to the trading system. However, the caps needed for setting up an emissions trading market are hard for governments to implement because of factors such as vested interests and the industry's aversion to new regulation – in particular to absolute caps.

Most European countries already have existing energy (rather than carbon) taxes. Since governments already have experience with levying these taxes, it will be easier for them to implement further such taxes to meet their goals than to introduce new ones. However, there are difficulties with both the level and the basis of these taxes. First, it proves difficult in a liberalized market to increase taxes, since this could disadvantage domestic market players compared with those from outside. It is also difficult to levy the taxes on a different part of the consumption cycle from that on which taxes bear in a neighbouring country. For example, levying a tax on the input fuel could greatly disadvantage a domestic generator compared with foreign imports from a home market where the final customers pay a consumption tax. Countries are therefore reluctant to levy any taxes which could give rise to competitive disadvantage, resulting in a shift down the fuel cycle to the final customer only. The fuel input tax in the Netherlands, for example, was shifted to electricity output, both to reduce the competitive disadvantage for Dutch generators and also as a concession to counterbalance the draconian measures on coal-fired power plants introduced by the government. However, especially in the electricity market, the final customer often does not respond to these price signals.

A carbon-based tax levied on the input fuels of the electricity producers could bring about large-scale fuel-switching. The fuels are a direct input for the electricity generators, and in some cases constitute the largest part of the total running costs of a plant. Fuel is the main component of the marginal costs, and sets the lowest possible market price for which the plant can run. Any tax on these fuels could therefore have a great effect on the behaviour of the power producers. A pure energy tax on fossil fuels would not influence the merit order of the input fuels much; the main effect would probably be a simple increase in fuel costs, making renewables relatively cheaper. A perfect carbon tax would favour the low-carbon fuels, such as natural gas, and make them relatively cheaper than the high-carbon fuels, such as coal. Of course, renewables would also benefit in this case. However, for the final customers the situation is very different:

- It is unlikely that the energy bill will be a great part of the total costs. Therefore, the fuel choice will not be high on the list of priorities, and the difference it could make is possibly too small to be worth the time and effort involved in switching.
- The price signal will have been weakened. The cost of electricity for the final user is made up of much more than just the costs of the fuel. Customers connected to the lower-voltage network often pay half of the bill to cover the grid connection. Most of the electricity cost of small and medium customers will therefore not change as a result of the tax, and could not be influenced by switching fuels.
- All but the largest final consumers have little choice. Power companies do not offer separate fuel deals, but only the overall fuel mix of that particular supplier.
- Smaller consumers often have little control over their own demand. Who thinks about their electricity supply when switching on a light? Apart from using a few readily available energy-efficient technologies, it is difficult to reduce demand.

Elasticity of demand is simply so low that any price increase will be absorbed without measurable effect on consumption. This will certainly be the case when the very large energy-intensive industries are excluded, as they usually are. Therefore a tax on the demand side, even if the level of the tax is substantial compared with the total fuel costs, will not bring about much effect and is simply a revenue earner for government. Only when the tax is very high – a substantial element of the price for the final customer – and an alternative, such as tax-free green electricity (as, for example, under the UK climate change levy and the Dutch regulatory energy tax), is given, can a demand-side tax be used to meet a specific reduction target.

As argued earlier, it is difficult to implement taxes further upstream, where they would have some effect, for reasons of competitiveness – though this is a problem only when the levels of taxation in neighbouring countries differ greatly, which at present they do. Upstream taxes in power generation, therefore, are being scrapped by an increasing number of countries.

Equalizing the tax levels on fossil fuels and electricity across Europe has been a goal of the European Commission for many years. However, resistance is strong from many member states, mainly because of special circumstances pertaining in individual countries. For one country, energy taxes are great revenue earners for government; for another country hidden subsidies give an incentive to certain domestic fuels; in a third country current levels of taxation are particularly low, stimulating demand and exports.

The current single market for electricity requires at least an approach to equalization of taxes. The case studies carried out for this book showed the result of this pressure in some European countries: the tax burden shifts downstream, so that domestically generated electricity and imports can compete on the same footing. However, the result is a weakening in the environmentally beneficial effect of the tax, for the reasons set out earlier.

It is interesting to note that some countries propose a system where increased taxes on energy would be used to decrease taxes on employment. By making the revenue effect neutral, these governments hoped to receive support for their ideas. However, those who are hurt always shout ten times as loudly as those who benefit, and therefore any tax will end up being controversial. The revenue recycling was also aimed to yield a double political dividend by increasing employment. The Italian government went further, recycling part of the revenues generated into reducing the always unpopular taxes on transport fuels. However, higher double dividends in the climate field could be established by further stimulating energy efficiency and renewables. In the UK, for example, some of the funds from the climate change levy are recycled back into low-carbon technologies.

It is also worth noting that any energy or carbon tax with revenue recycling will decrease in effect over time when it is actually working. A carbon tax, designed to reduce emissions, will bring in less revenue when it achieves its aims, reducing the benefits of the revenue recycling. However, a rising tax is most probably needed, in order to accelerate emissions reductions in the longer term, even when the marginal costs of reduction might also be rising.

4.6   An increased share for renewables in electricity production

The EU and its member states are aiming for higher shares of generation from renewable energy sources in the electricity sector. Even in France, where 80% of electricity production is from nuclear power, and therefore CO_2-free, use of renewables is encouraged. The reasons for the increased use of renewables are set out best by the energy supply security green paper produced by the European Commission in November 2000. The need to diversify, with the prospect of a shift away from fossil fuels in the long term, and the marketization of renewables, improving their performance and lowering costs, are the drivers for investment.

The EU-wide target for renewables has been translated into many different national targets. (Table 3.2, in Chapter 3, sets out the domestic targets.) Of course, countries differ in their suitability for the new non-fossil fuel technologies, but other factors are also important:

• In nuclear France, the renewables target is modest. The problems France faces are different from those of most other countries. First, the renewables have to replace the scarce fossil-fuel plants to make an effect on GHG emissions. Second, intermittent renewables are difficult to control in the French system without load-following capacity; load-following sources, such as hydro and solar PV (for air-conditioning, which has not penetrated widely yet), would be welcome.
• In the densely populated Netherlands, renewables just don't fit. Early targets for wind capacity were met only in the least populated areas, because of restrictive planning procedures on the densely populated west coast. Despite the readily available technology to claim land from the sea, land area is at a premium, making biomass an unattractive option for large-scale application.
• In the long-liberalized UK market, current levels of renewables are far below the EU average. Despite five successful rounds of the non-fossil-fuel obligation (NFFO), not much renewable capacity, apart from some hydro – mainly in Scotland and Wales – is operating. The liberalization of the market also significantly reduced R&D expenditure, certainly for research in novel technologies such as renewables. The government has been reluctant to intervene with large-scale support schemes, such as those that created the 'wind-rush' in Denmark and Germany. Even though the UK has a massive potential – some wind parks in the best offshore areas could alone provide the UK with more than enough electricity – the starting position is very low.

The common threads in the case studies are several: subsidies, feed-in tariffs or guaranteed contracts, and the wish to move towards a green certificates system. However, there are also common difficulties, notably:

• the non-compatibility of some subsidies with the single European market and state aid regulations;
• the non-compatibility of the feed-in tariffs and guaranteed contracts with the liberalized market for electricity; and
• the definitions and targets for the green certificates market.

However, a recent European Court of Justice ruling has approved the German feed-in law as a justified measure to protect the environment through promoting renewable energy. This ruling may encourage other countries to introduce similar regulations.[9]

The European Commission has also extended the permitted period for various forms of aid by national governments to domestic industries when the aid is required for environmental purposes. The extension, from five to ten years, means that support programmes, or pilot phases, set up now could run at least until the Kyoto commitment period. However, this might not always be enough; and existing subsidies may not fit the criteria prescribed for permitted allowed government aid.

A fledgling market for green electricity is already in existence in many sectors. In Germany and the Netherlands, for example, many suppliers offer green power, even though they sometimes keep their prices artificially above the 'normal' electricity price. In most circumstances green power is priced at 1–2 eurocents above the 'normal' rate. The Netherlands has also given green electricity customers the option to enter the free market two years sooner. In Germany, many different 'green power' schemes exist with different definitions, sometimes rebranding already existing capacity, sometimes guaranteeing that new renewable capacity will be installed to meet customers' demand for 'green power'.

Renewable obligation certificates, or 'green certificates' are more problematic. Whereas the green electricity market is a completely voluntary market, where customers agree to pay a certain premium, green certificates are obligatory. Although not exactly the same everywhere, the basic premise of the scheme is that someone (a supplier, for example) has an obligation to have a certain percentage of renewables in their portfolio. This percentage can be achieved through generating more renewable energy, contracting an outside supplier to do so, or buying green certificates from a green electricity supplier, to 'wash normal electricity green'.

Once the principle of green certificates is established, a market will develop. This new market will set the mark-up price for renewable energy. The principle is identical to that underlying emissions trading; once the target is set, it will be met through the price mechanism of this green certificates market.

However, there are many and various problems facing this potential market. It goes without saying that effective monitoring is needed to track the

---

[9] 'European Court Backs Renewable Energy' (Brussels: SolarAccess.com, 20 March 2001).

electricity from source to use; for example, once the green certificates are sold, the electricity cannot be sold again as renewable. Generally, the definitions and criteria across countries have to be compatible in order to trade the certificates across borders. The list of technologies that qualify for certificates might be different from one country to another (for example, some might include or exclude municipal waste and/or large hydro). The eligibility of a renewables project could also depend on its feed-in contacts, subsidies or the vintage (year when the project was built). In the UK, for example, projects already running under the fixed-price NFFO scheme will not receive certificates, but the authority paying the high NFFO price does, using revenue from the sale of certificates to part-fund the running contracts.

In most countries a shift has taken place away from fixed-price feed-in tariffs for renewable generation towards a fixed-price premium or the introduction of green certificates trading, while leaving the price of the 'commodity' of a kilowatt hour to the market. However, in Germany, the opposite has happened. Feed-in prices used to be somewhat flexible and directly linked to past electricity prices, but have now been changed to 20-year fixed feed-in tariffs. This is because market prices for electricity have dropped so much that the renewables tariff would have fallen commensurately, undermining the economic viability of renewables. The option chosen in most other countries would be to give a (higher) mark-up on top of the market price, letting the market play its role. However, the German government decided to extend its – admittedly highly successful – feed-in tariff policy, and has set a high fixed price for the coming 20 years.

In Italy, the old system of renewables support has been altered to suit the newly liberalized market better. The progressive carbon tax has already stimulated a substantial shift towards low-carbon or non-carbon fuels. Utilities now have the right to sell 'green power' at premium prices. Supply companies (above 100GWh) will have an obligation of 2% green certificates, which will be given only to new or newly refurbished renewable capacity. Regions are also encouraged to write tenders for more renewable generation, and a separate support system for small renewable plants is being considered.

The renewables targets and certificates trading will interact with the Kyoto emissions targets and international emissions trading. In the UK, a fixed 'exchange rate' for using renewables as emissions reduction projects is set, potentially capping the price on the carbon market. A more fundamental interaction is that a renewables target reduces emissions, and therefore the national marginal cost of abatement, 'with consequent effects on the world market price'.[10] In perfect markets worldwide, this could indeed be a concern on cost grounds, albeit a cost that countries are willing to bear. However, energy markets and emissions markets will be far from perfect because of differential national circumstances, domestic policies and targets. The renewables impact on the carbon price is likely to be marginal.

Increased use of renewable energy is largely attributable to various fiscal measures, such as subsidies and tax breaks. However, in many countries regulations are more important in stimulating renewables through guaranteed feed-in prices and minimum renewable energy requirements, now often rendered more flexible by trading in certificates. Many countries already have positive experience with fixed tariffs. The EU directive on renewables has set targets for all fifteen EU member states to increase their output from renewable energy sources. Tradable certificates and feed-in prices are expected to deliver most of the EU targets, but some governments might write tenders to increase capacity.

4.7 Emissions trading

The basic idea behind emissions trading has already been explained in Chapters 2 and 3 (see especially section 3.4.2). Several European countries and the European Commission are implementing or investigating domestic ETSs. In Denmark, the act on emissions trading has entered into force, but no trading has yet taken place at the time of writing (see Chapter 6). In the UK, the last details are being agreed at the time of writing, and the initial auction of permits has not yet taken place, but the first trade has already been registered (see Chapter 11).

The European Commission is also proposing a directive on emissions trading. It has taken this step with several aims in view, including:

- reaping greater benefits of trading by broadening the coverage to the whole of the EU;
- reinforcing domestic action throughout the Union, to show internal and external commitment; and
- harmonizing ETSs throughout the Union, which might increase the acceptability of emissions trading and caps in particular for international business.

---

[10] A. Denny Ellerman, *Tradable Permits for Greenhouse Gas Emissions: A Primer with Particular Reference to Europe*, MIT JPSPGC report no. 69, Nov. 2000.

An EU-wide scheme would reduce the overall costs of meeting the Kyoto or burden-sharing targets. The Commission estimates that separate domestic schemes would be about one-third more expensive than a harmonized EU-15 trading scheme. Section 3.4.2 described this proposal in outline.

The implementation of an EU-wide emissions trading scheme would reinforce the emissions reduction efforts of the Union and its member states. This is necessary both from the point of view of the international credibility of the EU as the 'green broker', and also for domestic compliance with the targets. Most EU countries have emissions exceeding their 1990 levels and are not on their way to meet the targets, despite the generous reallocation of obligations in the burden-sharing agreement. Section 1.3 highlighted this point.

On harmonization, however, the argument is less clear-cut. On the one hand, industry would prefer to have a level international playing field, with competitors throughout Europe and indeed all the Annex I countries subject to similar restrictions on emissions. On the other hand, incumbent industries are used to the established national rules and systems; an ETS that is incompatible with these established rules and that is imposed on them by an international body most likely would not suit them. The UK industry response to the EU proposal, for example, has not been very positive. German industry is hostile to any emissions caps, preferring the established voluntary agreements.

4.7.1   The impact of diverging models

Diverging emissions trading models might create various problems. These problems can be categorized in two groups: first, those related to the internal market, and ease of operating in different countries; second, the problems related to the compatibility of the systems.

Different emissions trading schemes in member states will create distortions in the (relatively) level playing field of the internal market. Industries across Europe will have to meet different standards; they will have different emissions targets and different mitigation costs. This could create potentially great advantages and disadvantages for industry in different member states. In some cases a sector is included in one ETS, but not in another. This could create unfair competition, with both sides claiming that they face costs higher than those across the border.

Different schemes across Europe would also complicate trading arrangements for the multinational industries. Factories across borders would have different rules to comply with; sectors could be included in the trading regime in one country but not in another. The electricity sector, for example, is excluded in the UK, but is the only sector to trade in Denmark; thus direct trade in power between these two states could result in Danish power with emissions already covered by quotas still having to pay the climate levy, or UK power being sold un-levied in Denmark.

There is also a big question about the compatibility of ETSs across Europe. Is a Danish tonne the same as a British tonne? Compatibility can be denied on several grounds, such as the inclusion or exclusion of sectors, the existence of price caps or the emissions targets in the market, such as absolute caps in Denmark and energy efficiency agreements in the UK. But maybe the worst incompatibility is between the EU system, counting only direct emissions, and the UK system, also counting indirect emissions – which means that responsibility for power sector emissions is passed on to the consumer of electricity.

The diverging emissions trading models and their correspondingly various compartmentalization of emissions trading will lead to excessively high costs in some countries or sectors that are not able to access cheap emissions allowances elsewhere in Europe. Theoretically, emissions trading is more economically efficient when the market includes a higher share of emissions, more sectors and more countries. Differences in abatement costs across the economies can be used to keep costs down overall.

Concern about the level playing field in competition has been one of the most important justifications for European environmental legislation. Indeed, a European directive would meet one criterion on which the subsidiarity principle rests: member states clearly cannot solve climate change alone, separate schemes could be incompatible and compartmentalize the market, and a Europe-wide scheme would bring greater savings. Thus the Commission would have competence to legislate on emissions trading. Also, the European bubble agreement, in which member states agree to fulfil their Kyoto commitments jointly, strengthens the case for the Commission.[11]

However, an academic response to the Commission scheme as outlined in the green paper on emissions trading argued that the fair trade and harmonization arguments are flawed.[12] It acknowledges some of the arguments about

---

[11] Farhana Yamin and Jürgen Levefre, *Designing Options for Implementing an Emissions Trading Regime for Greenhouse Gases in the EC: Final Report* (London: Foundation for International Environmental Law and Development (FIELD), 22 Feb. 2000); see www.field.org.uk.

[12] Laurent Viguier, *Fair Trade and Harmonization of Climate Change Policies in Europe*, MIT Joint Program on the Science and Policy of Global Change (JPSPGC) report no. 66, Sept. 2000.

Box 4.1: Allocations theories[a]

Two competing theories exist about allocation of emissions allowances and the impact on prices and competition. One theory says that initial allocation does not distort the relative prices and products. The other theory explains that the financial effects impact strongly on companies' performance.[b]

- The first theory argues that, whether permits are allocated through an auction or awarded gratis, for example, through grandfathering, firms will value the permits at the market price (cost price or opportunity cost, respectively). This would mean that in theory the relative prices of the product of a firm would not be changed. Consequently, there is no reason for demand to switch to products of those companies that were given their permits free. Grandfathering makes a firm wealthier, but does not change its competitive position.[c]
- However, the other theory does not believe in perfect markets and takes the financial positions of companies, the capital market and equity concerns into account. First, a company with grandfathered permits has gained a stronger financial position compared with a firm that had to buy all its permits. In a price war, for example, the former could undercut the price of the latter for a sustained period. Second, when capital markets are imperfect, borrowing to buy permits is very costly.[d]

The European electricity sector does not exist in a perfect market environment. In most European electricity markets, a few, very large companies are in competition with one another. The price cuts that took place in Germany are close to those occurring in a price war. Nor is it likely that ETSs will be set up with allocation systems as wide-ranging as full auctioning and grandfathering; they are more likely to use different formulas to distribute permits gratis. Sectors in all countries will lobby for a good deal and draw comparisons with neighbouring countries. This means that differences among the allocations in the various sectors will exist but will most likely be small, possibly negligible compared with other differences between them.

However, efficiency- or output-related targets, such as those often used in voluntary/negotiated agreements in Europe, change the arguments. A company facing an emissions cap, whether grandfathered or auctioned, values the permits at the market price. However, a company with an output related-target (say $0.4tCO_2$ per MWh generated[e]) will value a permit differently, since it will acquire the additional permit only if it produces additional electricity. Forgoing the additional production thus does not enable the firm to sell the permit, and therefore opportunity costs would be zero. However, if emissions reduction options, including non-emitting production, are taken into the equation, opportunity costs are non-zero.[f] Whether or not the output-related target is equal to the actual output-related emissions, the additional costs for emission permits will be lower than for capped sectors.

[a] I would like to thank Edwin Woerdman (University of Groningen, Netherlands) and Prof. ZhongXiang Zhang (East-West Centre, Honolulu, US) for their comments.
[b] A brief overview of these theories is also given in Edwin Woerdman, 'Organising Emissions Trading: The Barrier of Domestic Permit Allocation', *Energy Policy*, vol. 28 (2000), pp. 613–23; some of this summary draws on this article.
[c] ZhongXiang Zhang, 'Should the Rules of Allocating Emissions Permits Be Harmonised?', *Ecological Economics*, vol. 31, no. 1 (1999), pp. 11–28.

Box 4.1: Continued

[d] Edwin Woerdman, 'Developing a European Carbon Trading Market: Will Permit Allocation Distort Competition and Lead to State Aid?', paper presented at the workshop on Trade and the Environment in the Perspective of the European Enlargement, Milan, 17–18 May 2002 (Fondazione Eni Enrico Mattei).

[e] The IPCC's *Second Assessment Report* (Working Group II) indicates that the emissions from a highly efficient gas-fired combined cycle power plant are 110gC/kWh, that is 0.403tCO$_2$/MWh.

[f] The inclusion of emissions reduction options is my interpretation of disagreement over whether opportunity costs would really become zero for output-related targets.

---

the advantage of an EU-wide scheme, but disputes that the allocation of permits should be harmonized. The burden-sharing agreement already showed varying GHG utility functions (indicating the value of activities that cause emissions versus the value of avoided emissions) across the member states, and similarly they will allocate quotas according to their own priorities and marginal costs in each sector. 'This diversity of allocation rules in Europe would be fair and efficient.'

Harmonization or coordination of emissions trading will very useful in certain areas, such as establishing a common unit of trade, monitoring and verification, and enforcement regulation. These harmonized regulations would make sure that emissions trading systems are compatible. However, allocations in Europe cannot be harmonized for various reasons:

- First, some member states have already implemented climate policies that deliver the emissions reductions needed to meet the target of the burden-sharing agreement; in these cases there is no need for the costly implementation of an emissions trading scheme.
- Second, competitive distortions arising from differences in allocations are likely to be small compared with the impact of other, already existing regulation. Box 4.1 explains two conflicting theories on allocations.
- Third, the burden-sharing agreement was negotiated and renegotiated on the basis of the national reduction potential and 'willingness to pay', both in the sense of the value attached to GHG reductions, and in the sense of the willingness to do more or less than other member states, rather than economic cost. Harmonized allocations would thus deliver different targets from those agreed in the burden-sharing agreement, which could unravel as a consequence.

The European Commission proposal for an emissions trading directive does propose harmonized rules in several areas: for monitoring and verification, eligible and excluded sectors, penalties and the unit of trade. However, it leaves allocations to the member states, under guidance of the rules for state aid. The experience of the negotiations surrounding the renewables directive also recommends caution towards too much harmonization: the outcome of such an attempt is likely to be a messy political compromise.

4.8 Conclusions

Using the same or different economic instruments – regulatory, fiscal and/or flexible – there are many similar policy outcomes across European countries concerning emissions reductions in the power sector. This chapter has highlighted five likely outcomes: taxes, greater use of renewable sources, fuel-switching, energy efficiency measures and emissions trading.

Taxes on fuel input (for power generation) are not very popular in competitive markets. Most taxes would bear on the final consumer. This not only mitigates any competitive disadvantage of domestic generators for exports, but also allows taxes to be applied to imported electricity.

For fuel-switching and efficiency measures, competition works hand in hand with climate policy to some extent. Natural gas is the fuel of choice in all countries where there is easy access to it, on account of its flexibility and efficiency. Some efficiency measures are taken by power companies to compete in the marketplace. However, cogeneration is now often seen as a more expensive option and needs financial support.

Policies towards renewables are similar in many countries, with a clear move towards obligatory target levels and the possibility to trade 'green certificates'. Such a policy, in theory, leads to the target being met in a much more economically efficient way. However, feed-in tariffs also still exist. These premium tariffs stimulate renewable generation, but the levels of renewables that will be achieved are unclear from the outset, and tariff levels might have to be changed to meet targets. The clash between these two instruments is similar to that between carbon taxes and emissions trading. Because many European countries are moving towards green certificates, international recognition of traded certificates might not be a problem. However, some countries, such as Germany, have opted for higher or fixed feed-in tariffs, to counter reduced market prices.

The European Commission has proposed a Union-wide emissions trading scheme. However, some national governments have reservations about this scheme, either because they have already implemented a domestic scheme or because they do not wish to implement emissions trading at all. Emissions trading must be seen as the instrument most compatible with liberalized markets: the government sets the cap, but the market determines the price and how the reductions are achieved. Initially, it would be hard to harmonize the ETS(s) fully because of different starting positions, existing targets and existing policies in place.

Part II
Case studies of European electricity sectors

5 Introduction to the case studies

This second part of *Climate Change and Power* analyses the electricity systems and climate policies in six different countries in the EU. The case studies aim to show what is happening across Europe, how different or similar some of the measures taken are, and whether or not greater harmonization across Europe is required.

These six case studies are chosen to reflect a wide range of electricity systems and at the same time be representative for the whole of the EU. The electricity sectors in Europe have developed in very different ways. The generation mix is diverse, and the policy cultures are just as varied. However, the sectors are moving towards convergence through various European directives, as described in Chapter 3, in particular the liberalization directive.

The countries chosen are (in alphabetical order): Denmark, France, Germany, Italy, the Netherlands and the UK. The six case studies were prepared by national specialists.

Size

Together these countries represent three-quarters of the EU's power production (see figure 5.1). Germany and France each have a power production sector accounting for over 20% of the European market. Italy and the UK both have large sectors (over 10% of the EU total). The Netherlands and Denmark have relatively small sectors, (3.5% and 1.4% respectively). Apart from representing different market sizes, the six countries also represent a diverse set of locations, market structures, fuels and technologies.

Location

Denmark is connected with the Nordic market, but also has some connection to the south through Germany. France is in the centre of the European market, with interconnections to many countries which it uses to export substantial amounts of nuclear power. Germany is important for its size and relative central location; however, interconnections to the east are limited. Italy represents a south European country with some, albeit limited, interconnections. The Netherlands has a small power sector, but has large interconnection

Figure 5.1: Power sector shares in the European Union

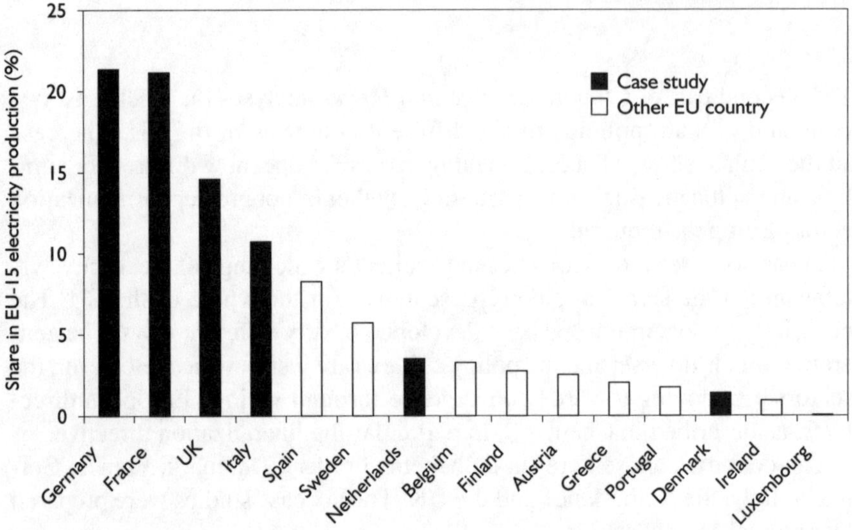

Source: Eurostat, Aug. 2001 (provisional data for 2000).

capacity with Germany and through Belgium with France. The UK, finally, is an island, with only very limited interconnections with France.

Market structure

The market structures of the case study countries are diverse. The UK and Germany have liberalized their power sectors completely. However, whereas the UK has a ten-year history with liberalized markets, the German sector was based on regional monopolies until recently. In France and Italy, the markets are still very much dominated by the traditional state-owned monopolists. In Denmark and the Netherlands liberalization has progressed to an intermediate level. In Denmark the power market is heavily interwoven with the heat market. Figure 5.2 gives an overview of the state of liberalization in the various case study countries.

Figure 5.2: Electricity liberalization in the case study countries

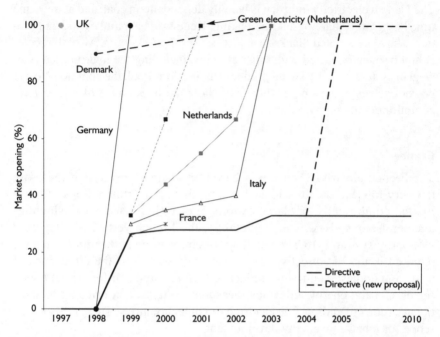

Source: Implementation reports on the EC website, see http://europa.eu.int/comm/energy/en/
elec_single_market/implementation/index_en.html.

Fuels and technologies

The fuels and technologies used in the countries are also radically different. In France, the sector is largely based on large nuclear power plants. In Italy, oil-fired power plants are still very important in the fuel mix, and much of the capital stock is old and in need of replacement. In Denmark, coal is the main fuel, but much of the sector is based on efficient CHP. The Netherlands has a very high fuel share of natural gas, also with a high proportion of (in particular industrial) CHP. The UK and Germany have a wide mix of fuels. The UK experienced a 'dash for gas' in the early 1990s, and the fuel mix is now nearly equally divided among coal, gas and nuclear. In Germany, local fuels (hard coal and brown coal) are important, as is nuclear; however, the government aims to phase out nuclear power. The share of renewables in the power sector is relatively high in Italy, France and Denmark (over 5%) and low in the Netherlands, Germany and the UK (~1%).

Denmark

The Danish electricity industry is heavily dependent on coal, and at the same time has a large share of district heating. Renewables, mainly wind and biomass, have penetrated thanks to a successful support system. Also, the sector is highly interconnected with other systems, including the hydro-based Norwegian system, and is a swing producer in the Nord Pool, the common Nordic power exchange. This case study will show the importance of a long-term commitment to energy policy.

France

The French electricity system is based on nuclear power, and therefore has very low carbon emissions. The emissions reduction options are very limited domestically, but large exports of electricity take place which reduce emissions elsewhere. Reluctantly, the French vertically integrated monopoly system is to be opened up for competition at the minimum level required in the EU directive. This case study will show the difficulties of achieving domestic emissions reductions with a large non-fossil-fuel power sector. General energy efficiency measures are taken that can lead to additional exports of carbon-free electricity to other countries. There is also large scope for renewable energy development.

Germany

The various vertically integrated regional monopoly suppliers in Germany are economically very powerful. Cut-throat competition has broken out among the companies, and prices have dropped since the opening of the market. However, competition is constrained and the utilities have to open their networks to competitors, creating a market structure which seems different from that of other European markets. With additional measures, the German Kyoto target is within reach, to a large extent because of the repercussions of unification. Despite the strong market features of the German market, it is full of contradictions. The system is highly dependent on government-subsidized coal, nuclear power is to be phased out before the end of its lifetime and fixed-price renewables support is preferred over market-based prices.

Italy

The Italian electricity system is taken as an example of a government-owned vertically integrated monopoly system, with a strong internal battle about introducing competition. A substantial share of its capacity uses heavy fuel oil. Carbon taxes and tariffs conducive to demand-side efficiency are in place. However, most of the emissions reductions are going to come from increased competition and generation efficiency. Competition is being introduced by requiring ENEL, the former monopoly, to sell capacity. It is agreed that substantial investment needs to be made in this capacity, both in fuel-switching and in increasing fuel efficiency.

Netherlands

This highly interconnected and relatively small electricity system is liberalizing rapidly and in its own direction. The high share of cogeneration and natural gas in the power sector poses challenges to achieving high reduction of emissions distinctly different from those applying in other countries, because the 'easy options' have already been taken. The Dutch government, for both national and international reasons, has decided to require only 50% of the Kyoto target to be met from domestic measures and to seek the other 50% from reductions abroad. Much of the domestic framework is based on experience with long-term voluntary agreements between government and industry. However, some of the domestic emission targets are still tough, such as those for coal-fired power plants.

UK

The system in England and Wales was opened up for competition at the retail level in 1998–9, ten years later than the wholesale market. It is one of the pioneering systems in liberalization and privatization of electricity in the world. The high level of competition presents extra challenges for effective climate policy. The power industry has already been actively involved in the emissions trading debate for many years, but will now be excluded from the domestic ETS. UK emissions have declined substantially since the beginning of the 1990s, mainly due to the 'dash for gas' in the power sector. Because of this historical 'lucky accident', the UK government has been able to put forward a more stringent domestic target of 20% reductions.

6 Denmark: long-term planning with different objectives

Poul Erik Grohnheit

Within the European context, the Danish electricity sector is small – accounting for only about 1.5% of European electricity production – but rich in experience that is important for this study. The long-term measures taken in Denmark over the last two or three decades, long before climate change became a political issue, could make a substantial difference in tackling current address issues of competition and climate change policy in the electricity sector.

The Danish power sector is heavily dependent on coal, with consequently high GHG emissions (see Figure 6.1). At the same time, emissions levels are moderated by the extremely high share of efficient CHP (see Figure 6.3), the favourable climate for biomass usage and Danish leadership in the market for wind power.

Two further issues make this case study of great importance. First, the Danish power sector has a significant role as swing producer in the Nordic

Figure 6.1: Fuel shares in Danish electricity production, 1999

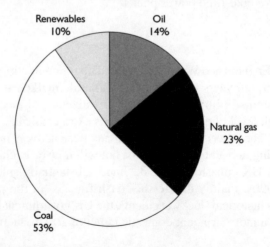

Source: Danish Energy Agency, *Energy Statistics 1999*; see www.ens.dk.

market, dominated by the hydro-based systems of Norway and Sweden. The emissions arising from the export of electricity now have to be accounted for under the Danish emissions target, within the framework of increased use of the common Nordic power exchange, Nord Pool. Second, the Danish CO_2 emissions trading law for the power sector has entered into force.

6.1 Organization of the industry

The electricity supply industry in Denmark has its origin in two separate traditions. In the towns, either the electricity supply was established by the municipality, or the privately owned electricity supply was taken over early in its development. In the countryside the electricity supply was established by consumer cooperatives. Since the Second World War the system has gradually become much more concentrated through mergers and co-operation. However, this centralization is still controlled from below; in 1995 the 103 distributing utilities owned the eight generating companies, co-operating in two regional associations that operate at either side of the Great Belt (the water separating the Danish mainland and the island Sjaelland on which Copenhagen is located). The organization of district heating at the local and regional levels is similar to that of the electric utilities; CHP for district heating is an integrated activity of the electricity utilities.[1]

During the current liberalization process, the two regional associations, previously known as Elsam and Elkraft, have been separated into companies responsible for transmission and system operation and companies responsible for commercial activities, and a similar separation between network and commercial activities has taken place in some distribution companies. However, the basic principles of ownership have remained unchanged.

6.2 Long-term energy policy

6.2.1 Energy policy after the first oil shock

At the time of the first oil shock in 1973, more than 90% of the Danish primary energy requirement was supplied by imported oil. The power generators had

---

[1] A more detailed description of the historical development of the energy sector in Denmark and the current liberalization process can be found in P. E. Grohnheit and O. J. Olsen, 'Denmark', in Gordon MacKerron and Luigi De Paoli (eds), *The Electricity Supply Industry of Europe: Organization, Regulation and Performance* (London: Earthscan, 2001).

also been increasing their dependence on oil. Most new power stations were built for oil combustion only, and they were often located away from heat demand. Until then the industry had resisted most attempts at state intervention.

In response to the oil crisis, the utilities changed the fuel mix dramatically, to a near-exclusive reliance on coal, within only a few years. Power stations under construction designed for oil were very quickly redesigned for coal, or rather dual coal–oil combustion, and several of the more modern power stations were converted from oil to coal.

In parallel with these industry activities a national energy policy review was initiated. A new electricity supply act was prepared and passed by parliament in 1976. This law provided the state with the powers to approve new large-scale power generation units. It was followed by reviews and energy plans from 1976 onwards. National energy policy and planning have remained high on the political agenda during the current process of liberalization.

Danish energy policy has had three main objectives:

1 security of supply;
2 economic efficiency; and
3 environmental protection.

The relative priority of these three objectives has changed over time. In the first energy plan (1976) security of supply had top priority, with the emphasis on substitution of other fuels for oil.[2] During the 1980s, after the diversification of energy supply and the exploitation of the Danish resources of oil and gas in the North Sea had gained momentum, priority shifted to environmental protection. This emphasis is clearly stated in the latter two energy plans (1990 and 1996).[3] Specific policies to promote economic efficiency have shifted over time from physical planning and infrastructure development in the mid-1990s to the current emphasis on competition and market organization.

Many other policy instruments have been introduced as means to address special interests or particular purposes. The promotion of natural gas combustion in the power stations, for example, supported the gas companies at a time when they were in financial trouble. Similarly, the combustion of straw in district heating boilers supports farmers, who have not been allowed to burn away the straw on the fields after harvest since the late 1980s.

---

[2] *Dansk Energipolitik 1976* (Copenhagen: Ministry of Commerce, 1976).
[3] *Energy 2000: A Plan of Action for a Sustainable Development* (Copenhagen: Ministry of Energy, 1990); *Energy 21* (Copenhagen: Ministry of Environment and Energy, 1996); see www-ens.dk.

Figure 6.2: Space heating demand in Denmark, 1972–1997

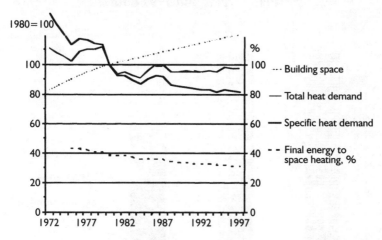

Source: Danish Energy Agency, *Energy Statistics 1999*; see www.ens.dk.

6.2.2 *The infrastructure for the space heating market*

In the mid-1970s the share of space heating in final energy demand was more than 40%. Space heating, therefore, was an obvious target for Danish energy policy from the start. Although there had been a significant development of district heating during the 1960s, these systems were supplied by heavy fuel oil in boilers, not efficient CHP. In some larger cities the district heating systems were interconnected systematically with heat supply from modern power stations. In central Copenhagen the larger district heating systems were supplied with steam from obsolete power stations.

Energy savings in buildings   Thermal insulation regulation was introduced in the building code in 1972. In the following years total heat demand was reduced by some 20% in spite of a significant increase in building space (see Figure 6.2). The most dramatic reduction came in the first period as consumers responded to the price increases of the oil shocks. This period saw little impact from technical improvement or targeted policy measures, but a significant reduction of comfort level and an increase in consumer awareness supported by public campaigns.

From 1980 onwards the impact of technological progress and a broad range of policy measures prevented specific heat demand, i.e. demand per unit of building area, from returning to the previous higher level and indeed

Figure 6.3: Space heating technologies in Denmark: 1981 Energy Plan targets and 1997 data

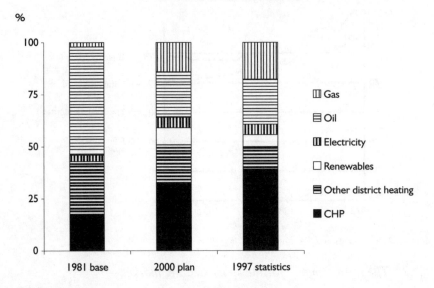

led to further reductions. During the 1990s the reduction has been more modest; nevertheless, over the 25-year period after 1972, specific heat demand was reduced by nearly 40%.

The most important instruments in bringing this about were stricter thermal insulation requirements in each new building code, taxes on delivered energy, and subsidies for energy savings targeting at both owner-occupied and ten-anted dwellings. New regulation was also introduced into the real estate market, requiring a declaration of heat expenditures in the sales contracts for owner-occupied dwellings. At the same time the trend to collective metering and billing of electricity and heat in multi-family houses was reversed.

Figure 6.3 compares the targets of the 1981 energy plan for the year 2000 with the 1997 statistics for the distribution of space heating technologies.[4] The figure shows that the penetration of both CHP and natural gas has already gone beyond the 1981 targets for 2000, leading to a further reduction of the demand for primary fuels. However, part of this gain in energy efficiency may have been achieved at the expense of economic efficiency.

---

[4] *Energiplan 81* (Copenhagen: Ministry of Energy, 1981).

Figure 6.4: Domestic supply of energy in Denmark, by type of production unit, 1999

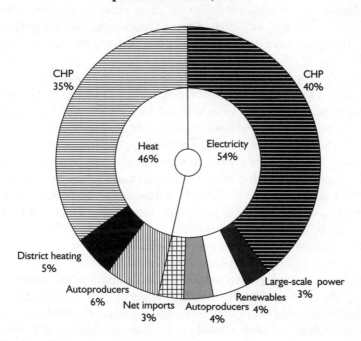

Source: Danish Energy Agency, *Energy Statistics 1999*; see www.ens.dk.

Heat planning with CHP and natural gas   On the supply side for space heating, CHP for district heating is an integral activity of the electricity utilities. A large share of the total electricity demand in Denmark is supplied by CHP, and district heating from all sources covers about half of the market for space heating and hot water. Nearly all the large Danish power stations now have heat extraction facilities with connections to large urban district heating grids. On the other hand, auto-producers of electricity and steam for industrial processes have never had a significant share of the market. Figure 6.4 gives an overview of the market share of production technologies supplying heat and electricity in Denmark.

Historically, Danish CHP production started early in the twentieth century, when waste heat from power stations was supplied to buildings in the immediate neighbourhood. In the 1950s and 1960s there was a shift away from solid fuels for both domestic heating and district heating systems. The preferred option was oil-fired boilers, but many cities and towns invested in district heating systems with a dual-fuel option of oil and solid urban waste. This infrastructure offered a very flexible response to the oil price shocks in the 1970s. Central boilers switched fuel to coal or gas, and many local district heating grids were connected to larger urban systems already supplied by CHP.

Outside the Copenhagen region, the municipal reform in 1970 had created municipalities that were consistent with the urban structure. In the medium-sized cities, such as Odense, local initiative had created large interconnected district heating systems by connecting many small district heating networks in the suburbs to the city network which was supplied from a large municipal power plant. Rivalry among cities of a similar size and competition among the utilities of different cities provided further incentives for innovative local initiatives and quick diffusion of new technologies. An additional motivation was the threat from the entry of natural gas technology, which was expected to be owned by the national government.

However, in the Copenhagen region several attempts during the last century to create a local governmental body failed, and the municipal rivalry within the urban region discouraged comprehensive urban and regional planning. Since the 1930s the suburban municipalities outside the city of Copenhagen had been very active in the development of centralized electricity supply, with large electricity-only power plants located away from urban areas – similar to the development in many other European countries. Even within the city of Copenhagen itself, little or no local effort was made to utilize the available opportunities for rational use of energy by CHP within the city limits. Consequently, the penetration of district heating in the Copenhagen region was substantially lower than in the other urban regions of Denmark.

National heat supply planning, introduced by the heat supply act of 1979, balanced centrally planned introduction of natural gas with incentives to expand local CHP systems. The impact of the latter was most significant in the Copenhagen region. By the mid-1980s the cross-harbour link for district heating in the city of Copenhagen was finished, and two inter-municipal companies were formed to handle the construction and operation of heat transmission grids. The interconnected district heating grid in the Copenhagen region is now one of the largest in western Europe, covering the suburban 'fingers' and satellite towns to the west and south within a distance of about 35km from the city centre.

Figure 6.5 shows the development of Danish electricity generation since the mid-1970s. The two main characteristics are the fluctuation in international

Figure 6.5: Danish electricity production and imports, 1975–1998

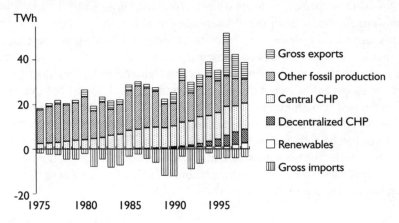

electricity trade and a steady increase in generation from large-scale and small-scale CHP, as discussed earlier, and – most recently – also from wind. The fluctuation in international electricity trade depends on the natural variations in precipitation and thus in hydropower generation in Norway and Sweden; in recent years these fluctuations have been substantial.

Development of natural gas and district heating grids   District heating and natural gas grids are competing in the market for space heating. However, important synergies can be found while developing the two types of grids. When natural gas was introduced in Denmark in the 1980s it was possible to build up a gas market without developing a costly distribution network to single-family houses or small housing units, because they were already connected in nearly all towns and larger villages. Often the natural gas grid connected the district heating plant, industry and buildings outside the district heating grids.

In the 1990s, when smaller CCGTs became available at competitive cost, it was easy to replace gas boilers with decentralized CHP units. Within a few years CCGT units of up to 100MW supplied a large share of the heat market in most mid-sized towns in Denmark; in many smaller grids gas motors were used. Biomass in the form of straw or animal waste was used where available.

Synergy of CHP and energy efficiency   It has been argued that a massive introduction of CHP, renewables and energy efficiency measures at the same time would give rise to conflicting effects and thus reduce the efficiency of these policy measures. Past experience does indeed show some Danish examples of such inconsistencies, but also shows how these instruments can be complementary or even synergetic.[5] Indeed, in the case of Denmark, the opportunities for synergy among the different measures during implementation are far more important than the risk of inconsistency. The development of new built-up areas and urban renewal, for example, offers the best opportunities for implementation of energy-saving technologies and district heating at the same time. However, the instruments by which such a synergy can be achieved are physical planning and appropriate regulation of property developments; national traditions influencing the application of these instruments vary widely across the EU, and there is little precedent for European harmonization of these markets.

6.2.3   The timing of energy taxes

Taxes on delivered energy – in particular on heating oil – have been very important in supporting the restructuring of the space heating sector in Denmark. The natural gas market in Denmark developed very quickly in the 1980s on the basis of supply from the oil and gas fields in the Danish sector of the North Sea. The gas tariffs were set on the basis of substitution pricing, i.e. the price of the substituted fuel including taxes.

When the price of imported oil fell drastically in 1986, it was met by increased taxation, which prevented the lower import prices from being transferred to consumers. An additional argument for the increase in taxes was that lower energy prices would lead to an undesirable macroeconomic expansion, which – most conveniently – could be neutralized by energy taxes.

Energy taxes in Denmark are generally high compared to other European countries. Several principles are applied. Fuels used for purposes other than power generation are taxed directly, whereas electricity is taxed at the point of consumption. Initially, only households and public institutions paid energy taxes, while business firms were exempted. Recently, energy taxes have been supplemented by 'green taxes', in particular for CO_2 emissions.

---

[5] The concern of the European Commission for such inconsistencies is reflected in the title of one of the volumes of the Shared Analysis Project; see P. E. Grohnheit, *Energy Policy Responses to the Climate Change Challenge: The Consistency of European CHP, Renewable and Energy Efficiency Policies*, The Shared Analysis Project, vol. 14; see www.shared-analysis.fhg.de/. Printed as Risø.R-1147(EN), Risø National Laboratory, Roskilde; see www.risoe.dk/rispubl/SYS/ris-r-1147.htm.

Businesses have also been exposed to the new green taxes, albeit at a lower rate than households.

6.3 Environmental considerations in energy policy

Total energy consumption has not increased in Denmark since 1972, which implies that energy intensity (energy consumption per unit of GDP) has decreased significantly during that period. The main explanation for this development is the massive introduction of CHP in heat supply and the reduction of heat consumption as a result of the insulation of buildings. However, Danish energy consumption causes relatively high emissions of CO_2 and NO_x, to which the electricity supply industry is a large contributor. SO_2 emissions have been reduced significantly.

6.3.1 New objectives for energy planning

The political objectives and instruments of Danish energy policy were presented in the two energy plans published by the government in 1990 (*Energy 2000*) and 1996 (*Energy 21*). The main goal is to secure sustainability of energy production and consumption under conditions of continued economic growth. Both plans also include national commitments to reduce CO_2 emissions by 20% in 2005 compared with the 1988 level. The 1996 plan contains stronger policy measures to reach this goal; it also outlines longer-term goals for 2030. In 2030, 35% of energy demand should be supplied by renewable energy sources; this target can be reached by an annual conversion of 1% of energy production from fossil fuels to renewables. However, the Kyoto Protocol and the European renewables directive set new targets for the energy sector.

Since the mid-1980s the two regional associations, Elsam and Elkraft, have been responsible for their emissions of SO_2 and NO_x. Maximum allowable quotas were fixed in accordance with international commitments and have been reduced over time. The industry can freely choose the instruments to meet the target: flue gas desulphurization equipment, low-NO_x burners, coal with lower sulphur content or fuel-switching. CO_2 quotas were introduced in 2000, but in compliance with the new market-based legislation these quotas can be traded as well as transferred from one year to another; more detail on the carbon market is given in section 6.6.

Integrated resource planning (IRP) was introduced by a new act of 1994. Elsam and Elkraft, were obliged to submit fifteen-year plans that specified how they intended to meet their obligations in environmental policy. It was stipulated that these plans should integrate construction of new plants with savings measures. However, the future of IRP is uncertain after the introduction of competition in the market for electricity.

Electric heating using simple resistance panels was attractive for developers of single-family houses, because the investment in the heating systems is very low. However, the technology is inconsistent with the energy policy objectives focusing on electricity savings and heat planning, and it has been discouraged by taxation on electricity. Also in the 1990s subsidies were introduced for conversion of electric heating to district heating or natural gas.

Agreements between government and industry, rather than legislation, have been very important instruments. The most recent energy plans, in particular, were implemented using agreements which include an obligation on the industry to construct small-scale CHP and wind turbines. Further incentives for renewables and cogeneration were provided by guaranteed prices for power sold to the grid: €0.01/kWh for gas-fired CHP; and €0.037/kWh for wind and biomass-fired CHP.

Several of these measures are inconsistent with the new competitive market and will be modified to meet the environmental targets. A green certificates system, for example, has been put in place for support of renewable energy.

6.3.2   The nuclear intermezzo

In the mid-1950s the Atomic Energy Commission and the Risø National Laboratory were established to look into the nuclear energy option. However, political and industrial support were not consistent. In the *Danish Energy Policy 1976* nuclear power was seen as an important option for substitution of oil and reduction of the heavy dependence on imports. As nuclear remained on the agenda, comparative studies of investment in nuclear energy instead of coal were published in 1976, 1981 and 1984.[6] These studies focused almost exclusively on costs: nuclear base load was cheaper then coal, given the fuel price forecasts of the early 1980s. However, the nuclear option was struck off the agenda in March 1985. Climate change did not become a political issue until the end of that decade.

---

[6] The utilities also studied the possibility of CHP supply from nuclear power plants to (future) interconnected regional district heating networks in Denmark and Sweden; see *Urban District Heating Using Nuclear Heat* (Vienna: International Atomic Energy Agency, 1977), proceedings of an IAEA Advisory Group Meeting, Vienna, 15–19 March 1976, IAEA-AG-62/3.

6.3.3 Accelerated penetration of wind power

Many energy policy programmes have been implemented during the last few decades to address environmental concerns, for example:

* the 100MW wind power programme (1985);
* the 450MW small-scale CHP programme (1986);
* a new 100MW wind power programme (1990);
* a new small-scale CHP programme (1990);
* the biomass-for-power programme (1993);
* the 200MW wind power programme (1996); and
* the 750MW offshore wind power programme (1998).[7]

The impacts of these programmes can clearly be seen in Figure 6.5; however, the penetration of biomass is behind schedule and wind is ahead of schedule.

The government's *Energy Plan 1981* proposed 60,000 small wind turbines and 5,000 biogas installations, which together would cover some 10% of electricity consumption by the end of the century. By 1997 wind power alone had penetrated about 6% of the Danish electricity market. The number of wind turbines was under 5,000, with an installed capacity at 1,100MW, but the size of new wind turbines has increased significantly (from an average of 100kW in the mid-1980s to 700kW in the late 1990s), and is still increasing. Development over the most recent years has been even faster; in 2000 the installed capacity had more than doubled to 2,300MW, and the leading turbine manufacturers (dominated by Danish firms) have launched commercial wind turbines of 1.5MW and more.

The system consequences of large-scale utilization of (intermittent) renewables, as targeted by the energy plan, amounting to 17TWh by 2030, nearly 50% of the total market today (35TWh), were studied in 1998.[8] The study analyses both the technologies and the market instruments necessary to regulate a fluctuating electricity generation of that magnitude.

Hydropower in the neighbouring regions offers a significant regulation capability, but some of the power-regulating capability will be available locally in the form of flexible CHP systems with heat storage and heat pumps.

---

[7] Sigurd Lauge Pedersen, 'The Danish CO_2 Emissions Trading System', *Review of European Community and International Environmental Law (RECIEL)*, vol. 9, no. 3 (2000).

[8] L. H. Nielsen and P. E. Morthorst (eds), *Fluktuerende vedvarende energi i el- og varmeforsyningen – det mellemlange sigt* (Roskilde: Risø.R-1055(DA), Risø National Laboratory, 1998); see www.risoe.dk/rispubl/SYS/ris-r-1055.htm.

Europe-wide introduction of wind power, covering different weather zones, will reduce the need for back-up power, provided that there is a reliable international trading mechanism. However, long-distance transmission of wind-generated electricity will not be able to respond to very short-term fluctuations. Load management options related to electric vehicles were analysed.

The target for wind power from the energy plan from was seen as radical when published. However, this target could soon become rather modest as a result of the ongoing development in wind turbine technology, transmission and regulation technology, the development of a European electricity market, and the European renewables directive.

Wind power development started with small-scale auto-producers and was followed by the utilities under agreements with the government for further development of wind power, mainly by offshore wind farms at the best locations for both wind resources and the electricity grid. There has been a very fruitful interaction between research and the industry, developing into a substantial export industry with a large share of the world market during the late 1980s and early 1990s. Research in wind power was started in the mid-1970s at Risø National Laboratory as a combination of initiative from individuals and spin-offs of nuclear research, in particular meteorology and materials research.[9]

6.3.4   Efficiency gains for coal-fired electricity

The attitude towards coal in Danish energy policy has been ambiguous and has shifted over the years. The *Energy Plan 1981* supported the shift from oil to coal for large-scale installations suitable for the application of advanced emissions abatement technology, and for smaller-scale plants for CHP in medium-sized towns and small and medium-sized boilers producing district heating or industrial steam. However, the current energy plan (from 1996) sets a target of a total phase-out of coal during the next twenty years.

Despite this shift in energy policy objectives, the utilities have consistently improved the efficiency of coal use for power generation. Over the last thirty years a series of medium-sized (250–350MW) extraction–condensing power stations has been built to supply the large, interconnected district heating

---

[9] H. Nielsen, K. Nielsen, F. Petersen and H. S. Jensen (eds), *Til samfundets gavn – Forskningscenter Risøs historie* (The history of Risø National Laboratory) (Roskilde: Risø National Laboratory, 1998).

grids in Copenhagen and five other city regions. The result of this policy has been that the base load of heat and power in all the CHP regions is generated by power stations of an appropriate scale and the newest possible vintage. There has been a consistent gain in thermal efficiency for each new power station. In the early 1970s the thermal efficiency of (electricity-only) generation from a series of 250MW stations was 39%; this was gradually increased to 47% by the commissioning of eight new power stations up to and including the last coal-fired unit, Nordjyllandværket.[10] (The last two units are steam turbines, which are designed for coal, but obliged to use gas in compliance with the current energy and environment policy). Thermal efficiency may reach 51% during the next decade, but much higher efficiencies can be reached only by using a new line of nickel-based material. This led to the start of a large European research project on 'The Advanced (700°C) PF Power Plant', led by a Danish engineering consultancy, Elsamprojekt (now Techwise). The EU-funded project, with forty participants from the European power industry, aims to reach an efficiency of 55% by increasing the steam temperature to 700°C.[11]

The phase-out of coal, substituted by gas, will lead to reductions in CO_2 emissions in compliance with the existing Kyoto targets and expected post-Kyoto targets. However, CO_2 emissions from natural gas combustion are still more than half those from coal, and gas is assumed to be more exposed to the risk of price increase than coal. The same emissions reduction target, therefore, may be achieved at the same price by a combination of advanced coal power stations and increased used of wind power.

At the global level, coal will remain the most important fuel for electricity generation for the foreseeable future. Thus efficient use of coal may have far more impact on global CO_2 emissions than the penetration of non-coal technologies. Additionally, coal technology is well suited for cofiring with biomass, which happens in many plants in Denmark, reducing emissions from these plants and making biomass use cheaper and easier.

6.4   The Nordic hydrothermal electricity market

The Danish electricity system is located in and between the hydropower-based market in the north and the thermal system in western Europe. (Mainland)

---

[10] These efficiencies apply to seawater-cooled power plants, wet cooling towers reduce net efficiency by 1–1.5%.

[11] For more details see www.techwise.dk.

Denmark is connected directly to the German electricity grid, and trades are taking place. Denmark is also connected to the Nordic market. In the four Nordic countries – Norway, Sweden, Finland and Denmark – hydropower covers more than half of total demand.

The total capacity of the interconnections is 3GW between Denmark and the other Nordic countries and 2GW between Denmark and Germany. Until the mid-1990s there were large transmission capacities connecting the Nordic countries, but very limited capacities connecting the Nordic countries with the rest of Europe. This situation is now changing: two 600MW high voltage direct current (HVDC) cables,[12] Baltic and Kontek, were commissioned around 1995, connecting Denmark and Sweden with Germany. Further cables are being constructed or planned between Sweden and Poland and across the North Sea from Norway to Germany and the Netherlands.

The hydro-based systems of Norway and Sweden offer very large capacity for diurnal and seasonal storage. However, the inflow of water varies significantly from year to year, impacting greatly on power production availability from year to year. The reservoirs can be used for peak production for the whole electricity system when rainfall has been plentiful, but the available thermal capacity (mainly in Denmark and Finland) will need to meet demand in these systems in dry years. Since the 1960s the Nordic countries have exploited this possibility through Nordel, the Nordic grid.

The natural variation in hydropower production in Norway and Sweden leads to very significant fluctuations in imports and exports for Denmark. In the very wet years 1989 and 1990 imports accounted for some 40% of Danish consumption; in the very dry year 1996 gross exports from Denmark exceeded 50% of national electricity demand. In most other years in the past decade there has been a small net export of electricity from Denmark (see Figure 6.5).

6.4.1   The organization of the Nordic electricity market

Before the liberalization of the electricity sector in Norway and Sweden in the early 1990s, trade between the Nordel countries was based on bilateral agreements on a split savings price principle, i.e. splitting the difference between known and agreed short-term marginal costs between the parties.

---

[12] HVDC cables are used to link different systems and can potentially carry large capacities. These cables do not require a complete harmonization of the two linked systems, as AC cables do. The west European and Nordic electricity systems, therefore, are still operating independently.

After liberalization, the power pool became the pricing mechanism for these international exchanges of power.

A short-term power market has been in operation in Norway since 1971. After liberalization, Stattnett Marked, the Norwegian power exchange, became the main price-setting mechanism. Then, in 1996, a common Norwegian–Swedish electricity exchange, Nord Pool, was formed by the two state-owned grid companies, and it became possible for power companies in neighbouring countries to trade in the pool. Nord Pool consists of a day-ahead spot market and a futures market covering the following three years. Finland's electricity exchange started in the same year, but was merged with Nord Pool in 1998. Elsam and Elkraft, the two main Danish companies, have traded in the Nord Pool from the start. Parallel markets for forward trading have been established by power brokers. Both the eastern and western parts of Denmark are now separate pricing areas within the Nord Pool.

Traditionally, electricity prices in Norway and Sweden have been much lower than in Denmark, and electricity demand per capita was twice or three times larger than in western Europe. A price rise, or increased energy efficiency in the northern European market, could lead to a significant reduction in CO_2 emissions through additional supply of hydropower to Denmark and into western Europe.

6.4.2 The new electricity act

The markets of Norway, Sweden and Finland are protected from competition by their geographical position and the existing infrastructure, in particular the limited interconnection with other systems. The Danish electricity market, however, is more open to international competition, with ample interconnection capacity to both Germany and Scandinavia. The pressure for liberalization coming from the Nordic market was therefore met with reluctance in the mid-1990s in Denmark. Despite a preference for the (slow) pace of Brussels rather than the speed of the other Nordic countries, the urgency of amending the 1976 Danish electricity act became apparent in 1996. The amendment was prepared hurriedly, and passed through parliament without time for thorough scrutiny.

Although it anticipated most of the provisions of the European electricity directive, which was passed later the same year, the amendment of the old electricity act was soon followed by an initiative to prepare a major reform of the energy sector. The objective of this reform was to combine Danish environmental and energy policies and the requirements of the energy market directives. Support for renewables and for small-scale CHP was to become a key issue in the review.

The work was concluded with a political agreement in March 1999; the new electricity supply act was put before parliament in April and passed in May 1999. The new law will come into force gradually, after the final decisions on matters such as the appointment of the regulator by the minister of environment and energy, and is to be fully implemented (full market opening) by 2003. It is accompanied by several bills on specific issues such as emissions, taxation and renewables support, and contains the following provisions:

- full (mandatory) third party access;
- an obligatory separation of monopoly activities (such as system operation, and the operation of transmission and distribution networks) and competitive activities (such as generation and supply) into independent companies;
- the introduction of an independent regulator;
- a temporary continuation of the present protection of renewables and local CHP by guaranteed prices and subsidies (the latter will no longer be financed by the taxpayers, but funded by a mark-up on the network tariffs); with respect to new renewable plant, the intention was to substitute the guaranteed prices by a market for 'green certificates', and indeed, this has now been agreed; see section 6.6.

The new electricity law redefines the organization of the electricity supply industry, and specifies which type of company is allowed to participate in which activity. The basic principle is a clear separation of monopolistic activities from companies in the competitive market. An additional principle is a continuation of the direct consumer influence in consumer cooperatives and municipal companies. The following types of companies are specified in the new act:

- *Generation, trade* and *supply* of power are free activities, in which any company can take part.
- *Grid* companies are responsible for operating the transmission and distribution grids. These activities require a licence from the minister of environment and energy, which is issued for a period of at least twenty years. Generation and trade companies are not allowed to own a distribution network. A licence will be given only to companies that have a majority of consumer representatives on their governing bodies.

- *Supply obligation* companies have the responsibility to cover the demand of the captive customers, i.e. those that are not yet eligible for third-party access or have chosen to continue to be supplied with regulated tariffs (this market will cease to exist in 2003, when the market is fully opened). The ministry of environment and energy issues licences for these activities. One-third of the board members of these supply obligation companies must be elected by consumers.
- The *system operator* is responsible for the transmission and overall system operation. This must be an independent company with state representatives on its governing bodies. It needs a licence from the ministry, which is granted for a period of at least twenty years. One of the duties of the system operator is to give priority to generators using renewable energy sources, waste or CHP.

6.4.3 Regulation

Regulation of the electricity sector is divided between the ministry of environment and energy, and the competition authorities. The ministry regulates energy and environmental policy, including the approval of new plants and licences for distribution. The competition authorities regulate tariffs and trade. Since the late 1970s energy policy has been a priority area, and the parliament's permanent energy committee has actively participated in decisions on energy policy issues.

In the framework of physical planning, local governments have substantial influence concerning the approval of new plants and other facilities. Local government, acting through its association, which also represents a large number of utilities owned by municipalities, is an important actor in Danish politics, in particular in the preparation of legislation. It is also traditional for business associations to participate in the making and implementation of policy. The electricity industry, for example, was represented on the Electricity Price Commission. However, the new electricity supply act is breaking with this tradition by introducing an independent Energy Supervisory Board, which will regulate tariffs and access rules for monopoly activities. Electricity trade and electricity generation (excepting those generators eligible for priority according to a public service obligation) will be regulated by the Competition Agency according to the competition act.

6.5   Planning failures: too much, too fast

Long-term energy planning since the 1970s in Denmark has been successful in creating both an infrastructure for a liberalized energy market and instruments for an effective climate change policy. However, there is also a long list of failures from which lessons may be drawn.

The large-scale introduction of different policy measures all with the same general aim could raise legitimate concern. The benefits of one policy, or the efficiency of a measure, could be offset by contradictory results of another policy or measure. The introduction of CHP, renewables and energy efficiency simultaneously, as in Denmark, could indeed reduce the effectiveness of the individual policies. The benefits of massive investment to reduce the space-heating demand, for example, could be small or negligible in buildings connected to district heating grids supplied by surplus heat from waste incineration or industry, or even efficient coal-fired CHP. This particular issue was indeed discussed in Denmark between the ministries of housing and energy during the preparation and implementation of the heat supply act in the early 1980s. However, the discussions never led to any explicit 'regionalization' of the energy conservation efforts; the economic advantage of saved investment did not outweigh the additional administrative burden. Planning failures are most likely to be found under the heading 'too much of the same thing too fast', of which numerous examples from the past may be cited.

In the 1960s, many towns introduced district heating systems at the same time. The speed of the introduction, unproven technology or shoddy construction work meant that many of the distribution networks were of poor quality. Consequently, some district heating grids were later completely refurbished, or given up when natural gas was introduced.

More recently, many small-scale gas-fired CHP schemes were introduced in Denmark over a short period. The CCGTs used were generally of the same vintage everywhere, and consequently could all be made obsolete by further technology development. Some new 'greenfield' district heating networks were developed in rural areas, where a surplus of biomass was available. However, at current prices for biomass and fossil fuels many of these systems have become far too expensive, even with subsidies.

The most likely candidate for a similar planning failure in the coming years is wind power. Expansion has been very fast in the last few years and is projected to continue at a similar speed in the coming years. However, much of this development is based on subsidies, which will be replaced in the near future with renewables obligations and other incentives.

6.6 Current issues: the development of green markets

The most important current issue in climate change policy in Denmark is the development of market-based instruments to support low-carbon or non-carbon technologies. It has been agreed that both tradable CO_2 permits and markets for 'green electricity' will be used.

6.6.1 Tradable CO_2 permits[13]

The new Danish electricity act of May 1999 introduced a CO_2 emissions cap on Danish electricity generators. The cap was set as a first step towards implementing the Kyoto Protocol, and meeting the Danish target of a 21% reduction in emissions. The CO_2 quota act was passed by parliament in June 1999. However, after some initial questions the European Commission approved the act only in April 2000; so, although the act originally included targets for the year 2000, implementation having been delayed by the Commission it entered into force only in January 2001.

The CO_2 quota act set targets to reduce emissions in 2003 by one-third compared with average emissions in 1994–8 (years in which emissions were particularly high due to high power exports). The emission caps were lowered by 1MtCO$_2$ each year from 2000 to 2003. Figure 6.6 shows the importance of Danish power sector emissions and the targets for 2000 to 2003. Although the act did not enter into force until eighteen months after its passage, the electricity companies had already reduced emissions to 3MtCO$_2$ below the indicative cap for 2000. Emissions caps for the years after 2003 have not been set.

The emissions trading system has been introduced unilaterally and is designed with a view to the current conditions for the electricity market in Denmark and the national commitments on CO_2 emissions. Because of the liberalized market in which the Danish power sector operates, the system includes a (low) price cap, which acts as a non-compliance penalty: DKK40 (€5.38) per tonne of CO_2 over the cap.

The level of the price cap is much lower than that considered in the Shared Analysis Project.[14] At the level of the price cap, production of electricity for the Nordic market in Danish coal-fired power plants is less attractive. According

---

[13] This sections also draws on Pedersen, 'The Danish CO_2 Emissions Trading System'.

[14] *The Shared Analysis Project: European Union Energy Outlook to 2020*, special issue of *Energy in Europe* (Brussels: European Commission, Directorate General for Energy, Nov. 1999); see www.shared-analysis.fhg.de/.

Figure 6.6: Danish emissions and power sector caps, 1990–2003

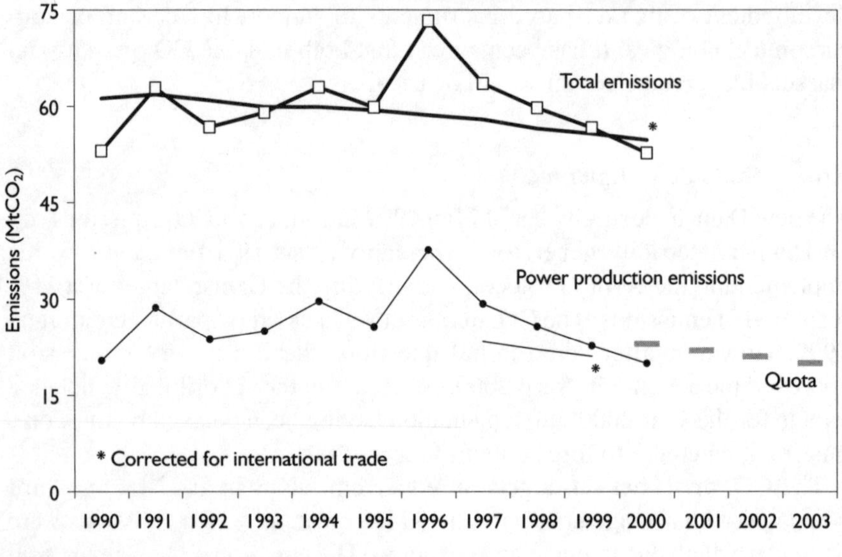

Source: Danish Energy Agency; see www.ens.dk.

Note: Emissions data for 2000 are provisional.

to some estimates, this CO_2 cap could reduce Danish electricity exports by as much as 50%. Indeed, the cheapest options for emissions reduction might well be the reduction of power exports, which were responsible for over $5MtCO_2$ of emissions in the period 1994–8.

A detailed study by the Danish energy research programme indicates that the introduction of the CO_2 caps could lead to a very rapid substitution of gas for coal, and penetration of some more carbon-efficient technologies.[15] However, the CO_2 permit system is not likely to be the major driver for new (renewable) technologies with no CO_2 emissions that face high investment costs. It is expected that the emission caps could be met at moderate costs (US$0–30/$tCO_2$).

The CO_2 emissions caps were 'grandfathered' to the existing power companies. However, as a result of consolidation in recent years, only two main

---

[15] S. Varming, P. B. Eriksen, P. E. Grohnheit, L. Nielsen, G. T. Svendsen and M. Vesterdal, *Tradable CO_2 Permits in Danish and European Energy Policy*, Risø.R-1184(EN) (Roskilde: Risø National Laboratory, 2000); see www.risoe.dk/rispubl/SYS/ris-r-1184.htm.

Figure 6.7: Danish emissions and distribution of emissions quotas, 2000–2003

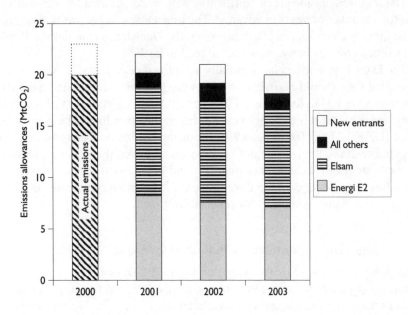

Source: Danish Energy Agency; see www.ens.dk.

players in the Danish market remain. The limited number of market players, and the relatively small size of the market, will reduce the liquidity of the market. Indeed, no trades have been recorded in the first few months of trading. Figure 6.7 shows the distribution of the emissions quota between the existing players, and possible new entrants. It also shows the provisional estimate of emissions in 2000.

6.6.2   Green certificates

The new electricity act also introduced a system of tradable certificates for renewables to replace the current subsidies and guaranteed prices.

All consumers of electricity in Denmark must purchase a certain share of their electricity from certified generators that use renewable energy technologies. Generators of renewable energy, i.e. wind power, biomass, photovoltaics, geothermal and small hydro plants, will receive a green certificate per unit of electricity generated. These certificates can be sold to distribution companies or other electricity consumers, who can meet their 'renewables obligation' in this way.

The requirement for green certificates will be determined by the authorities for a number of years in advance. The renewables target was initially set to be 20% of electricity in 2010; however, the Danish target under the European renewables directive was later agreed to be 29%.

The Danish authorities have initially set a fixed price range for the certificates, but they should be freely traded in the long run. On the one hand the minimum price (DKK0.10 or €0.013 per kWh) guarantees a minimum income for the renewable energy generators; on the other hand, the maximum price (DKK0.27 or €0.036 per kWh) limits the burden on the consumers. In September 2000, the European Commission approved the gradual phase-in of the system of renewables obligations and green certificates.[16] However, there have been delays in the development of the green certificates market, leading to a hiatus in support for renewables.[17]

6.7 Long-term commitment with limited foresight

This analysis of the climate change policy in the Danish electricity sector illustrates a paradox. Long-term commitments designed for purposes other than climate change mitigation have been the most effective measures in reducing emissions. There is no such thing as perfect foresight, but a long-term commitment to a broader set of objectives will be necessary to meet the specific targets that will emerge in the future.

Within a time horizon of several decades, political issues shift, fuel prices may go up and down, the structure of the main industries will change, and the positions of political parties and institutions may be turned upside down. However, climate change measures can be effective only over a period of several decades, which will require consistent long-term efforts.

Long-term efforts leading to development of infrastructure and restructuring of industries are required to achieve the goals of the climate change convention. The liberalization of the power sector and the introduction of emissions quotas and renewables obligations represent the next steps in long-term development. However, initial targets are likely to change substantially during the decades of their implementation.

---

[16] European Commission press release, 'Commission Approves State Aid in Connection with Electricity Reform in Denmark', IP/00/1027 (Brussels, 20 Sept. 2000).
[17] Gordon Edge, personal communication.

7 France: focus on non-fossil fuels

Christophe de Gouvello

The French electricity sector is of great importance within Europe. France lies at the centre of the market, with ample transmission capacity covering seven different countries. EdF, the French power company, has also been an active power exporter in the last decades before liberalization.

The French system is heavily based on nuclear power, and therefore has very low carbon emissions. Consequently, the emissions reduction options are limited domestically, but are substantial in respect of large exports of electricity elsewhere.

Reluctantly, the French vertically integrated monopoly system is now slowly being opened up for competition at the minimum level required in the EU directive. This raises a few issues for European climate policy, such as the continuation of carbon-free French electricity exports, and the survival of nuclear capacity in the liberalized market.

7.1 The current legal structure of the French electricity sector

The French electricity sector differs from that of most other industrialized countries, since it remains largely a public monopolistic structure. In 1946, just after the Second World War, the French government decided upon the creation of Electricité de France, a national vertically integrated public company.[1] Its main objective at that time was the reconstruction of the French electricity system. Since its foundation, EdF has benefited from a quasi-monopoly of generation, transmission and distribution of electricity in metropolitan and overseas territories.

A new law adopted in April 2000 by the French parliament separated EdF into three legally distinct entities: EdF Production; GRT, in charge of technical dispatching and transport grid management; and EdF Services, in charge of distribution activities.[2] With increased liberalization, power generation and trading in the wholesale market are no longer monopoly activities.

---

[1] Law No. 46-628 of 8 April 1946 on Nationalisation of Electricity and Gas.
[2] Law No. 2000-108, adopted 10 Feb. 2000.

On the other hand, the law confirmed the legal monopoly of EdF on transport and distribution to consumers not eligible for free choice of supplier. The final consumer market remains largely captive and supplied by EdF: the French have implemented only the minimum requirements of the European electricity directive. At present, only the largest consumers with an annual consumption over 40GWh have access to the free electricity market; this category includes only 440 consumers, or 26.4% of the national demand. The eligibility criteria will be lowered following the requirements of the directive.

In 1999, just before the adoption of the new law, EdF contributed 94% of national electricity production. The remaining 6% were produced by thermal and hydropower plants belonging to the national coal company, the national railways company (SNCF) and the municipalities.

In 2000, the electricity regulator, the Commission de Régulation de l'Electricité, was set up. However, the price of electricity for non-eligible consumers remains in the hands of the government. While prices on the free market are unregulated, government has set equalized prices on a national basis, including the overseas territories, for all non-eligible consumers.

In practice, there are some exceptions to the EdF monopoly on distribution that have been maintained by the new law and have introduced a degree of complication into the new institutional framework. Some municipalities own their own local distribution company: these distribution companies are legally not eligible to participate in the free market, but can purchase power directly on the free market on behalf of customers that are eligible. Almost all rural grids, serving more than 8 million rural consumers out of the national total of 30 million, belong to local authorities.

Two funds that already existed under the EdF monopoly have been maintained – the equalization fund and the depreciation fund – and one new fund has been created:

- The equalization fund, Fond de Péréquation de l'Electricité (FPE), gives financial compensation to distribution companies serving non-eligible users, to achieve equalization of prices for customers across France and the overseas regions. Before the opening of the market, the FPE was used to transfer only a very limited amount of money, just over €3m. Most cross-subsidies between final consumer groups (urban, rural, overseas territories) were achieved internally in EdF or through special rebates negotiated directly between EdF and the local distribution companies, probably reaching the tens of millions of euros.

- The depreciation fund, Fond d'Amortissement des Charges de l'Electrification (FACE), helps with financial depreciation of new investments in
  low-voltage rural grids. The FACE's turnover is currently over €300m.[3]
- The new electricity law has created an additional social tariff to address
  the problem of poor users.

All these redistributive mechanisms concern captive consumers only, and
are based on the integrated distribution revenues that include the tariffs for
energy and transport at low voltage.

To date, French market opening is limited and the essence of the French
public service approach to electricity remains unchanged. However, were
eligibility criteria to be widened, the basic republican principles that continue to define the philosophy of the French public service – in this case,
equity among French citizens regarding access to electricity – would be
challenged. A more radical reform of the institutional framework would then
be needed.

7.2 The current structure of power production and electricity demand

In 1999, the national production of electricity was nearly 500TWh. Figure 7.1
shows the breakdown of production sources. Three-quarters of production is
from nuclear power plants, 14% from hydropower, and only 10% from conventional fossil-fuel plants.

There is currently an overcapacity of installed power generation that
allows net exports of 64TWh a year (around 13% of total production), mainly
directed to the UK (15TWh), Italy (15TWh), Germany (7TWh) and Spain
(7TWh).

7.2.1 The current structure of electricity demand

The structure of electricity demand is characterized by a high share of the
residential sector (see Table 7.1). This is the result of the combination of
aggressive marketing by EdF in the 1970s and 1980s, and demand incentive from price equalization in the whole French national territory.[4] In
previous decades EdF was looking for rapid demand growth that would

---

[3] C. de Gouvello, 'Public Services, Equity and Innovation: Some Lessons from the
French Rural Electrification Regime', *Energy Studies Review*, vol. 8, no. 1 (1996), p. 13.
[4] Ibid.

Figure 7.1: Fuel shares in French electricity production, 1999

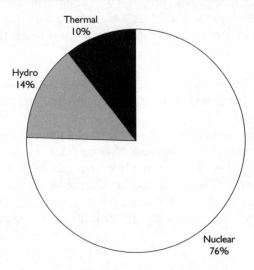

Source: Electricité de France, *Bilan Environnement 1999* (Paris: EDF, 2000).

Table 7.1: Structure of French electricity demand by sector

	Electricity share in sectoral energy consumption, 1999 (%)	Structure of electricity demand, 1997 (5%)	Consumption of sector, 1997 (TWh)
Residential	53.3	35.7	124.6
Industry	53.1	37.8	132.1
Services	67.0	26.5	92.4
Transport	4.3		
Total		100	350

Sources: 1997 data: DGEMP-MEFI, *Observatoire de l'Energie* (Paris: Ministry of Economy, Finance and Industry, 1999); 1999 data: DGEMP-MEFI, *Rapport 1999 de la DGEMP* (Paris: Ministry of Economy, Finance and Industry, 2000).

yield economies of scale in the development and maintenance of the nuclear power programme.[5]

---

[5] J. C. Hourcade, 'Calcul économique et construction sociale des irréversibilités: leçons de l'histoire énergétique récente', in *Les Figures de l'irréversibilité en économie* (Paris, Editions de l'EHESS, 1991), pp. 279–310.

Figure 7.2: Final uses of electricity in residential consumption in France, 1997

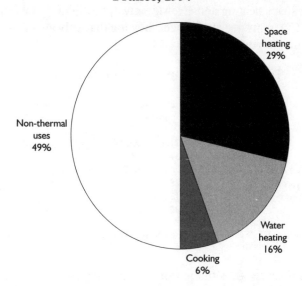

Space heating 29%

Non-thermal uses 49%

Water heating 16%

Cooking 6%

Source: DGEMP-MEFI, *Observatoire de l'Energie* (Paris: Ministry of Economy, Finance and Industry, 1999).

The large demand for electricity in the domestic sector is mainly due to the high penetration of electrical space heating, sanitary water heating and electrical cooking; Figure 7.2 shows detailed shares of residential consumption of electricity. To date more than 30% of residences and more than 20% of service buildings use electrical space heating. Because space cooling is not yet widespread in France, the national load curve is subject to very important seasonal variations, with a distinctive winter peak.

7.2.2   Greenhouse gas emissions from the French power sector

The share of power sector GHG emissions is very low in France, because of the very significant shares of nuclear and hydroelectricity. Only 10.5% of electricity is produced by conventional thermal power plants. Consequently, the carbon content of electricity is much lower than in other European countries: 20gC/kWh in France, against 120gC/kWh on average in Europe. Over 60% of the thermal capacity in France is fuelled by coal; fuel oil accounts for 15%, and natural and industrial gas together for about 20%.

The high penetration of electricity also reduces emissions from the residential and to a certain extent the transport sector, because of the importance of electrical space heating and electric railways in France. Table 7.2 details the sectoral CO_2 emissions in France, showing that only about 12% of emissions are from the power sector.

Table 7.2: CO_2 emissions in France, 1997

Sector	Emissions MtCe		Absorption
Industry	27.4	20.7	
Transport	37.7	28.4	
Residential and services	26.5	20.0	
Agriculture and forest	25.5	19.2	−43
Electricity production	15.5	11.7	
Total	132.6	100	89.6

Source: Interministerial Task Force on Climate Change, *National Programme for Tackling Climate Change* (Paris: ITFCC, 2000).

This quite idiosyncratic situation of the French power sector and overall energy use contributed to the current level of commitment agreed by France under the Kyoto Protocol. Whereas the EU as a whole has committed itself to an 8% reduction over the 2008–12 commitment period, in the burden-sharing agreement France committed itself to returning its emissions to the 1990 level of 144MtCe (528MtCO$_2$e). In 1990, electricity sector emissions were 42.4MtCO$_2$/year (11.6 MtCe/year); by 1999, they had risen to 49MtCO$_2$ (13.4 MtCe). Figure 7.3 shows the development and share of the energy sector in French GHG emissions.

7.2.3   The carbon content of exports

In 1999, electricity exports from France to other European countries were roughly 64TWh, about 13% of national production. In total, 52TWh of electricity was produced using conventional thermal plants.

Considering the load curve regularity of these exports and the present CO_2 content of electricity produced in France and in the European importers, it is possible to calculate the impacts of these electricity trades for the different parties. Table 7.3 shows that the exports have increased French emissions by over 4.5MtCO$_2$ annually, but reduced emissions in the importing countries by over 30MtCO$_2$, saving about 27MtCO$_2$ a year compared with a situation

Figure 7.3: French greenhouse gas emissions, 1990–1999

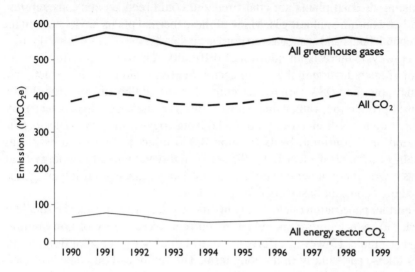

Source: European Environment Agency, EU emissions inventory; see www.eea.org.

without French exports.[6] If these emissions saving could be used to meet the Kyoto target, virtually no other measurers would need to be taken in France. Indeed, this situation highlights the importance of the interaction between the unified European electricity market and the future European emissions trading mechanism.

Table 7.3: Impact in terms of CO_2 of French electricity exports in EU

TWh	$MtCO_2$/year	
	for France	for European importers
63.7	+4.6	−31.3

7.3 The role of electricity in reducing emissions

7.3.1 Introduction

Because the share of the power sector in GHG emissions is quite low in France, the sector plays only a minor role in the national programme for tackling climate change.

---

[6] EDF, *Rapport Annuel 1999*.

The main potential for emissions savings comes from fuel-switching. Most existing thermal plants are coal-fired and could reduce emissions substantially by burning natural gas. Many of these thermal plants are located on the French islands and overseas territories.

However, there is an additional difficulty regarding opportunities for emissions reduction in the power sector. Fuel-switching, the introduction of renewables and DSM will reduce emissions only if they displace fossil-fuel-based production, rather than substituting for nuclear or hydroelectricity. Three-quarters of electricity produced from cogeneration in France is generated on a continual basis (around 8,000 hours per year), substituting mainly for nuclear electricity. Similarly, the development of energy from waste would not generate significant emissions reductions if it were generated on a constant basis, displacing nuclear.

Further penetration of electricity in different sectors could also be sought in order to reduce emissions, given the current overcapacity of non-emitting power plants. However, efforts to control electricity consumption are not worthless, particularly in the long term. The future carbon content of electricity and overall emissions will depend on both the future of nuclear production and the increasing share of thermal power capacity.

France has successively drawn up several national programmes to combat the greenhouse effect. In 1995, an initial programme to prevent climate change was published in the first national communication to the FCCC. In 1997, a second plan was drawn up and presented in the second national communication to the FCCC. Both of these programmes contain measures aimed at controlling GHG emissions from the power sector at both production and consumption levels.

The new commitments accepted by France in Kyoto have necessitated reassessment of the measures to be adopted to limit national emissions and comply with the new target. The existing measures adopted before Kyoto will be insufficient to bring emissions down to the level stipulated to 2008–12, namely a return to 1990 emissions levels. Therefore the Interministerial Task Force on Climate Change (ITFCC) elaborated a national programme for tackling climate change, which was adopted and published in April 2000. This programme is discussed in more detail in section 7.4.

7.3.2   Pre-Kyoto measures

A number of measures aimed at reducing the GHG emissions of the power sector had already been adopted before COP-3:

- *Nuclear:* Investment in an additional 13,600MW of nuclear power for the 1990–2000 period.
- *Cogeneration:* An objective of an additional 4GW was set for the period 1995–2010, compared with the 3.2GW already installed in 1994. This development is made possible thanks to a regulation that obliges EdF to buy freely the electricity generated by installations smaller than 8MW. Above this threshold, ministerial authorization is needed. However, the ministry of industry has committed itself to agree on 1GW cumulatively of such projects by 2000.
- *Wind:* The 'Eole 2005' plan was set up to install a production capacity of 250–500MW by 2005.
- *DSM:* A 'time of use' tariff and other DSM measures were introduced to reduce the peaks in the load curve, in particular the winter peak when conventional thermal plants are required to cover demand. The special tariff and other DSM measures are expected to reduce emissions by 0.5MtCe each annually by 2010.
- *Waste:* The incineration capacity for household industrial waste would be doubled. An additional GHG emissions reduction associated with energy from waste is in the order of 0.25MtCe/year.
- *Price:* A special budget line was established within the existing financial mechanism for rural grid development, with a specific annual budget of €15m (FF100m) since 1995, to counteract the adverse effects of price equalization in the French overseas departments and territories, Corsica and sparsely populated metropolitan rural areas.
- *Electrical equipment:* The directives 92/75/CEE and 96/57/CEE have been implemented. These directives prescribe that energy efficiency labels must be shown, and prohibit the sale of inefficient fridges.

The second national communication forecasts that full implementation of these measures would lead to a reduced level of national emissions of 160MtCe in 2010, compared with 175MtCe without measures. With measures, emissions from the electricity sector would rise from 10.6MtCe/year in 1990 to 11.6MtCe/year in 2010. This is due mainly to the increasing share of conventional thermal electricity, rising from 11.5% in 1990 to 14% in 2010.

7.4   Post-Kyoto measures: the national programme 2000–2010[7]

The measures taken before Kyoto reduce projected emissions substantially. However, the agreed Kyoto target is still lower than these measures are projected to achieve, at 144MtCe. Therefore the National Programme for Tackling Climate Change (NPTCC) has been put together to set out the tools which the government needs to use to enable France to meet its commitment of limiting its emissions to 144MtCe by 2010.

The programme sets out the objective of avoiding the projected 2010 excess emissions of 16MtCe. Through a raft of measures, the programme would allow France to meet its Kyoto obligations domestically, without the use of international mechanisms. As a result of this programme, France might find itself in a position as neither purchaser nor seller of emissions permits. However, if the growth were to be different from the projected annual 2.2% – or indeed, the policies are less effective than anticipated – the programme must ensure the necessary adaptations, by means including that of buying emissions credits. With economic growth 0.6% higher than forecast, emissions are projected to reach 171MtCe in 2010, rather than the 160MtCe referred to earlier.

The French government aims to achieve the additional 16MtCe reduction by a combination of economic mechanisms and sectoral measures. The economic mechanism of choice is the carbon/energy tax. Price signals are also used in sectoral measures. The tax amplifies the effect of measures already taken, and it creates a new range of measures that were too costly initially, but seem more profitable in view of the new tax conditions. However, the price signal will deliver reductions only if mechanisms do indeed exist by which users can respond through reduced or more efficient energy use.

7.4.1   The carbon/energy tax

On 20 May 1999, the French government decided to extend the general tax on polluting activities (GTPA) to energy consumption. In order to maximize the impact of the GTPA the revenues will be fully recycled into the reduction of social security contributions on low wages.[8]

A carbon/energy tax could be applied both on energy production and at demand side in order to guide the technological choices at both ends of the

---

[7] *National Programme for Tackling Climate Change* (Paris: ITFCC, 2000).

[8] An analysis of this double dividend can be found in E. Fortin, 'Effets redistributifs d'une écotaxe: présentation et analyse des résultats du modèle IMACLIM' (Paris: CIRED, 1999).

Table 7.4: Summary of the measures in the *National Programme for Tackling Climate Change* (CO_2 emissions reduction, MtCe)

	1st category	Carbon tax	Long term	Total measures	Share (%)
Industry	1.12	2.3		3.42	21.4
Transport	1.15	1.1	1.75	4	25.0
Buildings	1.34	1.2	0.12	2.66	16.6
Agriculture	0.55	0.2	0	0.75	4.7
Waste	1.1			1.1	6.9
Refrigerant gases	1.05	0.4	0	1.45	9.1
Electricity sector[a]	0.73	1.5	0.4	2.63	16.4
Electricity measures as % of total	*4.6*	*9.4*	*2.5*	*16.4*	
Total	7.04	6.7	2.27	16.01	100.0

[a] Other energy products (gas, coal) are addressed through intermediary energy consumption taxation, and corresponding CO_2 emissions reductions are accounted for by sector.

Source: Interministerial Task Force on Climate Change, *National Programme for Tackling Climate Change* (Paris: ITFCC, 2000).

energy chain. However, on the basis of initial discussions, and in so far as voluntary GHG emissions control programmes will be implemented, the government retains the principle of exemption of certain uses of energy, in particular energy used for electricity production.[9]

Regarding electricity consumption, the government indicated in a memorandum on the community directive on taxation of energy products that it was in favour of dual taxation on electricity by adding a price signal according to the carbon content of fuel used by the producer,[10] as well as a non-carbon related tax on electricity to encourage moderation in electricity consumption. Such moderation is considered necessary over the long term to enable the sector to face any modification, whether voluntary or obligatory, in the future structure of French electricity generation.

Because of the (partial) exemption of electricity, the carbon/energy tax would bear more heavily on energy-intensive companies. Such a tax could thus hamper the competitiveness of some of these industries. The government is considering tax reductions for these firms. However, such reductions

---

[9] Coal and heavy-fuel-oil-based power plants would not benefit from this exemption. Energy could also be exempted when used for chemical reduction, in metallurgical and electrolysis processes, and as a raw material.

[10] Contribution from the French government on the draft directive for restructuring the European community taxation framework concerning energy products; memorandum of the French government, April 1999.

would reduce incentives to cut energy consumption. These industries, therefore, must negotiate and implement voluntary, quantified, measurable and sanctioned energy efficiency programmes in return for the tax cuts. According to the NPTCC document, these programmes could incorporate, when the time comes, the possibility for the industries concerned to take part in trading emissions credits, in return for emissions reduction objectives.

On the basis of forecasts from two different economic models,[11] the government has set the reference rate of taxation at €75.8/tCe (FF500) in 2010. In the shorter term, the tax will start in the range €22.7–30.3 (FF150–200). According to the models, a tax level between €75.8 and €90.0/tCe (FF500–600/tCe) would deliver over half the reduction effort in the electricity sector (see Table 7.4).

7.4.2   First category measures

Following on from the carbon/energy tax, a number of specific measures, called 'first category measures', have been adopted in the NPTCC. Around 100 different measures have been adopted, addressing all sectors. Eight main measures address the power sector directly, on either the supply side or the demand side. Table 7.5 displays these measures and their impacts.

Measures on the supply side   Three key measures are developed on the supply side of the electricity sector:

* replacing traditional coal and heavy-fuel-oil-based power stations with CCGTs and cogeneration (CHP);
* reducing energy use related to transmission, distribution and the nuclear fuel cycle;
* developing renewable energy sources.

❏   Fuel-switching: Most of the conventional thermal power plants that are projected still to be in use in 2010 are coal- and heavy-fuel-oil-fired plants built before 1980. A complete substitution of these plants by CCGT and CHP could potentially reduce emissions by 4MtCe/year (out of projected emissions of 7.5MtCe/year in 2010). The fuel substitution could be aided by the lifting of

---

[11] GEMINI-E3, a general equilibrium model developed by the French Ministry of public works, transport and housing (METL) and the Commission for Atomic Energy (CEA); and POLES, a partial equilibrium model of the world energy sector, developed by the Institute of Energy Policy and Economics (IEPE) at the University of Grenoble.

Table 7.5: NPTCC emissions reduction measures in electricity sector (MtCe)

	1st category	Carbon tax	Long term	Total measures	Share (%)
Replacement of the existing thermal energy base: gas combined cycle and cogeneration		1.5	0.4	1.9	72
Overseas territories NRE programme	0.13	–	–	0.13	5
Total measures on production	*0.13*	*1.5*	*0.4*	*2.03*	*77*
European directive on energy-saving equipment	0.35	–	–	0.35	13
Reduction of VAT on energy-saving products	0.25	–	–	0.25	10
Management of state buildings and collective lettings	–	–	–	0	0
Electricity saving in new buildings	–	–	–	0	0
Electricity saving in old buildings	–	–	–	0	0
Ecotax effect on electricity demand	–	–	–	0	0
Total measures on demand	*0.6*	*–*	*–*	*0.6*	*23*
Total electricity sector	*0.73*	*1.5*	*0.4*	*2.63*	*100*

Source: Interministerial Task Force on Climate Change, *National Programme for Tackling Climate Change* (Paris: ITFCC, 2000).

the minimum threshold of national production of coal by 2005. However, care is required because CHP would normally replace base-load nuclear production and therefore increase rather than reduce emissions.

The NPTCC aims to equalize the marginal costs of this policy of fuel-switching and plant replacement with the carbon/energy tax (€75.8/tCe, or FF500/tCe). At this marginal cost, the programme calculates that 1.5MtCe per year could be saved by replacing the existing plant. This measure could be achieved through an extension of the carbon/energy tax. Additionally, the NPTCC proposes that the electricity industry should be allowed to take part in trading of emission credits.

❑ Reducing energy losses: In 1997 the nuclear fuel cycle consumed around 17TWh, and grid losses amounted to 28.5TWh. Together, the energy use of the power sector amounts to nearly 10% of national production. No concrete measures to address these issues have been adopted, but the NPTCC proposes to examine – with EdF Production and the GRT – actions likely to reduce these energy losses in the future.

❑ Developing renewable energy: The national programme proposes a new objective of 3,000MW of wind power to be installed by 2010. The programme estimates the GHG saving from the additional wind power to be 0.4MtCe/year; however this level depends strongly on the production replaced (whether nuclear, hydro or fossil). The NPTCC projected emissions avoided at 0.05–0.15kgC/kWh in 2010. At the same date, the net additional cost of production (production cost minus avoided cost) is estimated to be around €0.014–0.018/kWh (FF0.09–0.12/kWh). Consequently, the corresponding cost of carbon would be €90–360/tCe (FF600–2,400/tCe), which is higher or substantially higher than the level of the carbon/energy tax proposed.

Specific instruments, on top of the tax, are desirable to develop wind energy production in France. To date, France has used a tender procedure (Eole 2005), which has the advantage of selecting projects closest to profitability, without allocating an excessive allowance to the more economical projects. However, in the context of opening up the electricity market, implementing the tender procedure may prove to be more difficult. According to the NPTCC, it could be replaced with the instrument of 'green certificates', which allows the criterion of economic efficiency to be satisfied. 'Green certificates' enable the least expensive technical solutions to be selected, whatever their geographical location. The implementation of such a scheme at the European level, as has now been agreed in the European renewables directive, could be particularly profitable because France has attractive sites for producing electricity from new and renewable energy (NRE). France could become an important supplier of green electricity for the European market.

In the French overseas departments and territories and on Corsica electricity is mainly produced with diesel generators. Therefore any additional development of renewable energy in these territories will result in reductions of CO_2 emissions independent of the production it is replacing (it will not replace nuclear). However, this market represents less than 1% of the national power production.

The objective set by the ADEME and presented in the NPTCC for the year 2010 is to reduce emissions in these territories by around 0.13MtCe/year in 2010, through the following measures:

• the installation of 80,000 square metres of solar collectors for domestic water heating;

- the electrification of 500 sites with small photovoltaic systems;
- the additional production of 600GWh/year from renewable energy sources (100MW wind, 50MW geothermal, 20MW small hydro);
- the development of biomass energy to the level of 10,000toe/year.

Measures on the demand side   Any DSM measure to reduce GHG emissions faces the same difficulty as renewable energy sources: only demand avoided in the winter peak when fossil-fuel plants are in operation reduces emissions.

DSM can be implemented in two different ways: first, by the energy sector itself, with or without government incentives; second, by government measures that change the behaviour of the final consumers. Traditionally DSM programmes were implemented by the distribution companies, which have easy and systematic contact with the final users. However, liberalization has made this more difficult: the costs and benefits from a DSM programme often fall to different players in the energy chain. Since vertical separation has cut the chain, this creates serious obstacles to exploitation of the DSM potentials.

As the main shareholder of EdF, as regulator and through its specialized public agency, ADEME, only the state can create incentives or constraints on both supply and demand sides to promote DSM. Two such measures are being taken forward:

1   substitution of electrical space heating;
2   promotion of highly efficient appliances.

❏   Electrical space heating: As the main EdF shareholder, the government can directly negotiate specific commitments. These commitments can be registered in the multi-annual *contrat de plan* signed by both parties. Electrical space heating is one of the possible areas for such negotiations regarding measures to be taken to address climate change. Electrical space heating has reached a very high level of penetration in the French market, and any replacement of this kind of heating by a less polluting energy than the coal and heavy fuel oil burnt in the conventional thermal plants will theoretically reduce CO_2 emissions. In response, EdF has committed itself to promote high-performance wood-fuelled installations in combination with electrical heating, within the scope of the 'time of use' tariff.[12] However, the situation

---

[12] *National Programme for Tackling Climate Change.*

might be more complex, since statistical studies have shown that in France, the energy consumption for space heating by households using gas is more than twice the energy consumed by households using electricity for the same use. Therefore, at present the gas solution emits more CO_2 than the electrical one.

❑ High-performance appliances: ADEME, the public agency for rational use of energy and environmental protection, will be responsible for the implementation of the public policies aimed at controlling the development of electricity demand as a way to limit GHG emissions. While the carbon content of electricity in France is relatively low today, it may increase by 2010, especially in the absence of measures to control the demand for electricity.

Improvements in the energy performance of equipment and other demand-side management measures will reduce consumption during the decade 2010–20 and the future need for additional thermal-based production. However, the additional costs associated with more efficient appliances, even if they could be recouped quickly, makes them unattractive to many domestic consumers.

The market for the appliances is largely European, and the right level at which to draw up minimum efficiency standards legislation is most probably the European Union. The NPTCC is proposing European rules, but at the same time it is developing national legislation on thermal standards in buildings, efficiency of electrical motors used in new buildings, etc.

The NPTCC also proposes to negotiate with the European Commission to add a supplementary option to the provision relating to applying a lower rate of VAT on products or services that help to control the greenhouse effect.

The NPTCC is also considering initiatives for raising awareness and training on efficient appliances with key players in the distribution and installation chain. Finally, information campaigns will be implemented to explain in particular the role of energy labelling for electrical household appliances and labelling on electronic and computer equipment, and also the importance of reducing the consumption of appliances on standby, etc.

7.5 Conclusions

The share of the power sector in GHG emissions is very low in France, because of the significant shares of nuclear and hydro-electricity. The current overcapacity creates an incentive to look for CO_2 reductions through a higher penetration of electricity in different sectors. Still, efforts to control electricity consumption are worthwhile, especially because the carbon content of kilowatt hours depends on both the future of nuclear production and the increasing share of thermal electricity. However, opportunities to achieve CO_2 reductions in the power sector by additional renewable energy or demand-side efforts will be effective only if they reduce the need for fossil-fuel-based electricity, rather than substituting for nuclear or hydroelectric power.

Consequently, the potential of the French power sector to contribute to GHG emissions reduction is very dissimilar to that of other countries. First, in the short term this contribution is limited in volume. Second, the strategic view on this contribution concentrates on the long term, through the control of electricity demand development, in order to limit the future need to resort to fossil-fuel-based generation. Finally, the French electricity sector can best address climate change issues at the European market level, either through export of carbon-free nuclear electricity or through the huge potential to generate 'green certificates' in the future.

8 Germany: unification and contradiction

Joachim Schleich, Regina Betz, Frank Gagelmann, Eberhard Jochem and Dirk Koewener

The German electricity market is by far the largest in the EU with the power sector producing around one-fifth of total EU demand. The power sector is heavily dependent on coal and other solid fossil fuels, but also has a large share of nuclear production. Consequently, the German power sector accounts for a large share of EU emissions: 35% of all those from the EU electricity sector, and nearly 10% of all EU CO_2 emissions.

The German market was liberalized in one big step in 1998. Power prices have since dropped dramatically; many companies have merged and are taking over smaller companies across Europe. However, in this liberalized market, the companies have to reduce emissions, phase out nuclear power, and increase use of renewables and cogeneration.

Its size and its impact on the rest of Europe render the German market of crucial importance for the whole of the EU. However, German emissions reductions to date, to a large extent due to reunification, also guarantee easier targets for the other countries (see Figure 8.1).[1]

8.1 Description of electricity sector

8.1.1 Electricity demand

German electricity consumption is estimated to be 566TWh in 2000. This level is less than 3% above demand in 1990. However, since 1993, when the drop in consumption in the new *Länder* had come to a halt, electricity consumption in Germany has risen by 7.5%. Even so, over the last decade, electricity intensity – measured as the ratio of total electricity consumption to GNP – has decreased by about 13%.[2]

---

[1] The EU's overall 8% reduction target requires emissions reductions of around 250MtCO$_2$, while Germany's 21% target alone would deliver 200MtCO$_2$.

[2] *Stagnierender Primärenergieverbrauch im Jahre 2000*, DIW-Wochenbericht 5/01 (Berlin: Deutsches Institut für Wirtschaftsforschung, 2001); see www.diw.de.

Figure 8.1: German greenhouse gas emissions, 1990–1999

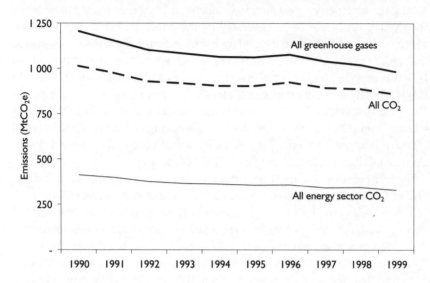

Source: European Environment Agency, EU emissions inventory; see www.eea.org.

The industrial sector is by far the largest electricity consumer in Germany. In 1997, almost 42% of total final electric energy was consumed by industry, about 28% in households, and 27% in the tertiary and agricultural sectors.[3] Within industry, five sectors account for more than 70% of electricity consumption. The chemical industry alone consumes about a quarter, with the largest share of this for the basic chemicals. Other major electricity-consuming subsectors are iron and metal processing (18%), pulp and paper (10%), iron and steel (10%), and non-ferrous metals (8%).[4]

Total electricity consumption is expected to increase over the next two decades, but annual growth rates are very likely to be below 1%. All sectors are expected to grow, with the highest growth rates in industry and the tertiary sector. In 2020, electricity consumption is expected to be around 13% higher than in 1998.[5]

---

[3] *Die längerfristige Entwicklung der Energiemärkte im Zeichen von Wettbewerb und Umwelt* (Basel: Prognos/ewi, 1999).
[4] VDEW press release, *Industrie in Deutschland 1999: Chemie größter Stromverbraucher*, 3 July 2000; see www.strom.de.
[5] *Die längerfristige Entwicklung der Energiemarkt im Zeichen von Wettbewerb und Umwelt*.

8.1.2   Electricity supply

Total gross electricity production in Germany in 1999 is estimated to be about 564TWh.[6] Nearly 90% was generated by the public power supply industry, which supplies electricity to the grid for use by industry, households, commerce and trade, the public sector, transportation and agriculture. In addition, about 10% was supplied by industrial power producers and the German railways. In 2000 Germany was a net importer of electricity, but trade balances were almost zero, since imports of 40.5TWh were about equal to exports of 39.5TWh due to seasonal comparative advantages with neighbouring countries. Total installed capacity is about 116GW. The electricity sector contributes about 1.5% to German GDP and currently employs *c.*150,000 people.

Nuclear energy is the most important energy carrier for electricity generation in Germany, with a share of 32%. Lignite and coal are next with 27% and 24%, respectively. Lignite is particularly important in the new federal states (*Bundesländer*), where its share in electricity generation is more than 80%. However, the shares of coal and lignite have declined over the years. By contrast, natural gas has increased its share to 7%. All other energy carriers together account for no more than 10% of electricity production in Germany, notably hydro with 5% and fast-increasing wind energy with 2%. Figure 8.2 shows the fuel shares in the sector.

In 1998 electricity from cogeneration in the public power and district heating supply industry amounted to 5.4% (28.1TWh) of public electricity supply compared with 4.1% (18.7TWh) in the early 1990s;[7] and about three-quarters of this was generated in municipal utilities. In the same period, electricity generation from cogeneration in industry has been fairly constant at about 40TWh (18–19% of electricity consumption in the industrial sector). However, with the decline of electricity production in the industrial sector between 1991 and 1998, the share of electricity from cogeneration increased from 53% to almost 79% in 1998.[8] In total, electricity from cogeneration in industry and in the public power supply industry in 1998 accounted for about 12% of generation in Germany.

Generation of electricity from renewable energy sources (RES) increased from 19TWh in 1990 to 29TWh in 1999.[9] Over the same period, its share in

[6] *Stagnierender Primärenergieverbrauch im Jahre 2000.*
[7] *Strategien einer pluralistischen Fern- und Nahwärmeversogung in einem liberalizierten Energiemarkt unter besonderer Berücksichtigung der Kraft-Wärme-Kopplung und erneuerbarer Energien* (Frankfurt: Arbeitsgemeinschaft Fernwärme, 2000).
[8] Ibid.
[9] 'Deutlicher Zuwachs bei Ökostrom', *Stromthemen*, no. 3 (2000), p. 6.

Figure 8.2: Fuel shares in German electricity production, 2000

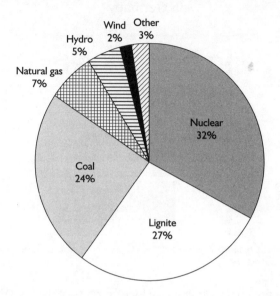

Source: Verband deutscher Elektrizitätswerke, *Drei Prozent mehr Strom erzeugt* (Frankfurt am Main: VDEW, 5 Feb. 2001); see www.strom.de.

total electricity production grew from 4.0% to 5.9%. Hydropower and wind are by far the most important renewable energy sources, followed by waste and biomass, which combined produce just under 3.8TWh. Wind power has been growing particularly strongly, with a total installed capacity of 6,113MW at the end of 2000.[10] By comparison, electricity from solar energy accounts for less than 0.06% of total electricity production in Germany.

8.1.3   Structure of the German electricity supply market

Prior to 1998, the structure of the German electricity sector had arisen from the German energy law of 1935 (*Gesetz zur Förderung der Energiewirtschaft* or *Energiewirtschaftsgesetz*) and its ordinances, and the federal anti-trust law (*Gesetz gegen Wettbewerbsbeschränkung*). These laws resulted in delimited areas of supply, guaranteed by demarcation and concession contracts. Electricity supply was essentially exempted from competition, resulting in the

---

[10] www.ewea.org.

Figure 8.3: The structure of the public electricity supply industry in Germany

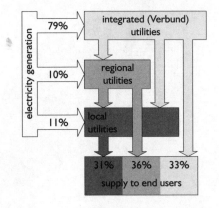

Source: Hans-Wilhelm Schiffer, *Energiemarkt Bundesrepublik Deutschland*, 6th edn (Cologne: Verlag TUEV Rheinland, 1997).

emergence of regional monopolies under the roofs of the big electricity suppliers (integrated so-called *Verbund* utilities). Within a certain region, one dominant large and many small and typically vertically integrated electricity producers and distributors were the only suppliers. Historically, the centralized structure of the German electricity production industry has further been shaped by public policy, which included high subsidies for the hard coal and nuclear power industries. The general electricity tariffs were subject to approval by the ministries of the individual federal states (*Länder*).

Over the last fifty years, the total number of utilities has been steadily declining. In the mid-1950s the public power supply industry sector consisted of about 3,500 companies; by 1999 this number had declined to under 1,000. These companies vary considerably in terms of size, ownership and the degree of vertical integration. With respect to their functions, three types of suppliers can be distinguished (see Figure 8.3).

1   In 2000 six *Verbund* utilities were planning, operating and coordinating the use of their power plants and the high-voltage transmission network. They were responsible for the supra-regional management of electricity reserves and trade with neighbouring countries. *Verbund* utilities directly supply regional utilities as well as local utilities, and in some cases also final electricity users. The *Verbund* utilities directly account for more

Figure 8.4: Market shares in German generation

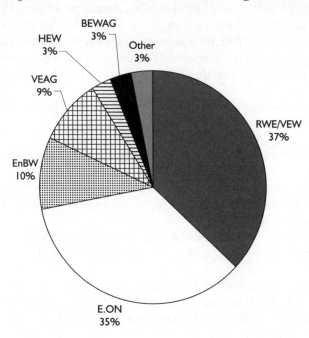

Source: 'The Geman Energy Market', *Emerging Markets Online*, Feb. 2001; see www.emerging-market.com.

than three-quarters of total electricity production in Germany. This share increases if their capital shares in other (regional and local) utilities are taken into account. Also, some of the *Verbund* utilities are linked via inter-locking financial arrangements. The east German VEAG is entirely owned by the other *Verbund* utilities or their mother companies. All *Verbund* utili-ties are joint-stock companies.

2 At the *regional level*, at the end of the 1990s about sixty utilities distrib-uted the electricity generated by themselves or by the *Verbund* utilities to local utilities or directly to the end users. There are close links between the regional utilities and the *Verbund* utilities through interlocking finan-cial arrangements or through long-term supply contracts. The regional corporations are mostly stock corporations or limited liability com-panies.

3 At the *local level*, at the end of the 1990s around 900 local utilities dis-tributed the electricity generated by the *Verbund* utilities, by regional

suppliers and by themselves, or by small independent power producers (IPPs). Most utilities at the local level are municipal utilities. Often, these are organized as combination utilities dealing also with natural gas, district heat, water and public transportation. Only large municipal utilities are limited liability companies (GmbH); most are owner-operated municipal enterprises set up as special funds without legal independence.

A survey of the ownership structure of 740 utilities in 1995 came up with the following findings:[11]

- In 62% of these utilities, the share of public ownership was at least 95%. These utilities delivered about 19% of total electricity.
- In 23% of these utilities, the share of public ownership was between 95% and 25% (semi-public). These utilities accounted for about 59% of total electricity supply.
- In about 14% of the utilities, the share of public ownership was less than 25%. These utilities supplied about 22% of total electricity.

This structure of ownership and electricity supply mirrors the facts that most utilities are municipal utilities owned by the local municipalities, and that most semi-public utilities supply electricity state- or nationwide.

8.2   The new energy law

In April 1998 the German legislature passed a new energy law (*Energiewirtschaftsgesetz*), which replaced the old law of 1935 and adapted German energy legislation to the European directive on electricity and gas. Along with the modified anti-trust law, the new energy law prohibited exclusive concession contracts and demarcation agreements, and effected a 100% opening of the electricity and gas markets to all consumers. Market liberalization in Germany, therefore, was instantaneous, without a transition period. Competition regulation is carried out by the federal anti-trust office (*Bundeskartellamt*) rather than a specific electricity regulator.

For the transmission system, the negotiated third party access (nTPA) system was introduced. However, for the distribution network an nTPA system with an optional transitional single-buyer system was allowed. Unlike in other countries, in Germany there is no law or ordinance governing the use

---

[11] Hans-Wilhelm Schiffer, *Energiemarkt Bundesrepublik Deutschland*, 6th edn (Cologne: Verlag TUEV Rheinland, 1997).

of the grid. Instead, grid use is regulated by a pan-industry voluntary agreement on transmission tariffs and conditions between the Federal Association of German Industry (BDI), the Association of Industrial Energy and Power Industry (VIK) and the German Electricity Association (VDEW). This so-called *Verbändevereinbauung* (VV) applies across the electricity sector unless the government decides to regulate.

The first agreement of this kind, the VV I of May 1998, linked transmission prices to costs and included a uniform tariff (stamp rule). At high voltage only, TPA beyond 100km was charged with an additional fee per kW and per km, applied at the point of extraction only. However, complaints led to a modified agreement, VV II, in January 2000. Lack of transparency, high administrative costs and prohibitively high rates (in particular for longer-distance transmission) were the main targets of protest. At the core of VV II is a point-of-connection tariff at the high-voltage grid of the *Verbund* utilities, which replaces the old system of individual agreements for every supply transaction. Grid users now pay a single charge for twelve months, which depends on the capacity required, and are then free to decide their trading partner, independent of its location.

The trading point for power is the high-voltage grid. Provisions in the new VV II allow a strict separation between grid usage and power delivery, which is a prerequisite for short-run contracts and for using power exchanges.

8.3 The consequences of liberalization

The electricity market in Germany is still in a transitional phase of market adaptation and restructuring, the duration and final consequences of which can only be guessed. The emergence of new players and existing excess capacity of about 10GW in the German electricity generation sector have led to fierce competition for market share in a nearly stagnant market. The final outcomes of the market restructuring will depend on national policies, such as public support schemes for cogeneration, RES and lignite; but also on the implementation of ecotaxes and on international developments, such as the planned emissions trading scheme for the EU.[12] The latter include in particular the further opening of the electricity markets in other EU countries, which have estimated additional excess generation capacity of about 40GW, and eastern Europe. Further strengthening of the international targets on GHG emissions could also have a great impact.

---

[12] For details on the European proposal see Chapter 3.

8.3.1 Electricity prices

Historically, electricity prices in Germany have been above the European average. High technical standards guaranteed reliable energy provision and the higher costs were passed on to the final consumers. Although electricity prices had already been falling moderately since the early 1990s,[13] the most important result of liberalization was the dramatic drop in electricity prices for all end users, wholesale rates falling by about 42% in real terms within eighteen months.[14]

Large industrial customers were the first to benefit from price decreases of up to 40–50%, but since the summer of 1999 private households have enjoyed significant price cuts of up to 30% as well. According to the Bureau for Statistics (Statistisches Bundesamt), electricity prices (including taxes) between March 1999 and March 2000 fell by 15.5% on average.

Given the excess production capacity of about 15%, electricity generators compete on the basis of short- to medium-term marginal costs, while transmission and distribution are charged at full costs as negotiated in the VV. In 1999 total electricity costs for industry decreased by €5.6bn and for private households by €2bn.[15] Despite a small increase in electricity sales by 0.7%, total revenues have declined by 10–15% between 1998 and 1999 as a result of the price cuts.[16]

Market studies indicate that 40–50% of the households would be willing to switch electricity suppliers, but two years after the formal liberalization fewer than 5% have actually done so, and recent polls show that the propensity to switch is declining. In general, the benefit of lower prices was felt not only by end users but also by many regional and municipal utilities, which, as distributors, managed to get better deals purchasing electricity without passing on the full savings to the end users. In many cases, however, incumbent utilities have charged (illegal) switching costs and excessive administrative and transmission fees, and delayed transmission, in attempts to avoid losing customers. Increasing complaints have resulted in formal investigations; the

---

[13] Prices for large industrial customers fell by 20% in real terms between 1991 and 1996; see E. Jochem and E. Tönsing, 'Die Auswirkungen der Liberalisierung der Strom- und Gasversorgung auf die rationelle Energieverwendung in Deutschland', *UmweltWirtschaftsForum*, vol. 6, no. 3., Sept. 1998, pp. 8–11.

[14] 'German Prices at Cash Cost', *Financial Times Energy Economist*, no. 223, 15 May 2000.

[15] Verband deutscher Elektrizitätswerke [German Electricity Association], *VDEW-Jahresbericht 1999: Wettbewerb im Strommarkt erfordert veränderte Rahmenbedingungen* (VDEW, June 2000).

[16] Ibid.

federal minister of economics and technology has threatened to create a regulatory agency, and the Cartel Office is examining the possibility.[17]

New entrants and incumbent utilities alike pursued an aggressive pricing strategy to gain or maintain market share in a stagnant market. In the light of the excess capacity, some producers are selling electricity below full cost – a strategy that may make sense in the short run, but cannot be sustained in the long run. Competition, and therefore loss of monopoly rent, is not the only reason for the price drops in Germany; improved productivity has also played a role. From 1998 to 1999 labour productivity increased by over 7%.[18] As a consequence, employment in the traditional electricity supply sector continues to decline. Between 1991 and 1999 employment in this sector decreased by 30% from over 217,000 to 150,000, despite consumption growth of 7%.[19] Almost 10% of the jobs were lost in the last two years of the decade. On the other hand, liberalization has created some additional employment in marketing, energy services, call centres, etc.

8.3.2 Market structure

The instantaneous liberalization of the electricity market has dramatically altered and will continue to change the structure of the electricity sector in Germany. Companies were forced quickly to reorganize their production, transmission, distribution and marketing activities in the face of increased national and international competition.

On the one hand, traditional utilities are trying to adapt through strategic alliances, cooperation and mergers. On the other hand, new national and international players, such as electricity traders and brokers, electricity marketers and electricity service companies, have entered the market. Because of its excess capacity, the German market proved particularly attractive for electricity traders, more than 100 of which had emerged by mid-1999.[20] German utilities are facing increasing competition form foreign firms. Firms from the

---

[17] Dr Werner Mueller, 'Die Energiepolitik der Bundesregierung', speech given by the federal minister of economics and technology at the VDEW Congress, 'Strommarkt Deutschland – Energie für Europa' 31 May 2001; *German Cartel Office Investigates Double Contract Model* (London: Platts, 18 Oct. 2001); see www.platts.com.

[18] *VDEW-Jahresbericht 1999.*

[19] Verband deutscher Elektrizitätswerke [German Electricity Association] press release, 'Stromversorger 1991–1999: Stromverkauf stieg um sieben Prozent', May 2000.

[20] E. Meller, 'Die Elektrizitätswirtschaft lässt ihre Flügel hängen', *Handelsblatt*, 8 June 1999.

United States, Britain and Scandinavia seem well positioned, since they already have experience with power trading. However, existing excess capacity, stagnant demand and low retail prices will have deterred many potential new entrants.

In general, liberalization has led to increased horizontal and vertical concentration in the German electricity market and has resulted in increased national and international competition.

On the supply side, examples for horizontal integration at the level of *Verbund* utilities include the mergers between VIAG AG and VEBA AG, whose subsidiaries Bayernwerk and PreussenElektra integrated to form E.ON Energie AG. The second example at the *Verbund* level is the merger between RWE and VEW. The European Commission and German anti-trust agency have approved both mergers, despite their large market shares (see Figure 8.4). Further, BEWAG has plans to take over the east German power utility VEAG together with the US company Southern Energy, which already owns 26% of BEWAG. Currently, VEAG is controlled by VEBA, VIAG and RWE, which are being forced to sell their stakes on competition grounds.

At the level of regional and local utilities, mergers generally take place between firms with adjacent supply areas or between firms using the same supplier. Examples for companies created through regional mergers include AVACON AG, Energie Nord AG and Energie Sachsen Brandenburg AG. At the local level, Mainova AG, Niederrheinische Versorgungs und Verkehrs AG and Emscher-Lippe-Energie GmbH emerged as new companies. Besides pure mergers, there is an increasing number of cooperations, networks and alliances for energy trading, distribution, energy services, marketing and, in some cases, the coordination of electricity generation. Examples include Entaga GmbH – a subsidiary of the Stadtwerke Mainz AG and HEAG Versorgungs GmbH – and EnetKo, which was founded by six networks of municipal utilities.

Foreign utilities have started to invest in German power companies. Direct investment by foreign firms is facilitated by sales of shares by many municipalities (often to consolidate their budgets), the German national anti-trust laws (which make further consolidation of German companies more difficult), and the desire for strategic partners with experience in liberalized electricity markets. Most notably, at the beginning of 2000, Electricité de France bought 25% of one of the big *Verbund* utilities, EnBW, from the State of Baden-Württemberg for about €2.4bn. Also, the biggest electricity producer in Scandinavia, Vattenfall (Sweden), bought 25% of HEW (Hamburg) for €0.87bn. Prior to that, Vattenfall and the Hamburger Projektentwicklungsgesellschafts Kommunalfinanz GmbH had formed a joint venture, VASA Energy GmbH, which bought 12.5% of the Stadtwerke Rostock AG, and operates as an IPP.

Some *Verbund* utilities also tried to gain access to foreign markets through IPP projects (RWE in Spain and Portugal), or through follow-the-customer strategies (RWE and BASF). They also made acquisitions and embarked on cooperation with foreign suppliers (PreussenElektra AG in eastern Europe and Scandinavia; EnBW acquiring 24.5% of Swiss utility Watt AG and 51% of Norwegian power trading company Skandinavisk Kraftmegling).

However, most consolidation and further integration is taking place within Germany. *Verbund* utilities have increased capital links and cooperation with regional and municipal utilities on all fronts in the attempt to secure market share; the smaller utilities are looking for strong partners in the competitive liberalized electricity market. As mentioned earlier, E.ON, now the second largest power company in Germany, came into existence by the merger of VEBA and VIAG. EnBW (Energie Baden-Württemberg AG) and the Neckarwerke Stuttgart AG have agreed to cooperate and bundle activities in generation, grid operation, fuels and customer management, while EnBW will take the sole responsibility for energy trading. Many utilities, primarily the *Verbund* utilities, have outsourced or bought in the expertise of electricity traders and energy service companies. Utilities are also developing new marketing channels, for example, retail stores.

On the one hand, utilities try to integrate vertically; on the other, liberalization has accelerated their efforts to diversify and become multi-utility companies offering electricity, district heating, gas, water, telecommunications and waste services under the same roof. Most new capital linkages have been between electricity and gas companies. In the long run, such a strategy is likely to be more attractive, since the benefits of vertical integration tend to vanish as the markets become more competitive. However, the separation between horizontal and vertical integration is often not clear-cut, because vertically integrated companies cooperate and merge with other vertically integrated companies.

Similarly, on the demand side, distributors and end users bundle activities to achieve better deals. This strategy is pursued not only by big companies with many stores or outlets, such as banks or retailers, but also by small and medium-sized companies within the same subsector or region. More than 5,000 craftsmen from the state of Baden-Württemberg, for example, pooled their electricity demand and struck a deal with an energy broker which saved the average company 47% on its electricity bills.

These dynamic market transformation processes have been fostered by the opening of two *power exchanges*. In the summer of 2000 the LPX (Leipzig Power Exchange) started with a spot market, and the EEX (European Energy Exchange AG, Frankfurt) started with a futures market.

At the end of this process of restructuring and market adaptation, the number of utilities is expected to be significantly lower. The number of utilities in Germany by 2005 may be only half that at the beginning of liberalization in 1998; on the basis of the Dutch experience, it may be that only 100 utilities will survive in the long run.[21]

8.3.3 Privatization

The liberalization of the energy markets has also accelerated changes in the legal form of utilities from entities organized under public law to entities organized under private law. The proportion of utilities which are organized under public law (as owner-operated municipal enterprises or special-purpose associations) has fallen from about 48% in 1994 to 45% in April 1998 and 40% in February 2000. Formal privatization of organizations is pursued primarily to gain independence from the local authorities and municipal administrations, to gain flexibility in the operative management and in labour markets, and to facilitate cooperation and negotiations with other market partners. It is also a precondition to attract private capital from direct investors.

The liberalization of the electricity market has also pointed to the weaknesses of other outdated regulations. Recently, some state parliaments have put pressure on the federal government to abolish the legal requirement that general electricity tariffs be approved by the *Länder*. Similarly, state regulations which prevent municipal utilities organized under public law from operating beyond the municipal borders have come under pressure, since they put the utilities at a severe competitive disadvantage.

Historically, municipal utilities have used profits from their electricity companies to cross-subsidize other areas of public services (in particular transportation); total cross-subsidies accounted for about €1bn annually. These financial resources have not been invested in the supply infrastructure, and – unlike in other utilities – are not available as reserves to overcome the

---

[21] 'Stromversorger unzureichend auf Kundenabwanderungen vorbereitet – Studie der MSR Consulting Group zur Standortbestimmung der deutschen Stromversorger', *Elektrizitätswirtschaft*, vol. 98, no. 25 (1999), p. 1.

current period of low electricity prices. However, utility profits are no longer available to municipalities to cross-subsidize other public services.

8.3.4 Investment and fuel mix

Uncertainty about market development, and the necessity of cost-cutting caused by the liberalization of the market, have resulted in lower investment levels. Total investment in the electricity supply sector in 1998 fell to €5.3bn, an 11% drop from the previous year.[22] Investment in plant dropped by 9%, while investments in transmission and distribution equipment declined by 11%. It is expected that investment will continue to decline to just under €3.6bn in 2003, while total installed capacity will remain at the same level.

The persisting market uncertainty and a liberalized market demanding flexibility and shorter contract periods have a profound impact on the production technology of choice. Traditional production technologies with high investment and low operating costs are being replaced by more flexible technologies with low investment and higher operating costs. Building new nuclear power plants in Germany is highly unlikely to be profitable in the future – quite apart from the complete phase-out the government and the power industry have negotiated (see section 8.4.1). Combined cycle gas turbines are expected to become increasingly important because of their flexibility and high efficiency. Thus, even before the phase-out of nuclear energy had been agreed, the share of nuclear power was expected to decrease substantially from almost 31% in 2000 to 9% in 2020, while during the same period the share of gas was projected to increase from 9% to 20%.[23] A substantial growth is projected for wind power, but market share will remain small. The share for coal will remain about constant; however, with the phase-out of nuclear energy coal could regain market share for base-load production in the longer term.

8.3.5 Cogeneration

Prior to liberalization, it was assumed that electricity from cogeneration could be doubled by 2010.[24] However, the restructuring of the electricity

---

[22] A. Seeliger, 'Investitionen in der deutschen Elektrizitätswirtschaft nach der Liberalisierung', *Elektrizitätswirtschaft*, vol. 98, no. 26 (1999), pp. 40–4.

[23] *Die längerfristige Entwicklung der Enrgiemarkt im Zeichen von Wettbewerb und Umwelt.*

[24] *Zweiter Bericht des Interministerellen Ausschusses für Klima* (Bonn: Bundesministerium für Umwelt, Naturschutz und Reaktorsicherheit, Bonn, 1997).

market following liberalization and fierce price competition have seriously threatened the existence of cogeneration in Germany. In the public power sector, only modern CHP plants or plants that are already written off are competitive under the new conditions; many utilities were considering halting production in these plants. Industrial CHP, however, can be operated with higher flexibility, since capacity is usually optimized to meet heat demand and electricity can be bought on the market. Nevertheless, the existence of 60% of industrial CHP plants is threatened, and by mid-2000 about 1,000MW of CHP had been switched off.[25]

8.3.6 New products and services

Energy services are perceived as a good strategy for municipal utilities, enabling them to retain customers, diversify risks and, most importantly, avoid pure price competition in a liberalized market. The main business areas are heat services and CHP projects, which account for roughly 80% of the energy services market. Only a small fraction is used for demand-reducing technologies such as efficient lighting, insulation or control engineering, or for other supply technologies such as compressed air and process heat. The total market for energy services in Germany had reached €1.8bn in 1998.

Whereas the drop in electricity prices has made some energy services less profitable, the liberalization process has opened up the natural monopolies, allowing energy service companies to establish an energy service market. It is now possible to bring energy services not only to a single customer but also to a group of customers using the existing infrastructure. Despite the setback for many CHP plants, the possibility of selling electricity to other customers proved to be a strong driver in the case of some projects. The tendency of industry to outsource capital-intensive investments such as CHP and compressed air systems also favours the emerging energy services market. It is expected that the energy services market in Germany will grow by 20% per year.

In an attempt to differentiate the market and cater to environmentally sensitive customers who are willing to pay a premium on electricity generated with renewable energy technologies or from cogeneration, most utilities are now offering green electricity.[26] The most common pricing scheme is a green

---

[25] *Elektrizitätswirtschaft*, vol. 99, no.11 (2000), p. 60.
[26] M. Dreher, S. Grähl, M. Wietschel and O. Rentz, 'Grüne Angebote – Die aktuelle Situation in Deutschland', *Elektrizitätswirtschaft*, vol. 99, no. 16 (2000), pp. 6–8.

tariff, where customers pay a premium (often about 30%) over and above the standard rates. Utilities offering these schemes either produce the electricity themselves from renewables or cooperate with a green electricity producer or trader. To date, the market share for green electricity is still very small, below 1%, but the market potential is estimated to be 5–10%. However, the emergence of about a half a dozen different certification schemes, each applying different standards for granting a green label, has created confusion and may even be counterproductive.

8.4 Environmental policies

8.4.1 German environmental targets

The Kyoto target With the Kyoto Protocol in 1997, the EU accepted an 8% reduction target from the 1990 base-year levels for the six 'Kyoto gases', to be achieved in the period 2008–12. Within the EU, this reduction was allocated among the member states under the burden-sharing agreement, in which Germany accepted a 21% reduction commitment. Consequently, Germany has to reduce overall emissions of these gases from about 1,200MtCO$_2$e a year to about 960MtCO$_2$e a year, which is by far the highest absolute reduction requirement of any member state and accounts for roughly three-quarters of the required reductions for all member states. According to the ministry for the environment, emissions in 1999 were 990MtCO$_2$e.[27] The substantial emissions reduction represented by this figure are attributable to the economic downturn and restructuring in the new *Länder* following German reunification in 1990, as well as to major reductions in CH$_4$ and N$_2$O emissions.[28] Recent estimates suggest that compared with a business-as-usual scenario, about 50% of the reductions in all GHGs in Germany after 1990 are due to reunification, the so-called 'wall-fall' profits, and 50% are due to policies.[29]

---

[27] *Nationales Klimaschutzprogramm – Eckpunkte für ein Anspruchsvolles Ziel* (Bonn: Bundesministerium für Umwelt, Naturschutz und Reaktorsicherheit); see www.bmu.de/klima/klimaschutz, accessed 20 May 2000.

[28] Eichhammer, W. et al., 'The Kyoto Target of the EU: Implications of the Burden Sharing and the Greenhouse Gas Basket for CO$_2$ – Emissions in the Member States', in *The Shared Analysis Project. Economic Foundations for Energy Policy in Europe to 2020*, vol. 11 (Karlsruhe: FhG-ISI, 1999); see www.sharedanalysis.fhg.de/index.htm.

[29] J. Schleich, W. Eichhammer, U. Boede, F. Gagelmann, E. Jochem, B. Schlomann and H.-J. Ziesing, 'Greenhouse Gas Reductions in Germany – Lucky Strike or Hard Work?', *Climate Policy*, vol. 1 (2000), pp. 363–80.

The national CO$_2$ target   The national GHG target is even more ambitious. In the early 1990s Germany committed itself to reduce its CO$_2$ emissions by 25% compared with 1990 levels in 2005. This goal was maintained throughout the subsequent years and renewed by Chancellor Schröder at the fifth conference of the parties (COP-5) in November 1999 in Bonn. The target means that Germany has to reduce annual CO$_2$ emissions by around 250Mt, of which 150Mt has been achieved by the end of 1999. Thus, about 100Mt still need to be taken off the annual total within the next five years.[30]

The climate protection programme unveiled by the German government in 2000 also involves policies and measures to fulfil the national 25% target.[31] For the first time, this plan allocates sub-targets to the main emitting sectors: transport (15–20MtCO$_2$), residential (18–25MtCO$_2$) and industry/energy supply (20–25MtCO$_2$). The respective ministries are charged with the responsibility of achieving the sub-targets in their own areas of influence, in principle using political instruments of their own choice. If a ministry feels unable to fulfil its sub-target, it will need to motivate another ministry to achieve higher reductions than allocated.[32]

While Germany is expected to meet its Kyoto target, the more ambitious national target is likely to be missed unless additional measures are implemented in the near future.

Phase-out of nuclear energy   One of the prime objectives of the new German Social Democratic–Green coalition, which came into power in autumn 1998, was gradually to phase out the production of electricity from nuclear energy in Germany. On 14 June 2000 negotiations between the government and the nuclear power industry (RWE, VIAG, VEBA und EnBW) ended in an agreement allowing the nineteen active nuclear power plants an additional combined production of about 2,500TWh of electricity. This amount can be allocated across new and older plants and is equivalent to an average total running time of about thirty-two years per plant. Given this timing, the phase-out of nuclear energy will have little impact on national or international climate objectives in the short term. However, in the long run nuclear energy will have to be replaced by other energy carriers, or by imports, so

---

[30] *Nationales Klimaschutzprogramm – Eckpunkte für ein Anspruchsvolles Ziel.*

[31] *Germany's National Climate Protection Programme* (Berlin: Bundesministerium für Umwelt, Naturschutz und Reaktorsicherheit, Oct. 2000).

[32] *100.000-Dächer-Solarstromprogramm* (Berlin: Bundesministerium für Umwelt, Naturschutz und Reaktorsicherheit); see www.bmu.de/fset800.htm, accessed 4 Sept. 2000.

that future emissions reductions may become more difficult to achieve. The emissions targets may become particularly challenging if electricity demand grows rapidly and coal-fired power plants are substituted for nuclear power.

8.4.2 Policy instruments

The German national climate protection programme is aimed at achieving the domestic target of -25% by 2005, and overshoots the -21% Kyoto target substantially. Table 8.1 gives an overview of the contributions to emissions reductions from various sectors. The energy industry will deliver an important part of the overall reductions. Table 8.2 gives a more detailed overview of the contributions of specific actions in the energy sector in the framework of the German national programme. Some of these actions are discussed next.

Table 8.1: Sectoral emissions reduction contributions of the new climate programme in Germany ($MtCO_2e$)

Sector	2005	2010
Energy industry	20	
Renewable energy sources	13–15	c.20
Ecological tax reform	10	20
Buildings	13–20	
Private households	5	
Industry	15–20	
Traffic	15–20	
Waste management	15	20
Agriculture	Impossible to quantify	
Total	90–95	

Source: Bundesministerium für Umwelt, Naturschutz und Reaktorsicherheit, *Germany's National Climate Protection Programme* (Berlin: BMU, Oct. 2000).

Coal subsidies　The climate policy goals conflict with interests seeking to preserve employment and electricity supply based on hard coal and lignite, which historically have formed the backbone of electricity supply in Germany. In particular hard coal, over 70% of which is used in the generation of electricity, has enjoyed substantial subsidies and protection from imports through a system of quotas and levies. Under pressure from the European Commission, import restriction were abolished in 1995.

Until 1996, subsidies to the German hard coal industry were, to a considerable share, paid indirectly by electricity consumers in the 'old' (western)

Table 8.2: Actions taken to reduce emissions in the German energy sector (MtCO$_2$e)

Action	2005	2010
Energy industry		
Addional use of CCGT	5–10	15–20
Aid programme for CHP	No additional effect[a]	
Long-term CHP policy	10	23
Contracting and other energy services	2	5
Renewable energy sources		
Renewable Energy Act	10	15
Market launch of renewables	2.5	6
100,000 roofs programme	0.2	0.2

[a] Aids the survival of existing CHP plant that are already taken into account in the baseline emission projections.

Source: Bundesministerium für Umwelt, Naturschutz und Reaktorsicherheit, *Germany's National Climate Protection Programme* (Berlin: BMU, Oct. 2000).

Länder, which had to pay a levy of 8.5% of their electricity bill, the so-called *Kohlepfennig* (coal penny). Revenues were passed on to the coal producers to offset their price disadvantages compared to foreign competitors.[33] At the same time, the German power industry had committed itself in 1980 with the so-called *Jahrhundertvertrag* (contract of the century) to buy a certain amount of German hard coal. In 1994 the federal constitutional court declared the *Kohlepfennig* unconstitutional, arguing that the general burden of energy supply security was to be borne by the general public and not only by the electricity consumers. As a consequence, since 1996 these subsidies have been paid directly out of the federal government budget and two *Länder* government budgets to the coal producers.

As laid down in the so-called *Hüttenvertrag* (steelworks agreement) covering 1989–2000, the German government subsidized the difference between import and domestic prices for hard coal to be used in the production of steel. Demand from this sector accounts for more than 20% of the hard coal use in Germany. However, in 1997 the EU did not allow an extension of this contract.[34]

Today, federal and state governments pay direct subsidies independent of the volume of production. In the early 1990s annual subsidies to German coal producers amounted to €5–6bn; in 1996 they ran to €102 per tonne of

---

[33] *Energy Policies of Germany: 1998 Review* (Paris: IEA/OECD, 1997).
[34] Ibid.

coal produced, and the direct subsidies are projected to decline to €2.8bn in 2005.[35] Still, at least 40% of demand in 2005 is expected to be supplied by imported coal, and only ten of the eighteen currently operating hard-coal mines are likely to survive.

Production of lignite is not subsidized in Germany. However, in the 1990s aid was given by some of the new eastern *Länder* for the construction and modernization of power plants running on lignite. In addition, under the new energy law, from 1998 until 2003 the 'right of access' to the grid can be denied in the new *Länder* if it threatens lignite-based power.

In contrast to the subsidies for coal and indirect aid for lignite, natural gas and oil are subject to mineral taxes for use in power production.

Ecological tax reform   In April 1999 Germany took the first step towards the long-discussed 'ecological tax reform'. The objective of this reform was to impose a tax on energy consumption to reduce emissions and, at the same time, use the tax revenues to lower labour costs and increase employment (the double dividend). The reform was planned to take place in five successive annual steps starting in 1999.[36]

The major components of the ecological tax reform in Germany are:

• The introduction of a general tax on electricity consumption of 1e/kWh in 1999, followed by four annual increases of 0.26e/kWh until 2003.
• An increase of the mineral oil tax on several fuels (the rates are given in Table 8.3). In contrast to the electricity taxes, these levies are increased only once, and the rates in terms of energy use are still far lower than those in the transport sector, which are also increased.[37]
• Tax revenues are primarily used to lower the pension insurance contributions of employers and employees; employer contributions previously

---

[35] Ibid; Schiffer, *Energiemarkt Bundesrepublik Deutschland.*

[36] *Primärenergieverbrauch im Jahre 1999 rückläufig,* DIW-Wochenbericht 4/00 (Berlin: Deutsches Institut für Wirtschaftsforschung, 2000); *OECD Economic Surveys: Germany 1999* (Paris: OECD, 1999); Hans-Wilhelm Schiffer, 'Energiesteuern klettern', in *VDI Nachrichten,* 3 Dec. 1999; *Die ökologische Steuerreform: der Einstieg und ihre Fortführung* (Bonn: Bundesministerium für Umwelt, Naturschutz und Reaktorsicherheit); see www.bmu.de/aktuell/index.htm, accessed 12 Jan. 2000.

[37] From April 1999 petrol and diesel taxes rise by 3.1e/litre each year until 2003. This increase comes on top of the already existing taxes (55e/litre leaded fuel, 50e/litre unleaded fuel, and 32e/litre diesel fuel). For natural gas the tax is increased from 0.96e/ kWh by 0.06e in each of the next five years, up to 1.24e in 2003. Liquid gas tax goes up by 0.75e annually from 12.3e in early 1999. See Schiffer, 'Energiesteuern klettern'.

amounted to 20% of total personnel-related costs. After five years these contributions will have been lowered by 1.8 percentage points.

For political reasons, and contrary to ecological reasoning, coal remains completely exempted from taxation in the power sector. The key reason for this is the preservation of employment in the coal-mining sector. Gas and oil are exempted from the tax increase only if they are used for electricity generation, in order to avoid 'double taxation' because of the introduction of the electricity tax.[38] Total tax exemptions on fuel inputs are now granted for efficient cogeneration (if efficiency is at least 70%), and temporarily for highly efficient CCGTs for electricity generation (if efficiency is at least 57.5%).[39]

Renewable energy sources are exempted from the electricity tax only if they are used for auto-consumption, since EU legislation prohibits a general exclusion. Several renewable energy sources are therefore promoted by other laws (discussed later in the chapter).

Several tax reductions have been introduced for public transport and industry. Because public transport is considered to be environmentally friendly, the tax increase on electricity for public transport is halved in each of the successive steps.[40] The manufacturing sector (as well as the agricultural and forestry sectors) pay only 20% of the general tax increases, i.e. 0.2e/kWh for electricity, 0.41e/litre for oil, and 0.033e/kWh for gas. These reduced tax rates apply only for firms with an annual electricity consumption of more than 50MWh. In addition, those companies whose additional tax payments exceed the reductions in the social security payments by a factor higher than 1.2 will get this excess burden reimbursed. However, the reduced tax rates, implemented to avoid putting German companies at a competitive disadvantage in the international market, are of a temporary nature only.

Taxing electricity 'output' rather than the fuel 'inputs' according to their carbon content does not encourage generators to use low-carbon fuels, but does allow the taxation of electricity generated by nuclear power plants. Apart from the politics surrounding power from nuclear power, there are two important reasons for taxing the electricity rather than the fuels. First, several other European countries do not tax fuel inputs either, and German power producers would therefore have been put at a competitive disadvantage in the

---

[38] *OECD Economic Surveys: Germany 1999.*
[39] Schiffer, 'Energiesteuern klettern'.
[40] Ibid; *Die Förderung des Umweltschutzes im deutschen Abgabenrecht* (Bonn: Bundesministerium der Finanzen); see www.bundesfinanzministerium.de/finwiber/auswahl.html.

European market by an input tax. Second, taxing electricity imports according to the fuel mix in the producing country is not compatible with either EU or World Trade Organization (WTO) rules, which do not, in principle, allow for discrimination according to production methods. Until an EU-level agreement has been reached, therefore, an electricity tax is used as the 'second best' solution. Table 8.3 summarizes the tax changes resulting from the ecological tax reform.

Table 8.3: Tax rates resulting from the ecological tax reform in Germany (eurocents)

Fuels	Before April 1999	From April 1999	2000	2001	2002	2003
Light heating oil[a]	4.1	6.1	6.1	6.1	6.1	6.1
Light heating oil for industry[a]	4.1	4.5	4.5	4.5	4.5	4.5
Light heating oil for CHP[a, c]	4.1	–	–	–	–	–
Natural gas[b]	0.18	0.35	0.35	0.35	0.35	0.35
Natural gas for industry[b]	0.18	0.22	0.22	0.22	0.22	0.22
Natural gas for power generation[b]	0.18	0.18	0.18	0.18	0.18	0.18
Natural gas for CHP[b, c]	0.18	–	–	–	–	–
Electricity[b]	–	1	1.3	1.5	1.8	2
Electricity for public transport[b]	–	0.5	0.64	0.77	0.89	1
Electricity for industry[b]	–	0.21	0.26	0.31	0.36	0.41

[a] e/l.
[b] e/kWh
[c] Only for CHP with an efficiency exceeding 70%.

Source: Schiffer, Hans-Wilhelm, 'Energiesteuern klettern', in *VDI Nachrichten*, 3 Dec. 1999.

The effectiveness of the ecological tax reform, in terms of raising the costs for electricity use, has been hampered by the dramatic drop in electricity prices following the liberalization of the electricity market in Germany. In general, the tax rates were not high enough to compensate for the price cuts; this is true in particular for industrial users, who enjoyed the largest decreases in electricity costs.

Promotion of renewable energy sources   The German government aims to double the share of RES in power production from about 5% in 2000 to 10% in 2010. Apart from the benefits of increased diversifiation and improved energy security, a reduction in CO_2 emissions of 20–30MtCO$_2$ is expected as a result by 2010.[41]

---

[41] *Erneuerbare Energien und Nachhaltige Entwicklung* (Berlin: Bundesministerium für Umwelt, Naturschutz und Reaktorsicherheit, 2000).

The main instrument to stimulate the development of renewable energy in Germany was the 'Electricity Feed Act'. However, the liberalization of the electricity markets has been a major driver for the change in this law. The old Electricity Feed Act required grid operators to pay a certain percentage of average historic electricity retail prices as feed-in prices for electricity generated by certain RES; these payments were to be continued until the share of renewables had reached 5%. This regulation affected the utilities operating the grid asymmetrically; wind turbines, which benefited most under the Electricity Feed Act, were concentrated in northern Germany, so grid operators in the North were therefore set at a (slight) competitive disadvantage in the liberalized electricity market. More importantly, falling electricity prices would have resulted in lower feed-in prices for electricity from renewable sources under the old law, undermining the economic basis of the renewable energy industry.

Consequently, in February 2000, the German legislature passed the new renewable energy sources act (EEG), which came into force on 1 April 2000.[42] Under the new law, feed-in prices are no longer linked to electricity retail prices, but are fixed for twenty years – in contrast to developments in most of Europe. The cap on the share of renewables was also abolished. Furthermore, for the first time, electricity generated by utilities from renewables is also covered by the law – unless the *Länder* or federal government owns more than 25% of the utility's shares.

Feed-in prices for some technologies (wind, photovoltaics and biomass) are set to fall for plants installed after 1 January 2002. Table 8.4 shows that feed-in prices vary across technology types and sizes, ranging from 6.65e/kWh for hydro to 50.6e/kWh for solar PV. In the case of wind power, price within the band specified is determined by location. The new feed-in law is expected to cost utilities and end users about €1.23bn compared with €0.67bn under the old law, and to increase electricity prices for consumers by 0.05–0.1e/kWh.

Additional promotion measures at the federal level   The '100,000 roofs' photovoltaic programme of the Reconstruction Loan Corporation (KfW) began in February 1999 with zero-interest loans as well as reductions in price for photovoltaic systems, adding up to an overall subsidy equivalent to 40% of the investment costs.[43] The programme aims to support the installation of an

---

[42] *Erneuerbare-Energien-Gesetz* (Berlin: Bundesministerium für Umwelt, Naturschutz und Reaktorsicherheit); see www.bmu.de/fset800.htm, accessed 2 Aug. 2000.
[43] *Erneuerbare Energien und Nachhaltige Entwicklung.*

Table 8.4: Feed-in tariffs under the German Renewable Energy Sources Act, 2000 (e/kWh)

Plant type	0–0.5MW	0.5–5MW	5–20MW	>20MW
Wind	6.2–9.1	6.2–9.1	6.2–9.1	6.2–9.1
Biomass	10.2	9.2	8.7	–
Photovoltaics	50.6	50.6	–	–
Geothermal	8.9	8.9	8.9	7.2
Hydro	7.7	6.6	–	–
Landfill gas	7.7	6.6	–	–
Mine gas	7.7	6.6	6.6	6.6
Sewage gas	7.7	6.6	–	–

additional 300MW of capacity on top of the existing 50MW, with an average capacity of 3kWh per unit.[44]

Schemes eligible for support under this programme can also benefit from other promotional programmes (such as the EEG), but only up to the point where public support equals the costs for the system owner. After the entry into force of the EEG the demand for the programme increased so much that in May 2000 slightly less favourable terms had to be worked out (see Figure 8.5).[45] Apart from the payments under the EEG, some municipal utilities pay even higher prices for electricity from renewables, in particular from photovoltaics.

In September 2001 the total capacity for which subsidies were granted exceeded 100MWp. Figure 8.5 shows the total capacity subsidized, the number of applications and the total number of subsidies granted. By August 2001 the total number of successful applications had reached a quarter of the target 100,000 roofs. The average installed capacity per application is just over 4kWp.[46]

The market introduction programme for renewable energy sources (*Markteinführungsprogramm Erneuerbare Energien*) was launched in September 1999. It focuses on the use of solar thermal and biomass energy. Financial

---

[44] *100.000-Dächer-Solarstromprogramm* (Berlin: Bundesministerium für Umwelt, Naturschutz und Reaktorsicherheit); see www.bmu.de/fset800.htm, accessed 4 Sept. 2000.
[45] *Wiederaufnahme des 100.000-Dächer-Programms* (Münster: Internationales Wirtschaftsforum Regenerative Energien); see www.uni-muenster.de/Energie/re/iwr/arch0700, accessed 17 July 2000.
[46] www.uni-muenster.de/Energie.

Figure 8.5: The 100,000 roofs programme

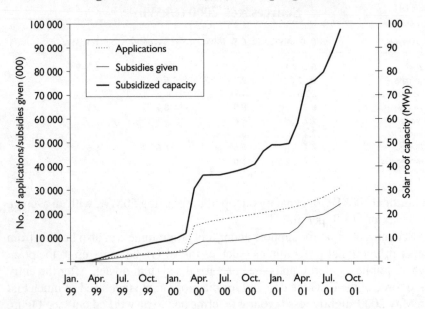

Source: Data from www.uni-muenster.de/Energie.

support is provided through direct payments and low-interest credits. The funds, €102m, are recycled from the revenues of the ecological tax reform.

The solar campaign 2000 (*Solarkampagne 2000*) aims to increase the use of solar heating by providing better information and advisory measures. The campaign is cofinanced by industry and environmental associations.[47]

The use of renewable energy was further promoted by changes in building regulations, including the payment and tax system for architects and building engineers.[48]

Support for cogeneration   As pointed out earlier, low electricity prices in the wake of liberalization have already led to the closure of several CHP plants and are seriously threatening the profitability of others. To provide temporary support for cogeneration in the public electricity supply sector, and to avoid stranded investments (investments that will not provide a return under

---

[47] *Erneuerbare Energien und Nachhaltige Entwicklung.*
[48] Ibid.; architects' fees are not freely negotiated, but legally regulated according to their honorarium code.

market conditions), government passed the so-called *KWK-Vorschaltgesetz* in spring 2000. Under a provision similar to that in the Electricity Feed Act for renewables, municipal power producers may receive a minimum compensation of 4.6e/kWh from the grid operator for electricity generated by CHP if this accounts for at least 25% of capacity, and at least 10% of the total power production of the utility. The subsidy is scheduled to decrease by 0.26e per year. The total costs for this support scheme are expected to be around 0.01e/kWh.

The ecological tax reform also supports efficient cogeneration by exempting oil and gas used for CHP from the tax. Users of CHP that do not reach the required 70% efficiency, but still exceed an annual efficiency of 60%, pay tax at a reduced level.[49]

According to the new energy law, utilities may block access to the grid if electricity generation from renewable energy sources or from cogeneration is economically threatened. However, in practice this law is powerless, in particular since the burden of proof rests on the clean electricity producer.

In the medium and long term further regulations were planned to achieve the goal of doubling electricity from cogeneration to 20% in 2010. In particular, the government was considering the introduction of a (tradable) quota system for CHP to substitute for the *KWK-Vorschaltgesetz*.[50] The response from power producers, which did not want to take on mandatory targets for a doubling of the current share of CHP, was less than enthusiastic. As an alternative to the CHP quota system, a detailed voluntary action plan was submitted to government. The industry acknowledged the importance of cogeneration in emissions reductions, but stressed that other measures could bring about further reductions, while being more in line with the competitive market now in place. In July 2001, government and industry agreed on a voluntary reduction target of $23MtCO_2$ by increased use of CHP. Whereas industry agreed to invest in CHP, government regulation will result in a premium for power from CHP. Until 2010, existing and modernized – but not newly installed – plants will receive a bonus of 1.53e/kWh; plants smaller than 2MW will receive 2.56e/kWh. Since only electricity which is fed into the public grid is subsidized, neither auto-generated CHP nor most industrial CHP will benefit. The agreement also includes additional support of €358m (DM700m) for electricity from micro-CHPs and fuel cells. Should industry

---

[49] *Die Förderung des Umweltschutzes im deutschen Abgabenrecht.*
[50] *Schutz der Kraft-Wärme-Kopplung* (Bundesministerium für Umwelt, Naturschutz und Reaktorsicherheit); see www.bmu.de/klima/index.htm, accessed 27 March 2000.

fail to meet its commitment, the government will introduce a CHP quota system.[51]

Voluntary agreements   The voluntary commitment of the German industry (1995/6) is based on individual declarations from nineteen industry associations grouped together under the BDI. German industry has stated its willingness to reduce its _specific_ energy consumption (i.e. per unit of output) by 20% from 1990 levels by the year 2005. The individual commitments varied considerably from industry to industry, with some setting absolute and others specific reduction targets. For example, the German Electricity Association (VDEW) agreed to reduce emissions by 8–10% in 2005 (23–29MtCO$_2$), and by 12% in 2010. In addition, the association of local authority public utilities (VKU), representing municipal energy suppliers, committed itself to reduce its CO$_2$ emissions by 25% (34MtCO$_2$) in the year 2005. By 1997, VDEW-utilities had already reduced their CO$_2$ emissions almost to the target levels for 2005. The VKU did not provide a quantitative assessment.[52] In 2001, however, the VDEW reported a strong growth in emissions in 2000 compared with 1999, leaving emissions at 7.6% below 1990 levels, compared with 10.7% below a year earlier.[53]

A new round of voluntary agreements have recently been negotiated between government and industry associations. The agreements have now been extended to all the Kyoto gases and higher reduction targets have been set.

Flexible mechanisms   Since 1995, the German government has supported projects under the AIJ pilot phase, establishing an AIJ coordination office and financing evaluations and research in this area.[54] To date, six German AIJ projects have been approved, and more than thirty are still in the process of approval or planning. Most of these projects are based on energy efficiency

---

[51] Bundesministerium für Umwelt, Naturschutz und Reaktorsicherheit press release, 'KWK-Förderung das richtige Signal vor der Klimakonfernz in Bonn', 132/01 (Berlin: BMU, 4 July 2001, www.bmu.de).

[52] Hans Georg Buttermann, Bernhard Hillebrand and Ulrike Lehr, 'Second Monitoring Report: CO$_2$ Emissions in German Industry 1996–1997', in _Nur zaghafter Einstieg in die ökologische Steuerreform, DIW Wochenbericht 36/99_ (Essen: DIW, 1999, pp. 652–8.

[53] Verband deutscher Elektrizitätswerke [German Electricity Association], _Electricity Suppliers Reduce CO$_2$ Emissions_ (Frankfurt am Main: VDEW, 18 June 2001, www.strom.de).

[54] _Second National Communication of the Federal Republic of Germany Pursuant to the United Nations Framework Convention on Climate Change_ (Bonn: Bundesministerium für Umwelt, Naturschutz und Reaktorsicherheit, 1997.

improvements or renewable energy supply and are financed by energy utilities like the former PreussenElektra, Ruhrgas, the former Bayernwerke and RWE. The six projects so far will reduce emissions by $8.65MtCO_2e$ over their lifetime. They are located in Russia (two), the Czech Republic, Latvia, Jordan and Zimbabwe; the last two projects are in cooperation with other Annex I countries.[55]

The German government is currently investigating the possibility of German industry participating in a national or EU-wide ETS. It has set up a working group, which includes government, industry and industry associations, and environmental groups, to look at the issue. While the environment minister Jürgen Trittin has said that 'emissions trading can contribute positively to climate protection', industry strongly opposes the Europe-wide scheme proposed by the EU.[56] One of the stumbling blocks is the relationship between the already agreed voluntary targets for industry and the mandatory caps required for trading. However, Hamburg utility HEW and state credit agency KfW (which also sponsors the 100,000 solar roofs programme) have responded positively. HEW has already embarked on international emissions trading, selling emissions rights to a Canadian generator and buying credits from Australia.[57] KfW has set up two funds to stimulate the use of the Kyoto mechanisms. One of the funds helps with investments in CDM projects; the other aims to encourage small and medium-sized companies to take part in national or international emissions trading.[58]

8.5 Conclusions

German emissions have declined substantially in the past decade. Since 1990 GHG emissions have gone down by nearly 20%, to a large extent due to the reunification; but a further decline of some percentage points is needed to meet the Kyoto target, and in particular the more ambitious domestic target. The government has set out a plan to meet the Kyoto target in 2010 and the 25% domestic target in 2005. Key to this plan are the ecological tax reform, support for renewables, and CHP; the ongoing and new voluntary agreements

---

[55] www.unfccc.int.

[56] Platts, London, 17 Sept. 2001; Reuters (Frankfurt), 'German Industry Slams EU Emissions Trading Plan', 29 Aug. 2001; see www.planetark.org.

[57] Reuters (Frankfurt), 'German HEW Urges Industry to Back Emissions Trading', 29 Aug. 2001; see www.planetark.org.

[58] Reuters (Frankfurt), 'German Credit Bank Proposes Emissions Trading Funds', 19 Sept. 2001; see www.planetark.org.

also bring substantial reductions. However, there are several contradictory elements in current German policies. First, coal and lignite are still being supported, either through direct subsidies to coal producers or through support for the building of new lignite-fuelled power plants. Second, the support scheme for renewables has been changed to give a guaranteed fixed price for twenty years not dependent on the (now very low) market price. However, whether this support scheme, and that for cogeneration, will survive the investigation under the state aid procedure set in motion by the EU is questionable. Third, the opposition of most German utilities and industry to emissions trading seems incompatible with the free market.

9 Italy: climate change policy and electricity liberalization

Marcella Pavan[1]

The Italian electricity sector is one of the largest in Europe. Traditionally it has been run by a vertically integrated state-owned utility, ENEL Spa. Emissions are relatively high, the capital stock is old and the major fuel is oil. However, the liberalization process, set in motion by the European liberalization directive, will have major repercussions in the sector.

Under law already in place, by 2003 no company in Italy will be allowed to have more than a 50% share of the electricity market. ENEL has already started reducing its capacity domestically to comply with this regulation. At the same time as introducing market forces, the Italian government also designed a strategy to combat climate change that relies heavily on emissions reductions from the supply side of the power sector.

9.1 The Italian electricity sector at a glance

Italy began the regulatory reform of the electricity sector from a position of very little competition. Since the nationalization of the electricity industry in 1962 the sector had been a public legal monopoly, with all electricity activities reserved to ENEL through a sole concession. In 1992 the power production market was opened to cogeneration and renewables. The independent power producers producing electricity by these means had to sell their output to ENEL at regulated premium prices. Auto-generators were also allowed to sell electricity they did not use themselves directly to ENEL. ENEL had a role in approving new entrants into the market and could therefore exert considerable influence. When Legislative Decree No. 79 of 16 March 1999 was enacted, implementing EC Directive 96/92 on electricity liberalization, ENEL still contributed 83% of Italy's electricity and owned 55GW of installed capacity. Until 1999 ENEL had also a de facto monopoly on imports and exports by concession from the ministry of industry.

[1] The opinions expressed in this chapter are those of the author only and do not reflect the views or decisions of the Italian Regulatory Authority for Electricity and Gas.

Figure 9.1: Fuel shares in the Italian power sector

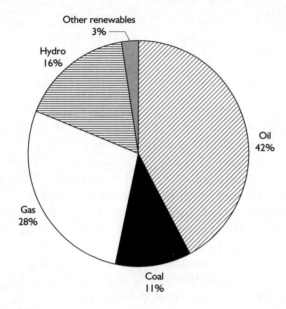

Source: IEA Electricity Information, 2000.

Note: Imports are not included.

Traditional thermal power plants represent 72% of the overall installed capacity and produce almost 80% of the total electricity generated in the country. Heavy fuel oil is the main fuel for electricity generation, primarily for base load, and accounts for more than 42% of the total electricity produced, followed by natural gas (28%), whose share in total electricity production has been constantly growing in the last decade, and coal (11%). Hydro represents more than 16% of total power generation, geothermal and other renewable sources accounting for the remaining 2.5%. The existing power plants in the Italian power sector are rather old, with an average conversion efficiency around 38%. Following a referendum in 1987, the government placed a moratorium on electricity generation from nuclear power. Figure 9.1 shows the fuel shares in the Italian power sector.

ENEL owns the transmission grid and 93% of the low-voltage distribution grid. However, following the implementation of the government decree on the liberalization of the sector, the TSO, a public company, operates, maintains and develops the national grid.

Total consumption in 1999 amounted to 262.7TWh. Net imports represents almost 15% of total electricity supply. The industrial sector's share in demand is 53%, the tertiary sector uses 22% and the household sector slightly more than 23%, the remaining 2% being taken by agriculture. The average annual electricity consumption per capita is below the EU average at 4,638kWh compared with 5,697kWh.

9.2   Liberalization of the market

Following Legislative Decree No. 79 of 16 March 1999 implementing EC Directive 96/92, the sector is being radically reformed. The major elements of this liberalization process are described below, and the new power sector structure is depicted in Figure 9.2.

9.2.1   Key elements of the liberalization process

The structure of the sector is changing to promote competition in generation and supply to customers:

Figure 9.2: The liberalized electricity sector in Italy

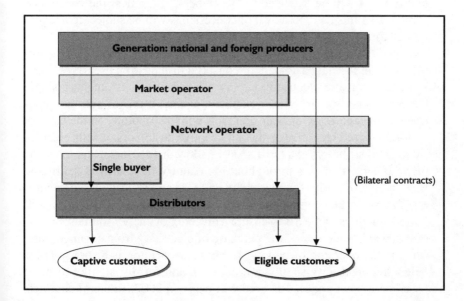

- Legislative Decree No. 79 of 16 March 1999, implementing EC Directive 96/92, requires functional unbundling of the electricity industry.
- A newly established publicly owned company is charged with the management and dispatch of the national transmission system. The network operator's responsibilities include the non-discriminatory management of the network; the provision of ancillary services; and taking decisions on maintenance and development. ENEL will retain legal ownership of the transmission network. In cooperation with the Regulatory Authority for Electricity and Gas, the network operator is in charge of issuing regulations to ensure equal access to the network and priority in dispatch to renewables and CHP. Network access can be refused only on the grounds of lack of capacity and, for imports, where reciprocity conditions are not met.
- Generation and import by any single company is limited to 50%, from 1 January 2003. By that date ENEL will have had to divest at least 15,000MW of its generation capacity.
- New generating plants are granted authorization according to a standardized procedure for each category of plant. Just one authorization covers the building of the whole plant and associated facilities, in contrast to the previous system in which several authorizations were needed. A thirty-year limit is set on ENEL's concessions for hydro plants. Other concessions for hydro plants will be extended to December 2010, unless the concession expires after this date. Renewal of concessions will be subject to a tender procedure.
- The electricity market is to be opened gradually to competition, beginning with industrial customers or consortia of industrial users.
- In order to ensure electricity supply to all captive customers, a single buyer (SB) is established as a public company. It makes purchase contracts with generators and sale contracts with distributors, on the basis of its forecasts of electricity demand by captive customers. It sells electricity to the distributors at a tariff so as to allow distributors to set the same price to captive clients throughout the country. The tariff is set by the Regulatory Authority for Electricity and Gas and is designed to encourage the SB to be economically efficient. The ministry of industry will issue guidelines to the SB to ensure a diversity of energy sources, the use of renewable sources and the purchase of electricity from cogeneration.
- The market operator, owned by the network operator, is responsible for balancing electricity supply and demand, and for dispatching of plant based on a power pool. The pool will begin in 2002. Bilateral contracts

between generators and eligible customers are subject to agreement from the network operator and authorization by the Regulatory Authority for Electricity and Gas.

- Concessions for distribution are granted by the minister of industry for a period of thirty years. The distribution tariffs are regulated by the Regulatory Authority for Electricity and Gas. Large municipal distributors, those with more than 300,000 final consumers, must have a corporate structure that separates their distribution activity from other activities.
- Imports from EU countries is unrestricted, subject to available grid capacity and reciprocity criteria. Imports from non-EU countries are subject to additional environmental protection considerations.

9.2.2 Impact on emissions

Figure 9.3 shows Italian GHG emissions for 1990–9. The electricity sector (including heat generation by public utilities and auto-producers) accounts for 30% of total CO_2 emissions from fossil-fuel combustion nationwide, making it the largest-emitting sector, followed by transport. Energy sector

Figure 9.3: Italian greenhouse gas emissions, 1990–1999

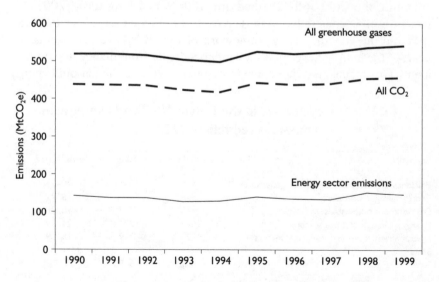

Source: European Environment Agency, EU emissions inventory 2000; see www.eea.org.

emissions in 1999 fell to only 2.5% above 1990 levels from higher levels in 1998.

Emissions per unit of output are significantly higher compared with the European average (511gCO$_2$/kWh against 425gCO$_2$/kWh). This is a consequence of the different fuel mix used in power generation (larger share of oil) but also of the rather low conversion efficiency of conventional fossil-fuelled power plants. Oil-fired thermoelectric power plants are responsible for more than 60% of CO$_2$ emissions, with coal-fired and gas-fired plants representing slightly more than 20% and 18% respectively. Accordingly, a large potential for emissions reductions exists.

9.3   The national climate programme

Under the Kyoto Protocol and the EU burden-sharing agreement, Italy is committed to reducing its emissions by 6.5% from 1990 levels by 2008–12. However, recent official national GHG emissions data show a 5.4% increase in 1999 over 1990. The target therefore represents a substantial reduction from business as usual.

In November 1998 the government adopted the second NCP, which singled out six 'key actions' that are set to deliver this emissions reduction target. Table 9.1 gives an overview of these measures, with the corresponding the short- (2002), medium- (2006) and long-term (2008–12) goals for emissions reductions. The overall reduction target, sectoral targets and the general policy framework of the NCP have been set at the heart of the national energy policy independently from the Kyoto commitment. This means that they have to be integrated into the national energy

Table 9.1: Key actions in the Italian NCP and consequent emissions reductions (MtCO$_2$e)

Key action	2002	2006	2008–2012
Efficiency improvements in power generation	4–5	10–12	20–23
Energy saving in transport	4–6	9–11	18–21
Promotion of renewables	4–5	7–9	18–20
Energy savings in end-use sectors	6–7	12–14	24–29
Emission reductions in non-energy sectors	2	7–9	15–19
Sinks	–	–	0.7
Total	20–25	45–55	95–112

Source: CIPE deliberation, 19 Nov. 1998, no. 137/98.

strategy for the next decade even in the event that the Kyoto Protocol does not enter into force.

Policies and measures in the electricity sector will play a key role in the reduction of GHG emissions nationwide. Over 20% of the reduction target will have to come from efficiency improvements in power plants; 18% will have to be delivered through increased use of renewable energy; policies and measures to promote energy savings in end-use sectors will deliver 26% of the target. Together, about 38% of the national target will have to be achieved through actions on the supply side of the electricity market. DSM programmes in the electricity sector could also make a significant contribution.

The NCP is based on three main principles. It will:

1 enhance the emissions reduction potential of policy measures that have to be introduced in order to comply with EU directives and regulations;
2 pursue the modernization of the industrial and energy sector and infra-structure and improve energy efficiency in a cost-effective way;
3 promote the development of innovative low-emission technologies.

As far as the electricity sector is concerned, these principles translate into the need to define, within a specified time-frame, specific policies and measures that will:

* promote a faster capital stock turnover, in particular of the most ineffi-cient power plants that will play only a marginal role in the new liberalized electricity market;
* favour the use of the best available technologies for the protection of the environment and the promotion of energy savings when authorizing the construction of new power plants or renewing the authorizations to pro-duce electricity for existing ones;
* promote the development of electricity from renewable sources;
* promote additional use of biomass in electricity production;
* promote energy savings in end-use sectors;
* diffuse information on climate change and its impacts to the general pub-lic; and
* define criteria for the promotion of initiatives in the framework of the Kyoto mechanisms (tradable permits, JI and CDM).

The great part of this package of measures should be of a 'no-regrets' nature: that is, apart from emissions reductions, the measures will deliver a number of secondary benefits in terms of efficiency improvements, enhancement of the competitiveness of the Italian electricity supply industry, and air quality improvements in towns and cities.

9.4 Implementing the NCP: supply

The development of the NCP gave new impetus to the political discussion about the 'best' package of policy tools to achieve the emissions reduction objectives in key sectors. The range of policy instruments relevant to the electricity sector include regulation, 'standard' economic instruments (fiscal measures), 'new' market instruments (voluntary approaches and the flexible mechanisms), and information and research programmes.

Two major factors have driven the choice of instruments to be implemented:

1 the relatively high marginal cost of abatement in Italy compared with other EU countries, due mainly to the low energy intensity of the economy; and
2 the gradual liberalization of the electricity market and the need to design policy tools consistent with the new market framework.

Because power generation in Italy is highly reliant on fuel oil in old and rather inefficient thermoelectric power plants, the policy measures introduced or under discussion aim to:

• modify the fuel mix in power generation, shifting away from carbon-intensive fuels to lower- or zero-emission fuels; and
• increase the conversion efficiency of existing thermoelectric power plants as well as investments in new capacity.

Three particular policy instruments are highlighted here: fiscal policy (tax), economic policy (competition and tariffs) and industrial policy (renewables).

9.4.1 Carbon tax

In order to promote the use of low-carbon fuels in the energy and transport sector, as well as aiming to proceed towards harmonization of energy taxation in the EU, the government proposed a carbon tax in 1998. The tax came into effect in January 1999 and will be progressively increased to reach target levels by 2005.

Table 9.2 shows the 1999 and 2005 target carbon tax levels for different fuels in power generation. These rates are the sum of two taxes. First, the existing excise duties on mineral oil products are increased; second, a new excise tax is introduced of €0.52 (L1,000) per tonne of coal, petroleum coke or orimulsion for use in combustion plants with a thermal capacity over 50MW.

The incremental increases of the tax will be decided annually by government. Taxes will increase by a minimum of 5% and a maximum of 20% of the difference between current and target tax levels. The rate of increase will be dependent on CO_2 emission trends and harmonization of EU energy taxes. However, in 2000 the government decided to leave tax rates unchanged, because of the strong increase in crude oil prices at the end of 1999 and the impact on inflation.

Table 9.2: Carbon tax rates in Italy, 1999 and 2005 (€/t)

Fuel	1999	2005 target level
Fuel oil	15.33	21.31
Diesel oil	12.73	16.63
Natural gas	0.45	4.49
LPG	0.68	6.82
Coal	2.63	21.61
Petroleum coke	3.52	30.59
Orimulsion	2.06	15.92

Generally speaking, the original structure of the tax reflected two components: an 'energy component' and an 'environmental component'. The first component was designed in order to correct existing taxation levels according to the minimum levels set out in the proposal of the European Commission to the Council on the harmonization of energy taxation within the EU (COM/97/30). Tax rates on fossil fuels used in power generation do not include this 'energy component' since electricity consumption in Italy is already taxed.

Contrary to the situation in most countries, the 'environmental component' of the new tax has a progressive structure, i.e. the (marginal) tax rate is greater the greater is the carbon content of the fuel. As far as fuels used in power generation are concerned, the tax rate per unit of carbon is much higher for coal than for oil products and natural gas. Figure 9.4 shows the progressive tax rates and carbon contents of the fuels used for power production. For industrial auto-producers or cogeneration, the tax rate on mineral

Figure 9.4: Carbon tax levels for different fuels in Italy, 1999

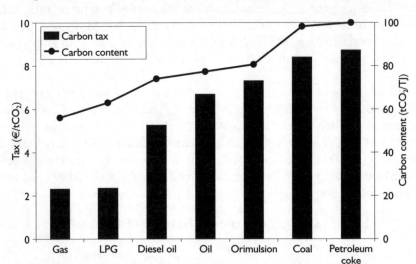

oil products is always equal to 30% of the rate applied to electricity production by utilities, while an equal rate is applied on the consumption of coal,
petroleum coke and orimulsion. Imported electricity is not taxed.

The government has estimated that the tax revenues could amount to €5.9bn
(L11,500bn) when fully implemented in 2005; in 1999, revenues would be
around €1bn (L2,000bn). Revenues from the electricity sector alone would
be €413m and €52m (L800bn and L100bn) respectively for 2005 and 1999.
The tax is designed to be revenue-neutral, with the revenues recycled back
into the economy through three measures:

1 Social security payments for labour will be reduced, in line with the
   government's aim of shifting the tax burden away from labour and towards use of environmental resources. Over half the revenues raised are
   recycled back in this way, and are expected to lower employment costs
   and increase the number of jobs.
2 Nearly 30% of the carbon tax revenue will be used to reduce excise duties
   previously charged on diesel oil for transport, compensating households
   for the increased heating costs. This part of the recycling will clearly not
   generate extra environmental benefits.
3 Various forms of incentives, such as direct subsidies and tax breaks, to
   promote investments in GHG emissions reductions, energy efficiency

improvements and renewable energy sources use up the remaining 13% of tax revenues. These subsidies cannot exceed 20% of total investment expenditures in the previous year or 25% of the total amount due under the tax.

The price effects of the new carbon tax on fossil fuels in power generation are relevant. At the 2005 target level of tax, taking the average conversion efficiency of existing power plants (in 1997), marginal costs are changed substantially. The cost of coal-fired power would increase by 40%. The increases for oil and gas are much less, at 6% and 3% respectively. The tax therefore clearly favours the shift away from coal and oil to natural gas. The total CO_2 emissions reductions expected to be achieved through the tax are around 12Mt, 12% of the total reduction target set out in the NCP.

9.4.2 The introduction of competition and the reform of the tariff system

Substantial incentives for efficiency improvements in existing power plants as well as for investment in new capacity are being introduced with the liberalization of the electricity market and with the recent reform of the electricity tariff system.

The reform of electricity tariffs   Historically, the level of electricity tariffs for final consumers in Italy reflected a stratification of objectives: social, industrial, environmental and revenue-raising. In November 1995 the government set up the Regulatory Authority for Electricity and Gas, an independent, statutory body whose remit is to regulate and control the electricity and gas sector. The authority operates within the policy framework laid down by the government and the parliament, with full regard for EU legislation. Its task is to promote competition and efficiency and ensure adequate standards of service in the regulated sectors.[2] It is required to pursue these policy objectives by ensuring the uniform availability of services in the country, by establishing a clearly defined tariff system based on set criteria, and by promoting the interests of users and consumers. The tariff system is also required to reconcile the economic and financial objectives of the industry with general social objectives, environmental protection and efficient resource use.

On these grounds the Regulatory Authority for Electricity and Gas set the reform of the existing electricity tariff system in motion in June 1997. The reform

---

[2] Law no. 481/95 of 14 Nov. 1995; available at www.autorita.energia.it.

has radically changed both the principles and the mechanisms of regulated tariff-setting. Key features of the new system include cost-reflectivity, flexibility in the contractual relationships between electric utilities and customers, and incentives for efficiency improvements in power generation and supply.

In June 1997 the mechanism through which the contribution to generator–distributor companies funded the part of the tariff which covers fuel costs was drastically reformed.[3] Fuel costs amount to about 50% of the overall cost of generating electricity in Italy. The new mechanism promotes efficiency in fuel use by replacing the previous 'pass-through' mechanism of actual fuel purchase costs borne by generators with one in which contributions are related to a standard fuel cost. This cost is linked to the international prices of a representative basket of fuels used in the Italian electricity supply industry (prices are converted into lire and averaged using fixed weights). Contributions are subjects to a two-monthly automatic adjustment on the basis of price movements in the previous four months.

The shift from the pass-through mechanism to a system based on standard costs introduced significant incentives for electricity companies to reduce their costs via efficiency improvements, since not all costs they incur will automatically be passed on to final consumers.

The new cost recovery system for fuel costs also works effectively in parallel with the carbon tax – both instruments aim at promoting efficiency improvements in power generation. The tax promotes fuel substitution towards low- or zero-carbon fuels, while the tariff allows generators to recover an average fuel cost corresponding to achievable efficiency levels.

Further incentives for efficiency improvements in electricity generation, transmission and supply have been introduced via the tariff system in the framework of the newly liberalized electricity market. The administered price regime remains in place for:

- the *transport of electricity* over the national transmission network and the local distribution networks, in which there is little or no scope for competition (the cost of transport currently accounts for 35% of the final pre-tax price paid by low-voltage electricity users; the percentage is lower in the case of large high-voltage customers); and
- the tariff for *captive customers.*

---

[3] Autorità per l'energia elettrica e il gas, *Deliberation 26 June 1997, no. 70/1997*; available in Italian only at www.autorita.energia.it.

In both cases, the authority sets initial tariff levels, defined as the maximum unit price, and the parameters for price adjustments, using a price-cap method on a multi-year basis. From 2000 the tariff for the supply of electricity to captive customers covers components for the costs of transmission, distribution and supply of electricity. It has been set gradually to approach a level reflecting 'allowed costs' for these activities as opposed to the pass-through mechanism of the previous tariff system.[4] Allowed costs have been set on the basis of an analysis of costs actually incurred by electricity companies.[5] Activities carried out in the public interest are also covered.[6] As in the case of fuel costs, the shift from a pass-through mechanisms to a system based on allowed costs gives companies an incentive to increase their efficiency.

In the reformed tariff system the tariff components covering transmission, distribution and supply of electricity are subject to annual variations within a four-year regulatory period. The price-cap mechanism provides electricity companies with a degree of certainty with regard to future tariff levels. Annual variations in tariff levels are dependent on:

- the annual variation in the consumer price index; and
- efficiency targets set in advance.

Quality of service, unforeseeable and exceptional events, as well as changes in the legal framework and cost related to DSM programmes are also taken into account when setting the tariffs.

During the first regulatory period (2000–4), the efficiency target has been set at 4% in real terms. Companies' profitability will benefit from any efficiency gains over and above the target level, encouraging them to improve their productivity. At the end of the first regulatory period a partial tariff-cost

---

[4] Consultation paper of 27 Nov. 1999 and Deliberation of 29 Dec. 1999, no. 204/99; available in Italian only at www.autorita.energia.it.

[5] The Regulatory Authority for Electricity and Gas analysed the average unit costs actually incurred by ENEL as the principal operator in all stages of national electricity production. These costs were compared with those of the other major companies in the sector, using data for the financial year 1997 collected by the authority in 1998. These data made it possible to define allowed cost levels for each stage of production. Allowed costs include costs of external sources – i.e. personnel, procurement of materials and services, depreciation and fair return on net invested capital.

[6] These include, inter alia, the promotion of renewable sources, the protection of low-income customers, the costs related to the phasing-out of nuclear plants following the 1987 referendum, the financing of special tariff regimes and the financing of R&D activities.

readjustment is envisaged. At the start of the second period productivity gains over and above the 4% target level will be shared between companies and users.[7] Investments aimed at increasing productivity are considered to be part of the net invested capital, on which return is guaranteed.

Liberalization of the market   Capital stock turnover and new additions to the existing capital stock offer important opportunities for increasing the use of cleaner, more efficient technology. The conversion efficiency of conventional fossil-fuel generation has risen from about 38% in oil-fired power stations to about 53% in the latest CCGTs. Efficiencies of up to 60% are promised in new designs. These developments, taken together with the lower carbon intensity of natural gas, mean that each unit of electricity generated from gas emits only about half the CO_2 of the same unit generated from oil, which accounts for over 40% of Italy's generation and 60% of power sector emissions.

Historically, the power generation sector in Italy has been characterized by a slow capital stock turnover. Therefore, policies that affect the speed of capital stock replacement, and the nature and efficiency of both replacement and new stock, will be central to the efforts to reduce GHG emissions. In addition to the incentives introduced by the recent reform of the tariff system, the operation of competitive market forces in electricity generation will be critical in this respect.

As discussed earlier, by 2003 no single operator will be allowed to produce or import more than 50% of the total electricity demand in Italy. To meet this requirement, ENEL will have to reduce its power generation capacity by about 15,000MW by the end of 2002. Only in case of adverse market conditions and following approval by the Anti-Trust Authority and the Regulatory Authority for Electricity and Gas can this date by postponed by a maximum of one year.

ENEL's divestment plan, approved by government in August 1999, groups the plants to be divested in three generation companies. The plan met detailed selection criteria set by the ministry of industry. Each generation company had to replicate as closely as possible the cost structure, merit order and geographical distribution of the remaining generation assets of ENEL, in order that all would possess sufficient capacity for technological innovation and the ability to compete at an international level.

ENEL's divestment plan also contains detailed investment plans, including deadlines, for each of the plants to be sold. In particular, it sets out required

---

[7] The companies' share of these gains should not exceed 50%.

investments in replacements for old generation units with CCGTs for about 70% of the capacity to be sold. Buyers of the three generation companies take on the obligation to follow ENEL's development plans as laid out. From a climate change strategy point of view, should these investments be completed by 2008, as indicated in the divestment plan, CO_2 emissions from the power sector would be cut significantly in the first commitment period.[8] It is important, therefore, to speed up the divestment process and to simplify procedures for entry into or expansion of generation, which are particularly lengthy in Italy.[9] In addition, binding investment obligations similar to those envisaged for the buyers of the plants divested should be imposed on ENEL itself in order to avoid distortions in competition and to further speed up the renewal of the existing capital stock.

Finally, incentives are needed to promote further new additions as well as a fast replacement of the existing capital stock. Even after completion of the divestment plan ENEL will retain a large share of the market (close to 50%), making competition unlikely.[10] A new power pool is planned to be in place in 2002, setting prices for generation through a competitive bidding process. However, in order to have effective competition in the pool, more market players are needed.

9.4.3   Incentives for renewables

In August 1999 the government's interministerial committee on economic planning (CIPE) approved the white paper on the use of energy from renewable sources that set the framework for the government's policy and programmes in the renewable sector. According to the white paper, the contribution of renewable sources should increase from about 11.7Mtoe in 1997 to 20.3Mtoe between 2008 and 2012. Intermediate targets are also defined for 2002 (13.9Mtoe) and 2006 (15.9Mtoe). Quantitative targets for each renewable source are set. The total installed capacity of renewables should rise from 17,100MW to 24,700MW in the same period. The most significant increases

---

[8]   According to the Regulatory Authority for Electricity and Gas's estimates, the cut in CO_2 emissions would be around 20Mt, close to the target assigned by the NCP to the 'key action' of efficiency improvements in power generation.

[9]   At the time of writing, the government is aiming at accelerating the selling-off process.

[10]   ENEL's market share is in fact understated, since much of the non-ENEL capacity is not immediately available for competition in the market. Instead, the output of much current non-ENEL production is sold at premium prices under the CIP/6 programme (formerly to ENEL, but now to the TSO).

are expected to be in power generation from biomass, followed by hydro, wind, geothermal, energy from waste and solar energy. Emissions reductions from the additional use of renewables in electricity production are projected to be more than $18MtCO_2$.[11]

Against this background, a number of policy measures have been introduced to promote renewables, and others are under discussion. The aim is twofold:

1 to correct as far as possible the shortfalls of the incentive mechanisms implemented prior to the opening up of the electricity market, which can still result in distortions of competition in the new liberalized market;
2 to design new policy tools consistent with a competitive environment.

The legislative framework in place before the liberalization of the electricity market provided for two main measures to promote renewables:

1 a system of favourable payback tariffs for renewable electricity; and
2 subsidies of 30–80% of the capital cost of a renewable energy plant.

Under the buyback system ENEL purchased renewable electricity at fixed subsidized prices for the first eight years of the plant's operation.[12] This financial support system was stopped for projects after the second half of 1995, in order to be adapted to the new electricity regulatory framework.

The generous payback tariff for renewables has been a key factor in their increased role in power generation. However, the buyback system does not fit the new organization of the electricity sector. Opening up of the electricity

---

[11] According to the white paper, an additional cut of about $5MtCO_2$ should result from increases in renewable-generated heat production.

[12] In 1991 Law No. 9 and Law No. 10 encouraged the development of RES-E, assimilated sources and CHP, allowing for a certain number of new plants to sell power to ENEL at regulated prices. A selection procedure was implemented every six months. Independent projects were proposed to ENEL which, considering how much new capacity could be connected to the network, proceed to select some projects for approval by the ministry of industry. In 1992 a government directive (CIP 6/1992) provided for the following buyback tariff to these plants: (a) a subsidy, granted for the first eight years of the plant's operation, the amount depending on the type of plant; (b) a sum equal to the avoided cost of using fuel by ENEL during the contractual period; and (c) a sum equal to ENEL's avoided cost of investment, operation and maintenance. The first two components of the buyback tariff are financed by electricity tariffs during the contractual period, while the third is paid by ENEL to the plants during the contractual period.

market to competition has made it necessary to introduce new incentive mechanisms which are less costly, less rigid and do not result in distortions of competition among electricity producers. The old payback tariff was very costly to electricity consumers: currently, the tariff increases the price to final consumers by more than 4%. The total price paid by electricity consumers for this support is estimated to be around €1.3bn (L2,500bn) per year and could increase further as new planned plants enter in operation. Moreover, a large share of the new renewables capacity approved under the 1992 government directive that established a buyback mechanism (CIP6; see note 12) has yet to be built or to enter into operation. At the end of 1998 only about 48% of the total new renewables capacity approved under CIP6 contracts had been built, although the number of cancellations was very low. Finally, after introduction of competition, ENEL cannot be solely responsible for promoting renewables.

Against this background, major changes are being introduced in the policy repertoire to promote the development of electricity from renewable energy sources (RES-E) within the new competitive electricity market framework.

Corrective measures on old incentives   The revision of the existing system for the promotion of renewables is limited by the illegality of breaching existing rights derived from long-term CIP6 contracts. However, from 1997, the Regulatory Authority for Electricity and Gas began to revise the buyback tariffs for renewables and cogeneration to make them more cost-reflective. According to the CIP6/92 provisions, the buyback tariff should have been regularly updated in order to reflect the decreasing costs to ENEL of generating electricity as a result of technological progress. However, this was never done. On the contrary, both the reference investment value and the reference fuel cost value used to calculate the 'avoided cost' components of the buyback tariff have constantly grown as a result of adjustments for inflation. In 1998 the authority revised the calculation for ENEL's avoided costs so as to reflect the utility's decreasing costs of generating electricity. The eight-year subsidy is being maintained for projects already approved.

In order to stimulate the actual realization of plants approved under CIP6 contracts – and to put an end to 'speculative behaviours' – the decree which liberalized the electricity market established a deadline for CIP6 contracts. Only plants that enter into operation within the date specified in the agreement with ENEL keep the right to incentives.

In the new liberalized electricity market, existing renewables plants built according to Law 9/91 sell their electricity to the network operator at prices set by the CIP6/92 regulation as revised by the authority. In order to ensure that the costs incurred by the operator are covered, the authority includes the costs of renewables support in the 'cost of the system charges'.

New incentives in the liberalized market   In order further to promote electricity generated from renewable sources in the new competitive marketplace, a number of additional measures have been envisaged:

- A new definition of renewable sources has been formulated, which includes solar, wind, hydro, geothermal, wave and biomass energy, and energy from organic and inorganic waste.
- Renewals of hydroelectric concessions are subordinated, inter alia, to the submission of plans aiming at increasing hydro production or installed capacity.
- Electricity from renewable sources and cogeneration will be granted priority in dispatch in the new electricity pool on the basis of specific criteria to be defined by the Regulatory Authority for Electricity and Gas.
- Generators and importers of 'brown electricity' (i.e. that generated from fossil fuels) with annual production or imports of more than 100GWh will be obliged to generate renewable energy up to a level of 2% of the generation above 100GWh. This 'renewables portfolio obligation' excludes electricity from auto-consumers and cogenerators, as well as exported electricity.
- Regions and provinces are allowed to promote new renewable energy capacity through tender procedures.
- Distributors will be allowed to sell green electricity at green (premium) prices to customers.

The renewables portfolio obligation is aimed at sharing the burden of renewable energy development among utilities. The government can decide to increase the 2% level in subsequent years. 'Green certificates' issued by the network operator will certify the source of energy, which must conform with the new definition. Only energy produced by renewable power plants that entered into operation after 1 April 1999 (including CIP6/92 plants that will be connected to the grid after this date, whose rights are transferred to the network operator) will be granted 'green certificates'.[13] The minimum value of one green certificate is fixed at 100MWh. The right to be granted green

---

[13] This definition includes plants entering into force after repowering, reactivation or rebuilding.

certificates expires after eight years of operation of the 'new plant'. No 'banking' of certificates is allowed. Producers and importers can comply with the 2% obligation by buying green certificates from other utilities (provided that they feed the renewable electricity into the national electricity system) or from the network operator at fixed prices corresponding to the costs of the incentives for the CIP6/92 plants. Green certificates will also be traded in the pool market. A secondary market of green certificates will therefore emerge, parallel to the electricity market. The price on the bilateral contract markets might differ from the price prevailing in the pool.

In order to compensate for annual fluctuations in production from renewables or insufficient renewable energy supply, the network operator is allowed to issue green certificates not linked to actual renewable electricity production, provided that the shortfall is compensated within three years. The price of these 'buy-out certificates' is equal to those owned by the network operator, acting as a sort of price ceiling. Penalties for non-compliance with the obligation include restrictions on access to the electricity exchange.

A reciprocity clause is envisaged whereby producers and importers are in principle allowed to meet the renewables portfolio obligation also by importing renewable certificates, as long as there is a corresponding physical electricity exchange. This electricity should be generated by plants that entered into operation after 1 April 1999, and located in EU countries where similar market mechanisms are implemented for the promotion of renewables and similar rights are granted to Italian renewable power plants. In the case of electricity imported from non-EU countries, a convention setting monitoring and verification criteria between the network operators in the exporting and importing country is required.

Eligibility criteria for green tariffs offered on the captive market will aim at promoting renewable electricity generation *over and above* (i.e. *additional to*) the renewable target set by the renewables obligation. One possible technical mechanism that could be used to achieve this aim is to link green power to the tradable green certificates; certificates should be held and cancelled to meet demand via the green tariffs. In this ways the same certificate cannot be used for two different purposes (green tariffs and renewables obligation) and double counting of certificates is therefore avoided.

As a result of the above provisions, small renewable power plants (i.e. those with annual production lower than 50MWh) are not entitled to apply for or to receive green certificates under the 2% obligation. The Regulatory Authority for Electricity and Gas is currently studying new mechanisms to promote the development of these plants in a cost-effective way.

To boost the development of small hydroelectric plants, the Regulatory Authority for Electricity and Gas has increased the price they receive from ENEL for electricity. The incentive involves plants up to 3MW for which the old price did not cover their relatively high production costs (compared with larger hydro power units).

The recent reform of electricity tariffs for captive customers introduced the possibility for electricity distributors to offer 'green tariffs' to their customers. In the previous tariff system this possibility did not exist: both the structure and the level of electricity tariffs were set by the government bodies in charge of tariff-setting and no distinction was made between 'brown' and 'green' electricity. In the new tariff system electricity distributors will be able to sell certified renewable electricity on the captive market at green tariffs. These tariffs will allow distributors to cover above-average renewable generation costs and, at the same time, to translate the existing willingness to pay for green electricity into actual consumption.

9.5 Implementing the NCP: demand

As noted on page 190, demand-side management in electricity is expected to make a significant contribution to the reduction of GHG emissions. The promotion of energy savings in electricity end-use sectors is being integrated both in tariff policy and in the design of the new competitive electricity market. The concessions for distributors in the liberalized market will contain provisions to increase the energy efficiency of end uses, according to quantitative targets to be set by decree of the minister of industry jointly with the minister of the environment. Similar provisions have been integrated into the liberalized gas market.[14] The government is currently working on the definition of these targets.

The recent reform of electricity tariffs for captive customers gradually removes several disincentives and introduces a number of incentives for utilities and consumers to improve energy efficiency. Generally speaking, however, electricity utilities are averse to DSM programmes because of their direct and indirect costs. The indirect costs take the form of reductions in electricity sales and associated loss of profit if the programmes are effective in reducing consumption. The new tariff regulation aims at tackling these disincentives in two ways.

In the first place, in the new tariff system electricity companies will be able to recover via the tariff mechanism the allowed costs incurred for DSM

---

[14] Legislative Decree No. 164 of 23 May 2000.

initiatives. To this end, a specific parameter is included in the price-cap formula for annual tariff adjustment, the value of which can be annually adapted to needs. This ensures that it will not be subject to automatic downward pressure as a result of the price cap. The criteria according to which electricity companies will be entitled to recover such costs have yet to be finalized.

Second, in the new tariff system utilities' revenue-drivers are partially modified to reduce the share of profits dependent upon electricity sales. In broad terms, the new tariff regulation is based on a system of tariff constraints, i.e. maximum price levels, that electricity distributors can charge to their customers. The constraints are defined for each customer class, excluding domestic customers connected to low-voltage lines: a first constraint places a limit on the company's overall revenue; a second one limits the revenue per customer. The two constraints allow a degree of flexibility in the contractual relationship between electricity companies and captive customers, while ensuring the protection of the latter. For domestic customers connected to low-voltage lines a compulsory tariff is defined by the authority which electricity distributors have to offer to their clients.[15]

The structure of both the overall revenue constraint for non-domestic customers and the compulsory tariff for domestic customers is such that the share of utilities' profits dependent upon electricity sales is significantly reduced compared with the previous tariff system. In particular, in the revenue constraint about 75% of the allowed costs for electricity distribution and 100% of the allowed costs for electricity supply to non-domestic customers

---

[15] The compulsory tariff aims at ensuring a greater degree of protection to domestic customers. The main novelty of the new tariff is represented by its linear structure. In the previous system the tariff for residential domestic customers with less than 3kW of contracted power was progressive with consumption. A more favourable (i.e. below-cost) price level was granted to low and medium–low consumption levels, while higher (i.e. above-cost) price levels were allowed for medium–high and high consumption levels to recover this 'social provision'. In order to ensure a gradual phasing-in of the new cost-reflective tariff system, two compulsory tariffs are defined (and updated on a yearly basis) by the authority: one applies to residential domestic customers with less than 3kW of contracted power, and a second has to be offered by electricity distributors to domestic customers with contracted power greater than 3kW and to non-residential domestic customers with less than 3kW of contracted power. The structure of the first tariff is initially similar to the 'old' progressive tariff and will gradually converge, with the second tariff, towards the unique, linear, compulsory tariff for domestic customers to be applied from 1 January 2003. The new linear tariff for domestic customer will eliminate, inter alia, the disincentive for utilities to realize DSM programmes targeted on medium- to high-consumption customer classes (which guaranteed the higher marginal profits).

depend on the number of customers served as opposed to the amount of electricity sold. As a result, for these customer classes the new tariff mechanism allows electricity distributors to make average tariff revenues which decrease as sale volumes increase. Similarly, the weight of electricity sales in total allowed costs as reflected in the compulsory tariff that electricity distributors have to offer to domestic customers has been reduced. A greater share of allowed costs is now dependent on the number of customers served and the amount of contracted power. The existence of a compulsory tariff for domestic customers reduces the degree of flexibility that electricity distributors have in defining alternative tariffs aiming at increasing electricity consumption. As a result of this partial decoupling of utilities' profits from electricity sales, DSM programmes are becoming more revenue-neutral.

From the consumers' point of view, the new tariff system introduces two major incentives to efficiency improvements in end-use sectors.

In the first place, in the new regulatory framework for the supply of electricity to captive customers, cost-reflective tariffs require the gradual phasing-out of the existing special arrangements, which imply tariff levels significantly lower than the cost of service, thus promoting wasteful use of electricity. The scope of application of below-cost tariffs is scheduled to shrink, and only one subsidized tariff band will be retained for low-income customers. This 'social tariff' will be applied to a smaller set of users than at present.

Second, positive effects in terms of increased efficiency in end-use sectors are likely to occur as a result of the greater availability of feedback information on consumption patterns for customers that are not eligible to choose their supplier. In the new tariff system, electricity distributors are required to report at least once a year on the electricity bill of the customer – in both physical (i.e. kWh) and monetary terms – the average daily consumption in the reference period and possible differences with respect to the previous period. The hypothesis underlying this provision is that a more informative energy bill will raise consumers' energy awareness or knowledge, thus contributing, together with an increased availability of DSM programmes, to bring about reduced consumption via more efficient energy use.[16]

---

[16] Some argue that the 'old' progressive tariff for domestic customers, originally introduced for social purposes, had a significant role to play in limiting average domestic consumption per capita. However, the real effectiveness of such a tariff structure in terms of price signals *effectively perceived* by consumers is uncertain due to the characteristics of the old electricity billing system, which was uninformative and not transparent. These features contributed to reduce significantly the price signal of this complex tariff *as effectively perceived* by consumers. It is therefore very difficult to understand what role, if

9.6 Conclusions

Market liberalization is not per se beneficial or detrimental to the environment. The impact of competition on the natural environment greatly depends upon the policies and measures that shape and go along with the liberalization process. These policies and measures will influence the market behaviour of the various actors in the electricity marketplace, whose actions have significant impacts in terms of GHG emissions.

The previous sections of this chapter have outlined a number of important steps that have already been taken at various policy levels to integrate environmental concerns into the liberalization process. Nevertheless, additional efforts are still needed to encourage and hasten behavioural changes on the part of electricity market actors that will bring about further reductions in GHG emissions. The promotion of cost-effectiveness and the consistency with a liberalized market framework will be key features of policies and measures designed with this end in view.

On the supply side of the market, policies that affect the speed of capital stock replacement and the nature and efficiency of both replacement and new stock will be central to efforts to reduce GHG emissions. Here additional policy interventions are needed in order to speed up the divestment process of the three generation companies as well as to simplify procedures for entry into or expansion of generation.

The promotion of electricity generated from renewable sources has to be achieved through the design and the implementation of policy instruments which are cost-effective, less rigid than formerly and do not result in distortion of competition among electricity producers. In this respect, the introduction of a tradable green certificates mechanism plus a quota system (renewables obligation) has the potential greatly to enhance the development of renewable electricity at the national level. For this potential to become effective the system as it is currently designed needs to be integrated and amended so that it provides substantial pressure on actors in the market without making it impossible to reach their goals; provides sufficient security for investors (i.e. a stable and predictable growing market for renewables over time); ensures liquidity and transparency of the green certificates market; and provides customers with sufficient information to allow them to make informed choices.

---

[16] (cont)
any, the existence of non-linear electricity prices played in the past in limiting electricity consumption of this customer class.

An important factor for investors attempting to assess whether renewables will be an attractive market (and therefore whether they will be deployed) is the development of the obligation over time. The longer the period for which the market induced by the obligation is known, the higher investor security will be. It is therefore extremely important for the effectiveness of the newly introduced tradable green certificates mechanism that targets are set (i.e. the profile of the obligation is defined) for a sufficient number of years – eight to ten at least – to give investors enough security.

In addition to this, for the green certificates system to be credible there must be appropriate penalties for non-compliance. The rules governing the non-compliance regime should be designed in such a way to allow obliged actors to quantify in monetary terms the consequences of not meeting the target, so that this factor will represent part of a reference framework for the definition of their market strategies and behaviour. Of course, the level of the penalty (together with the level of ambition of the obligation) will influence market expectations of potential investors in renewable generation. Several options can be envisaged for determining sanctions. For the first year of operation of the system the penalty could be a fixed price per certificate or per kilowatt hour and could therefore act as a ceiling price. For the following years this fixed level could be revised or, alternatively, the penalty could be set equal to the average market price of certificates in the previous year multiplied by a factor greater than 1. A condition for this option is that the body determining the penalty level should have access to market information to determine the average market price. This in turn means that there should be a highly liquid and transparent stock market, or that the control body should have access to price information on every transaction.

Last but not least, the tradable green certificates market will have to operate without distortions. In the system designed by the legislative decree of 11 November 1999 the upper limit on the price of certificates is likely to be equal to the fixed price at which both certificates related to CIP6/92 plants and borrowed certificates are sold by the network operator. These certificates (particularly the former) are likely to account for a significant part of the overall market, at least in the early years of its operation. From this it follows not only that the fixed price at which green certificates from CIP6/92 plants are sold on the market will act as a ceiling price, but also that it is very unlikely that the equilibrium price will significantly differ from (i.e. be lower than) this value.

For the green certificate to be a real market-based instrument, aimed at minimizing the cost to society of reaching a predefined renewables target while promoting fair competition, the price of certificates related to CIP6/92 plants should not be fixed but should be determined by market forces. If this distortion is not eliminated the tradable green certificates market introduced by Legislative Decree No. 79 of 16 March 1999 will turn out to be an old instrument with a new name.

As far as the demand side of the electricity market is concerned, it is very important that the quantitative targets to be set by the government for electricity (and gas) distributors according to Legislative Decree No. 79 (and Legislative Decree No. 164 of 23 May 2000) are realistic with respect to the estimated technical and economic potential in the sector as well as with respect to the actual level of experience of market actors in the design and implementation of energy efficiency programmes. In addition, mechanisms and procedures should be envisaged which ensure the additionality of these programmes as well as their cost-effectiveness, prevent distortions in competition and take into account the interest of low-income and disabled people. The definition of the rules governing the electricity pool will offer the opportunity to give electricity consumers the possibility of active participation in the market through, for example, demand-side bidding procedures.

10 The Netherlands: supplemental to domestic action

*Coos Battjes, Michiel Beeldman, Fieke Rijkers and
Gerrit Jan Schaeffer*

The Dutch electricity system is of medium size in the EU. However, it has
some special characteristics that make this case study of particular interest.
The past decade has been one of very economic growth for the energy-intensive Dutch economy, leading to rapid increases in emissions, despite
pre-Kyoto climate policies. Without many options to reduce emissions
domestically, the host of COP-6 decided to use the Kyoto mechanisms ex-
tensively; however, this also showed the host's commitment to the
mechanisms – important for the Umbrella Group countries – while still
inside the EU's supplementarity caps of a maximum 50% of reductions
coming from emissions trading. The highly interconnected electricity system reduces the policy options to those that do not make the industry
uncompetitive compared with imports. At the same time few possibilities
exist for increased use of renewables (because of the high population density)
or cogeneration or natural gas (because of their already high penetration
rates).

10.1 The electricity sector

Power production from large plants and long-term contracted imports have
remained relatively constant in recent years. Increased demand has been
covered mainly by a growth in decentralized capacity, in particular from cogeneration plants. Some of these plants are controlled by energy distribution
companies; some are managed by industrial end users. Total installed production capacity in the Netherlands amounts to over 20,000MW. However,
liberalization of the electricity market is projected to change these trends:
electricity imports will probably increase, and the growth of cogeneration
capacity will decrease.

Large-scale production of electricity in the Netherlands has historically
been carried out by four power companies. These companies combined
cover about 60% of the market (see Figure 10.1). Three of these companies

Figure 10.1: Overview of the Dutch electricity production sector

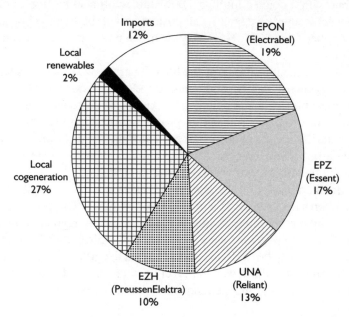

have now come under foreign ownership. UNA has been taken over by Reliant (US), EZH by PreussenElektra (Germany) and EPON by Electrabel (Belgium) with ING bank (Netherlands). The southern Netherlands energy supplier Essent is majority shareholder of the fourth generating company, EPZ. With its ownership of EPZ, Essent is striving for vertical integration of its supply and distribution activities. Interestingly, after initial problems with the market, the state decided to buy the high-voltage network of the producers.

The market share for decentralized capacity is almost 30%. This consists largely of electricity generated from cogeneration plants, owned by distribution companies and industrial end users. The share from renewable sources is derived mainly from waste incineration and wind power.

10.2 Liberalization of the energy markets

The new Electricity Act of 1998 set the liberalization process in motion in the Netherlands. The Dutch electricity market will be liberalized in three phases. Since January 1999 the electricity market has been open for large industrial customers (over 2MW). In 2002, medium-sized customers (under 2 MW, but with a connection over 3×80amp[1]) will also be free to choose their electricity suppliers. Finally, all customers will be free to choose their energy supplier from 2004. However, the green power market is open to all customers in 2002.

As a result of the phasing-in of the liberalization, two types of customers can be distinguished: captive and non-captive customers. Deliveries to captive customers may be made only by the existing Dutch energy distribution companies. In order to protect this group against high electricity costs, electricity tariffs are set by a special regulator on behalf of the ministry of economic affairs. Small electricity generators will also be subject to tariffs regulated by the ministry of economic affairs until 2002.

With the liberalization of the market, the electricity price is split into two components: the power price and the network tariff. The power price is determined by market forces, while the latter is strictly regulated by means of r-TPA. The transport tariffs are based on a so-called cascade point tariff system, under which the tariff depends solely on the grid level of the connection of the end user (the lower the level of connection, the higher the net tariff) and is, therefore, independent of the distance between supplier and user.

Electricity prices in the Netherlands are strongly influenced by the price of natural gas (for fuel shares, see Figure 10.4). The liberalization of the gas market, therefore, is of great importance to the electricity market liberalization process. The gas market will also be liberalized in three phases. With the entry into force of the Dutch Gas Act of 2000, large gas customers (over 10m m³ per year) are free to choose their suppliers from the beginning of 2000. Medium-sized customers (over 1m m³ per year) will be free to choose supplier in 2002, followed in 2004 by all customers.

Gas-supplying companies (Gasunie and the distribution companies) must separate their transport activities from their other energy service activities. In this way, gas prices are split into a transport tariff and a commodity price. Access to the gas network is defined by a negotiated third party access (n-TPA) protocol, under which the tariff is a result of negotiations between the customer and the gas producer. Generally, the tariff consists of a payment for connection, system costs and transport costs. As a result of the n-TPA

---

[1] The 3×80amp limit was chosen as this corresponds to the maximum connection of domestic consumers, and corresponds with the system applied for the regulatory energy tax (see page 218).

regulation and the strong market position of Gasunie,[2] gas prices in the short run will be dominated by the tariff system introduced by Gasunie, the so-called commodity/service system (CSS). In the CSS, the gas price no longer depends on the amount of gas purchased, as was the case in the previous 'zonal tariff system', but depends instead on the load factor – the ratio between the total annual volume purchased and the maximum volume used per hour (i.e. capacity).

10.3 Climate policy targets

Under the EU burden-sharing agreement the Netherlands has agreed a target for reduction of GHG emissions of 6% from 1990 levels. This corresponds to a reduction of approximately $50MtCO_2$ in 2010 compared with projected emissions under an existing policy scenario. In the agreement between the governing Dutch coalition parties it is laid down that (a maximum of) 50% of the required emissions reduction will take place through the use of the Kyoto mechanisms, outside the Netherlands. This results in a minimum required domestic reduction of $25MtCO_2$. The first part of the Dutch climate policy implementation plan examines the measures to be taken domestically to achieve this reduction.[3] These measures cover energy conservation ($10MtCO_2$), renewable energy ($4MtCO_2$), non-CO_2 GHGs ($8MtCO_2e$) and the electricity production sector ($6MtCO_2$). Taking overlap into consideration, the total reduction comes to about $25MtCO_2e$ (see Figure 10.3). The other half of the total 50Mt reduction target may be fulfilled through the so-called 'flexible instruments'.

The fuel mix of the Dutch electricity sector is shown in Figure 10.4. Electricity generated in the Netherlands comes almost entirely from fossil fuels; nuclear and renewable energy together cover less than 5% of the total. This leads to a relatively high rate of CO_2 emissions per kWh, despite the particularly high share of natural gas.

---

[2] Gasunie is the biggest gas supplier in the Netherlands. More than a third of gas supplied to large industries comes directly from Gasunie. Taking this together with the gas supplied to twenty-one power-generating plants, Gasunie accounts for 45% of the domestic gas market. In addition, Gasunie provides all the Dutch energy distribution companies with gas, which makes the total market share of Gasunie about 90%.

[3] *The Netherlands' Climate Policy Implementation Plan: Part I: Measures in the Netherlands*, developed by the Dutch ministry of housing, spatial planning and environment, was published in June 1999 and represents the ministry's plans to reduce GHG emissions in the Netherlands.

Figure 10.2: Dutch emissions and the contribution of the energy sector, 1990–1999

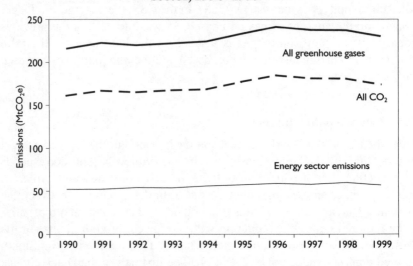

Source: European Environment Agency, EU emissions inventory 2001; see www.eea.org.

Figure 10.3: Contributions of measures according to the Dutch Implementation Plan

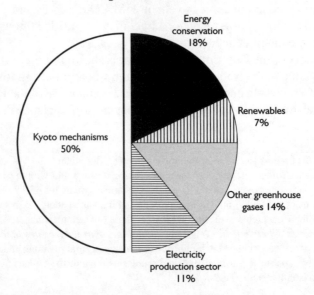

Figure 10.4: Fuel mix of Dutch electricity generation

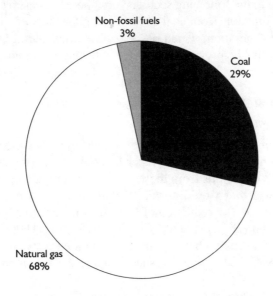

Non-fossil fuels
3%

Coal
29%

Natural gas
68%

10.3.1 Impact of liberalization on climate policy

With the liberalization and privatization of the Dutch electricity and gas markets, energy companies will become competitive market players and company strategies will shift from meeting public interest to making profit. Consequently, the Dutch government reconsidered its role in the energy sector and changed it from that of an 'active player' to that of a 'director'. The policy measures with respect to the reduction of GHG emissions and promotion of renewable energy have to change as well because government can no longer influence the strategies of the energy companies directly.

In order to meet the reduction targets for GHG emissions, the government is applying different measures to the different actors involved. It distinguishes two groups of actors. The first group consists of 'small customers' (mainly households). This group is faced with rather strict policy measures and high levies (ecotaxes). The second group includes large energy consumers and energy companies. For this group, policy measures are developed to be consistent with the 'new market thinking' approach of the Dutch government. Because this group of energy users and producers does not like strict and expensive measures, the government wants to realize emissions reduction in these sectors with the aid of benchmarking and voluntary agreements.

Climate policy related to the electricity sector addresses three issues, discussed in detail in the following sections: first, policy measures with respect to emissions reductions from coal-fired power plant; second, the further increase of CHP generation, which plays a substantial role in Dutch climate policy; and finally, the promotion of renewable energy to reduce emissions.

10.4   Coal-fired power plants

10.4.1   Background

The measures in the electricity production sector mainly concern coal-fired power plants. The government has reached a voluntary agreement with the sector to reduce emissions from these plants. The target is to reduce emissions to the level that would pertain if natural gas had been used. This corresponds with a 40% reduction of CO_2 and will lead to a total reduction from coal-fired power plants of $6MtCO_2$ (see Box 10.1). These measures for power plants thus satisfy about a quarter of the total domestic requirement for reduction of GHGs. This large share emphasizes the importance of the agreement.

However, the measures to be taken are generally not cost-effective, causing extra costs. In order to encourage the sector, the environment ministry (VROM) stated that the agreement was linked to the conversion of a fuel tax on power plants into an end-user levy. The fuel tax was being levied on the purchase of fossil fuels for power plants. However, because such a levy is lacking in other countries, under liberalization this would place the Dutch electricity sector at a competitive disadvantage. In order to maintain tax income for the state at the same level while abolishing the fuel tax, the levy

---

Box 10.1: Emissions from coal-fired power plants in 2010

It is expected that seven coal-fired power plants will be in operation in the Netherlands in 2010, with a total capacity of about 4,000MW, producing approximately 17TWh. The emissions of CO_2 by coal-fired plants depend on the efficiency of the power plant and the CO_2 emission factor of the coal used. Current efficiency of the coal-fired plants in the Netherlands is about 40%, and the emission factor of coal is 94kg/GJ. This means that for 1kWh of electricity there is a CO_2 emission of 0.85kg. Natural gas has a lower emission factor than coal (56.1kg/GJ). If gas were burned in the same power plants with the same efficiency, this would lead to a CO_2 emission of 0.5kg/kWh, a reduction of 40%. If emissions from all coal-fired power (17TWh of production) dropped from 0.85kg/kWh to 0.5kg/kWh, this would result in an emissions reduction of $6MtCO_2$.

Box 10.2: Level of the fuel tax

Coal for use in power plants is taxed at €10.83/tonne. The tax for the largest natural gas users, such as power plants, is 0.65e/m³. In 1998, gas use for power production plants amounted to about 7bn m³, while the coal use for coal-fired plants was 8.5Mt. The total fuel tax, on coal and gas, is therefore about €138m per year.

---

was transferred to electricity customers by increasing the regulatory energy tax (ecotax) on electricity.

For coal-fired plants, the fuel tax change reduces the annual tax burden by about €138m (see Box 10.2). The cost of the measures to satisfy the voluntary agreement is of the same magnitude. However, the costs are not interchangeable. First, the emissions reductions do not have to be implemented until 2008, while the fuel tax could be changed earlier. Second, such a tax reform should be probably be implemented anyway in light of the liberalized European market for electricity.

10.4.2 Technical possibilities

The power sector has a number of options at its disposal to reduce emissions from existing coal-fired power plants. The climate policy implementation plan indicates a number of these, based on the document of options published in 1998 by the ECN and the Dutch National Institute of Public Health and the Environment (RIVM).

Accelerated decommissioning The coal-fired power plants currently in use were built between 1980 and 1995. Based on an estimated lifetime of 25 years, the two oldest of these plants are planned to be decommissioned in the commitment period 2008–12. However, if current developments in the electricity market continue, competitive considerations will probably mean that these power plants remain in operation, because profits are at risk and few new investments are taking place. If these plants were decommissioned according to the original plans, CO_2 emissions would be reduced by $3MtCO_2$. Accelerated decommissioning of the other power plants would further reduce emissions, but writing them off before the end of their economic lifetime would entail higher costs.

Conversion to natural gas/fuel oil   All power plants in the Netherlands are equipped to use a second fuel. The two oldest coal-fired power plants can use fuel oil, while the five newer plants can use natural gas. Conversion of the plants to fuel oil would lead to a CO_2 reduction of 20–25%, while conversion to natural gas would lead to a reduction of approximately 40%. Conversion to fuel oil, even leaving aside the smaller CO_2 reductions it would achieve, is probably less cost-effective and has other (negative) environmental effects, such as an increase in SO_2 emissions. Conversion to natural gas for the five suitable power plants will yield a reduction in CO_2 emissions of about 4Mt.

Cofiring with biomass   Part of the coal could be replaced with biomass. Cofiring projects are already being developed at several power plants, but the full potential of this route has not yet been exploited. The document of options outlines the possibility of using about 2.5Mt of biomass annually in cofiring – about 10–15%, around the level of current projects. It appears possible to attain higher percentages but more research is necessary for this. To reach the emissions reduction objective, cofiring of 40% biomass would be necessary.

Cofiring with biomass, as one of the forms of renewable energy, is already supported through a few incentive schemes. The most important of these are the nil tariff (i.e. the exemption of green power consumers from the regulatory energy tax) and the discount for renewable energy. Together these could result in a maximum price reduction of 4.5e/kWh. These are important incentives for expanding activities in this area.

CO_2 removal and storage   The abovementioned possibilities require only limited investment. However, it would also be possible to provide the coal-fired power plants with equipment for the removal and storage of CO_2. Large investments are required for this option, which is therefore most suitable for relatively new power plants. For power plants with a shorter lifetime CO_2 removal is an option, but costs would be substantially higher per tonne of CO_2.

Efficiency improvements   The electricity generators participate in the covenant for benchmarking energy efficiency, under which the sector promises by no later than 2012 to be among the best in the world in terms of energy efficiency. A detailed analysis of the potential effects of this covenant for the power sector is needed. The Dutch government has been striving towards an increased share of renewable energy in the energy supply for many years. The climate policy implementation plan sets an objective of 5%. This objective and the accompanying policy instruments are important when considering the possible role of biomass in complying with the agreements of the benchmarking covenant, and the implications also for the coal power plants.

The current assessment is that by around 2012 the best coal power plants in the world will have an efficiency of 45%. The existing power plants in the Netherlands have an efficiency of 40%. An efficiency increase to 45% would mean a CO_2 reduction of approximately $1.5MtCO_2$. However, it appears nearly impossible to adapt the existing power plants in such a way as to attain the desired (efficiency) increase; the existing power plants would have to be virtually rebuilt. It is more likely that producers will focus their attention on compensation measures at other plants or on taking measures abroad.

It is also striking that some possible routes to achieve the CO_2 reduction, for example, the replacement of coal with natural gas, appear to conflict with the covenant, for if large volumes of gas were used in the coal power plants, the average efficiency of generating electricity with natural gas would decline. This might lead to the necessity of changing the covenant.

10.4.3   Voluntary agreement

In June 2000 the electricity generation companies agreed in general terms with the ministry of economic affairs and the ministry of housing, spatial planning and environment (VROM) on reducing the emissions of the seven coal-fired plant by $6MtCO_2$. Cofiring of biomass will cover a substantial part of this (about 2.5Mt); the rest will be met by improving energy efficiency (about 1.5Mt) and by CO_2 storage (about 2Mt).

10.5   Role of CHP

10.5.1   Background

CHP is assumed to play an important role in energy conservation, both now and in the future. The government assumes that the total Dutch capacity of CHP will grow and will therefore contribute to the reduction of GHG emissions. The emissions reduction targets mentioned earlier include this further growth of CHP. Therefore, the targets may become more difficult to meet if development of CHP is slower than expected. According to the climate policy implementation plan from the ministry of the environment, the total CO_2 reduction achieved through cogeneration should reach $5–10MtCO_2$ by

2010.[4] This is 5–10% of the total reduction necessary to reach the emissions level under the burden-sharing agreement. Considering the effects of the liberalization on cogeneration and, through cogeneration, on the CO_2 reduction target, it is worth exploring measures that might help cogeneration to overcome the uncertain period that it faces.

In the past two decades CHP capacity has developed considerably and now contributes about 30% of Dutch electricity generation. This contribution is one of the highest in Europe. The expansion of CHP is the result of a combination of (policy) measures taken in the past. As in Germany, the downward pressure of liberalization of energy markets on prices and tariffs is threatening the development of CHP capacity. Hence, it is becoming less certain whether the emissions reductions which are assumed to stem from CHP will be realized in fact. Policy measures may, therefore, be required to secure the future development of CHP.

10.5.2   The history of CHP

From 1980 to 1985 Dutch electricity generation was mainly based on natural gas. Because of high oil prices and the price linkage between gas and oil, electricity prices were relatively high, and high gas and electricity prices engendered a favourable rate of return for cogeneration. Nevertheless, the growth in the capacity of cogeneration remained modest, mainly as a result of overcapacity in central generation, the relatively low feed-in tariffs for excess electricity, and the fact that the size of cogeneration plants was planned according to electricity demand rather than heat demand.

Around 1985–7, the unbundling of production and distribution in the electricity sector encouraged the distribution companies to invest in decentralized cogeneration. Also, the feed-in tariffs of electricity were increased. As part of a promotion programme, specific tariffs for natural gas were also introduced for cogeneration. In addition, producers willing to invest in CHP received higher investment subsidies for building cogeneration plants. Finally, a new support office was established for the coordination and implementation of cogeneration. Obviously, the relatively clean combustion of new combined cycle plants created another argument in favour of cogeneration. In the late 1980s these favourable conditions caused a steady growth of industrial cogeneration of around 150MW per year.

---

[4] However, only good-quality cogeneration will reduce emissions compared with separate generation of electricity and heat.

In 1990 the government decided to cancel the financial debts of district heating projects, which gave the Dutch power producers, organized in Sep, the opportunity to launch the so-called 'heat plan' involving an investment in five combined cycle units (in total 1,250MWe) for district heating. Meanwhile, the number of small-scale cogeneration projects increased gradually, in particular in the greenhouse agriculture sector.

From 1990 to 1993 cogeneration increased strongly because of growing concern about increasing emissions of gases such as SO_2 and NO_x. A specific tariff system for electricity from cogeneration resulted in very good price conditions for cogeneration. Also, the government provided additional financial support to cogeneration projects because of its contribution to reducing these emissions. The power producers increased the target capacity of CHP to 2,500MWe. Industries and distribution companies also regarded cogeneration as the most important technology to reach the environmental goals formulated by government. Therefore, agreements were established with the government resulting in the objectives of the environmental action plan of the distribution companies and the long-term agreements of large industries involving the Dutch ministry of economic affairs, industries and energy distribution companies. In addition, cogeneration proved to be the best way for distribution companies to develop embedded production capacity, made possible with the introduction of the Electricity Act of 1989. Joint ventures between electricity distribution companies and large heat consumers proved to be very attractive, and were widely used for investments in cogeneration. Consequently, the capacity of cogeneration increased to 3,000MWe at the end of 1993. All actors had adjusted their capacity targets on cogeneration to a higher level than before and regarded cogeneration as the main route to realizing the environmental agreements with the government.

In 1994 measures were taken to slow down the development of cogeneration because of an increasing overcapacity in the Dutch electricity generation sector. The feed-in tariffs for electricity were decreased substantially, and subsidies were abolished as cogeneration proved to be an economically attractive option. Increased interest in climate policy at the end of the 1990s resulted in policy plans and measures to reduce energy use and mitigate GHG emissions. Subsequently, cogeneration did also benefit somewhat from these environmental policy actions.

The Dutch government adopted a new Electricity Act in 1998 and Gas Act in 2000, thereby implementing the directives from the EU concerning the liberalization of the electricity and gas markets. The newly liberalized markets have led to the dismantling of the specific gas tariff and specific feed-in

Figure 10.5: Development of CHP capacity in the Netherlands, 1980–1999

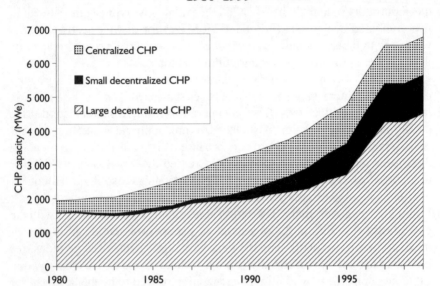

tariffs for electricity. Moreover, cogeneration will also have to cope with uncertainties associated with liberalized markets.

Figure 10.5 gives an overview of the development of cogeneration capacity through the past two decades. Government policies and market developments stimulated growth throughout the 1980s and early 1990s. Late in the 1990s, the governments measures to slow down capacity expansion started working.

10.5.3   Future threats to CHP

The effect of liberalization of energy markets on prices and tariffs has been noted as a potential threat to CHP. Results of studies on the future of CHP in the Netherlands show that the profitability of investments in CHP may substantially decrease in a liberalized energy market.[5] The main reason for this is

---

[5] A. W. N. van Dril, F. A. M. Rijkers, J. J. Battjes and A. de Raad, 'Toekomst warmtekrachtkoppeling: verkenning van de economische aantrekkelijkheid in een geliberaliseerde energiemarkt', ECN-C–99-086, Oct. 1999; A. W. N. van Dril, F. A. M. Rijkers and J. J. Battjes, 'Toekomst warmtekrachtkoppeling: actualisatie betreffende tarieven Dte and REB', ECN-C–00-022, Feb. 2000; see www.ecn.nl/unit_bs/main.html.

the strong competition on the electricity market and the uncertainty whether prices will cover more than just marginal costs of fuel in the near future. Moreover, the new gas tariffs do not favour CHP.

As noted earlier, with the liberalization of the electricity market, the electricity price has been split into two components, the commodity price and the grid tariff. The Dutch cascade point tariff system for network pricing is subject to criticism since its structure appears to be unfavourable to decentralized production, in particular CHP. In addition, the old system of rewarding CHP for lowering grid costs is abolished in the new Electricity Act.[6]

Commodity prices are determined by the market and are therefore, subject to uncertainties in the market. The Dutch electricity market is currently facing a situation of overcapacity, which according to economic theory will result in lower electricity prices: prices tend to marginal production costs in fully competitive markets. As long as this overcapacity persists, the electricity market is bound to be unstable. However, once the market has stabilized, producers will be able more easily to apply long-term contracts based on average production costs to include the fixed investment costs of an installation, assuring both producers and consumers a reasonable fixed price without great financial risk. Also, long-term investment, which is necessary to maintain reliable electricity production, will then be possible.

As with the electricity market, liberalization of the gas market will have a large impact on the structure of the energy market. In the old 'zonal tariff system' gas prices were differentiated on a volume-based system, giving CHP a special favourable tariff. However, this system is now abolished in the liberalized market, leading to much higher prices for CHP plants.

The uncertainty surrounding prices on the electricity market also applies to CHP since special feed-in prices have been abolished. However, the market may affect CHP disproportionately since it does not benefit from the economies of scale associated with centrally produced electricity. In addition, CHP is now subject to unfavourable gas prices compared with those applying for centrally produced electricity, having lost the special favourable gas prices of the old zonal system. This situation is likely to result in a stabilization or fall in the CHP share in the Dutch electricity production, if no preventive policy measures are taken.

The transmission tariff system of gas and electricity appears to be unfavourable for CHP, in particular for small-scale CHP. The new tariffs charge

---

[6] CHP lowers grid costs because embedded generation reduces the need for (interaction with) the high-voltage transmission network.

CHP relatively highly if it has fluctuating patterns of gas and electricity demand.

10.5.4 Policy measures to promote CHP

In the Netherlands, the development of CHP has resulted from a mix of measures, which varied over time:

- regulated feed-in tariffs;
- a special gas price for CHP;
- fiscal measures;
- subsidies;
- voluntary agreements on energy efficiency;
- joint ventures with the energy industry;
- the environmental action plan of the distribution sector.

Energy market liberalization raises questions of unfair competition, with certain policy measures favouring a particular technology or fuel. Regulated feed-in tariffs and special gas prices, two of the measures that stimulated growth of CHP capacity in the last two decades, will be abolished as incompatible with a liberalized electricity market.

Nevertheless, a number of policy measures in the Netherlands with respect to climate change still provide favourable conditions for CHP. Besides fiscal measures, the benchmarking energy efficiency covenant discussed earlier is a major policy measure to mitigate GHG emissions in the energy-intensive industry. For other industries, energy efficiency measures are a condition of being granted environmental licences. CHP appears to play an important role in benchmarking and improving energy efficiency since it is generally regarded as a cost-effective way to increase energy efficiency. In addition, taxes on energy use increased substantially, in particular for small customers. Since CHP is exempted from these taxes, the conditions for CHP, especially small-scale CHP, improve as they are raised. Finally, the Dutch government is considering the introduction of a special certificate for CHP, similar to the system of green certificates, which will enable end consumers possessing such a certificate to apply for a reduction in the energy tax.

The future of CHP in the liberalized energy markets is still unclear, and the Dutch government will observe the development of CHP with great care.

10.6 Promotion of renewable energy

10.6.1 Introduction

There has been broad interest in renewable energy for decades in the Netherlands. This interest originally arose from the idea that the reserves of fossil fuels are finite. Attention in the last few years has shifted to the prevention of environmentally harmful emissions, in particular CO_2. Initially, political interest in renewable energy resulted in the promotion of research and development activities; actual implementation objectives came later. However, the contribution of renewable energy to the Dutch energy supply is still marginal. This contribution has been stable for years at only about 1% of energy demand. Current policies are focused on achieving a domestic target of 5% in 2010 and 10% in 2020, but will have to be stepped up to achieve the EU renewables directive target of 9% of electricity demand in 2010.

10.6.2 Fiscal measures

The renewable energy targets were initially supported by measures aimed at a monopolistic, government-affiliated sector. Agreements were made with provincial governments regarding the placement of wind turbines. The government gave subsidies for investments in renewable energy, and energy utilities were urged to give a sufficiently high feed-in tariff for renewable energy generation, with a legally established minimum of 3.7e/kWh.

As part of a general 'greening' of the tax regime, a number of fiscal measures have been developed that can benefit the renewable energy sector:

- Investments in renewable energy can profit from a regulation for accelerated depreciation (VAMIL) and energy investment deduction (EIA), and can be financed from tax-free green funds.
- In 1997, the regulatory energy tax (REB, or 'ecotax') was introduced. However, the tax is not levied on energy generated from renewable sources. A payment of 1.4e/kWh must be given to the generator of renewable energy.
- Since 1995, energy utilities have been offering 'green electricity' to their customers, though under different names depending on the company. Since 1 January 1998 consumers buying green energy pay the special 'nil tariff' of regulatory energy tax. This means that energy utilities can offer green energy at prices that are barely higher than the prices for conventional energy.

Table 10.1: The Dutch regulatory energy tax, 1996–2001

	1996	1997	1998	1999	2000	2001
Natural gas (e/m³)						
0–800 m³	–	–	–	–	–	12.03
800–5,000 m³	1.45	2.90	4.32	7.25	9.45	12.03
5,000–170,000 m³	1.45	2.90	4.32	4.74	5.19	5.62
170,000–1 million m³	–	–	–	0.32	0.70	1.04
Over 1 million m³	–	–	–	–	–	–
Electricity (e/kWh)						
0–800 kWh	–	–	–	–	–	5.83
800–10,000 kWh	1.34	1.34	1.34	2.25	3.72	5.83
10,000–50,000 kWh	1.34	1.34	1.34	1.47	1.61	1.94
50,000–10 million kWh	–	–	–	0.10	0.22	0.59
Over 10 million kWh	–	–	–	–	–	–

Source: Dutch Ministry of Finance; see www.minfin.nl.

Since 1997, the 'ecotax' has increased considerably (see Table 10.1). In the energy report presented by the ministry of economic affairs at the end of 1999, it was announced that this increase would continue in the coming years. If indeed the nil tariff is maintained, this would represent substantial financial support for renewable energy.

However, the rising 'ecotax', the introduction of VAT on electricity and the lack of price reductions resulting from liberalization have led to substantial price increases. Indeed, inflation, already high in the Netherlands thanks to the rapidly growing economy, has been pushed up further by energy prices. Electricity became 17% more expensive in 2000, gas 12%. Together with the rise in transport fuels this pushed up price levels in the Netherlands by 1.1% out of the total inflation of 2.6%.[7]

10.6.3   Additional regulation

There are significant bottlenecks in increasing production of renewable energy. Contracts for domestic supplies of biomass are not at easy to arrange; biomass plants must comply with strict emissions requirements. Solar electricity is currently still very expensive. It is often very difficult to get all the required installation permits for wind turbines and solar boilers. Application procedures often fail at the local level. Even if city councils have a positive

---

[7] Central Bureau of Statistics press release, 'Inflatie in 2000 gemiddeld 2,6 procent' [Inflation in 2000 on average 2.6%], 12 Jan. 2001.

attitude, people living in the neighbourhood or environmental organizations that fear harmful effects on the local ecology often make complaints.

To remove the bottlenecks on the supply side, a number of measures are indicated. To this end, the government has the intention of abolishing the obligation to get a permit for solar energy installations in the built environment. Also, the permit procedure for wind turbines will be relaxed: once it has been decided to grant a permit, no further objection can be raised.

10.6.4 Green certificates

Renewable energy received special attention in both the new Dutch Electricity Act of 1998 and the Dutch Gas Act. In both laws the Dutch government retains the right, if necessary, to mandate customers to use a certain minimum percentage of electricity and/or gas from renewable energy sources. So-called tradable 'green certificates' can prove fulfilment of this obligation. A green certificate is a proof that a certain amount of energy has been produced in a renewable way. On 1 January 2001 the government introduced a green certificate system and a corresponding free-market system. Besides electricity, this system will also encompass renewably produced gas and heat. A simultaneous obligation for consumers to purchase a minimum amount of renewable energy is still under discussion. The lower house of the Dutch parliament has stated in several resolutions that it supports such a move. However, for the time being, the Dutch government does not want to introduce this obligation, preferring to focus instead on promoting voluntary demand by increasing the regulatory energy tax while retaining the nil tariff. The government finds freedom of choice to be better suited to the liberalized market.

The most important disadvantage of the current policy mix in the Netherlands is that it is unnecessarily complicated and opaque. For the moment, the preference appears to be for promoting voluntary demand by lowering prices. The advantages of this are that it is a clear, simple and transparent system. However, the size of the voluntary market is uncertain. As long as the nil tariff is combined with a high regulatory energy tax, there is a reasonable degree of certainty for potential investors. However, political uncertainty about the tax structure remains. The European directive on state aid prohibits more environmentally benign products being made less expensive with subsidies (at most, they may be made equally expensive as the alternative). Furthermore, the question arises as to how voluntary demand relates to an international market in green certificates. Other countries with green certificate systems and obligations will not be quick to accept Dutch certificates to fulfil their country's 'obligation', because there is no guarantee that additional renewable energy will then be generated in the Netherlands. Besides, confidence in voluntary demand is not compatible with the 'polluter pays principle'. Thus, for those involved, there is no equitable distribution of the burden.

10.6.5 Allocation of objectives

When countries enter into agreements about the conditions for trade in green certificates and the associated place of obligations and objectives, this will lead to a comparative evaluation of the objectives of the countries, just as has happened in the framework for international climate policy. At the EU level, discussion about a fair allocation of the EU's renewable energy objectives has now taken place among the member states within the negotiations on the renewables directive. The Netherlands' renewables target under the EU directive is 9% of electricity demand, lower than the initial allocation of 12% proposed by the Commission.

Because of international trade in green certificates, the production of green energy is no longer equal to its consumption in the same country, and the Netherlands and other EU countries will formulate objectives for production alongside objectives for consumption of green energy. The production objective may be translated into a requirement that a part of the purchase obligation will be realized with certificates from the Netherlands. It may also be required that municipalities realize a certain amount of renewable energy production within their borders, and that this obligation is tradable among municipalities.

10.6.6 Market for renewable energy

From 1 July 2001, the market for green energy in the Netherlands has been completely open. A green image for suppliers will be important to capture a good starting position in the small end users' market, because at first (only) 'green' consumers will be free (non-captive); not until 2004 will all consumers be free to choose their suppliers. However, not only Dutch companies will operate in this market. Foreign companies with renewable generating capacity and new (international) companies specializing in selling renewable energy will enter the Dutch market.

Only just over 1% of Dutch electricity is green. In just three months since the opening of the market for green power, 50,000 customers have switched to a green supplier. In total 630,000 customers in the Netherlands receive green power from their supplier and so do not have to pay the 'ecotax'.[8]

10.7 Using the Kyoto mechanisms

The Dutch government has also begun to work towards the 50% emission reductions that should be obtained through the use of the Kyoto mechanisms. Apart from being a member of the World Bank's Prototype Carbon Fund (see Chapter 2, section 2.4.3), the government, through its grants implementing agency, wrote a tender for emission reductions, named ERUPT 2000 (ERUPT standing for 'emissions reduction unit procurement tenders'). On 17 April 2001, the first contracts were signed for the sale of carbon credits as a result of ERUPT 2000.

ERUPT was set up to buy emissions reductions from JI projects in eastern Europe, learn by doing and kick-start a market in carbon credits. The projects allowed under the programme were subject to strict guidelines, in order to make them valid under any future JI rules. The emissions credits should count towards the Dutch Kyoto target. The Dutch energy sector plays a key role in the emissions reduction projects contracted, and may play an even more important role in future programmes.

Table 10.2 gives an overview of the five projects contracted under ERUPT 2000. Nuon, one of the largest distribution companies in the Netherlands, has played an important role, submitting three winning projects. The total amount of reductions from these contracts is $4.2MtCO_2$ over the five-year budget period, or $0.84MtCO_2$ annually: just over 3% of the required reductions through the mechanisms. The average price the government paid for of the reductions is €8.75/tCO$_2$e. This price is higher than market studies indicate, and higher than the World Bank's PCF is willing to pay. However, the Dutch government has accepted these prices for three reasons: first, the price is below the marginal cost of reductions in the Netherlands; second, no previous market existed and the price is considered to be a 'first movers' premium'; and third, the number of offers was limited, reducing competition.

After the successful completion of ERUPT 2000, the Dutch government has decided to continue, using lessons from the first experiment.

---

[8] See www.duurzame-energy.nl.

Table 10.2: ERUPT 2000 contracts

Project	Location	Emission reductions (tCO_2e)	Price (€/tCO_2e)	Contractor
Municipal 26MWe cogeneration plant	Targoviste, Romania	1,536,140	9.08	NV Nuon Warmte
Municipal 26.4MWe cogeneration plant	Cluj-Napoca, Romania	924,590	9.08	NV Nuon Warmte
55MW hydro power plant	Surduc-Nehoiasu, Romania	612,631	5.00	United Power Company[a]
60MW windpark	Skrobotowo, Poland	583,500	9.00	Nuon International Projects BV
A biomass energy portfolio (28 projects, 130MWt)	Czech Republic	522,320[b]	9.00	Biomass Technology Group BV

Source: Senter, www.senter.nl/erupt/projects.htm.

[a] To be created by SC Hidroelectrica SA, Bucharest, Romania (49%), and Harza Engineering Company International LP, Chicago, USA (51 %).
[b] Minimum 522,320tCO_2e, maximum 1.2$MtCO_2$e.

10.8   Conclusions

With the liberalization of the electricity market, the role of the Dutch government has changed from that of an 'active player' to that of a 'director'. Direct government interference in the electricity sector with respect to climate policy does not fit in the concept of a liberalized market, in particular in relation to strict regulation and high taxes.

Strict regulation with respect to reducing the emissions from coal-fired plants has been softened with several flexible measures to fit the market. The voluntary agreement between generators and government consists only of the cheaper options for reducing emissions, such as increasing the efficiency of the coal-fired plant, cofiring with biomass and storing CO_2; it does not include the more costly options such as the accelerated decommissioning of coal-fired plant or conversion to other fuels. In addition, the fuel tax hitherto paid by generators has been converted into an output tax on electricity; since consumers of electricity pay this tax, it will not bear on the generators.

Policy measures related to CHP are for the most part implemented to mitigate the market barriers in the liberalized energy markets, and mainly involve fiscal measures. CHP is heavily promoted by the Dutch government as it contributes substantially to Dutch electricity supply and also to energy conservation and reducing GHG emissions. A decrease in the contribution of CHP to power production could mean that the targets for reducing GHG emissions have to be strengthened.

In the case of renewable energy, the customer will be charged with the extra costs. The regulatory energy tax (or the price of green certificates) covers these extra costs and these are met by the customer, in particular the captive customer. Initially, the purchase of green certificates will be on a voluntary basis. As long as purchasers of green certificates are exempted from the high regulatory energy tax, there is a reasonable degree of certainty for potential investors. However, political uncertainty about the exemption and aid structure remains. If the targets for renewable energy supply are not met, a purchase obligation, rather than the current voluntary approach, may be implemented.

Overall, the (climate) policy measures related to the electricity sector do not appear to be very strict, in line with the liberalization of the sector. The measures implemented are mainly on a voluntary basis (e.g. those applying to coal-fired plants). The extra costs and responsibilities are passed on to the end consumer, in particular the small customer. Consequently, small customers will have to pay for the extra costs of renewables and adjusting the coal-fired plant by means of the regulatory energy tax or by buying green certificates. Also when a renewables obligation is implemented, it is anticipated that it will be put on the demand side, again placing the burden on consumers.

11 United Kingdom: power markets and market policies

Nicola Steen[1] and Christiaan Vrolijk

The Labour Party took office in 1997 and formed the first New Labour government. It is now in its second term. One of the few quantified targets in the party's 1997 election manifesto was related to its aim to reduce CO_2 emissions by 20% by 2010, relative to 1990 levels. This was taken from a policy report written for the then shadow environment minister, Chris Smith, in 1994.[2] The '−20%' remains one of the government's current environmental targets. Another target that soon came into the policy debate was to source 10% of electricity from renewable fuels. Environmental issues were high on the government's agenda.

The United Kingdom has the second largest electricity market in the EU after Germany. The market is also the oldest liberalized and privatized market in Europe, the process having begun with the Electricity Act of 1989. With the benefit of this experience, important lessons can be drawn from the UK sector for other countries that have only recently liberalized their electricity systems.

Directly following the start of liberalization of the power sector and a change in European regulation, opening the gas market for power production, the 'dash for gas' occurred, when many UK utilities shifted fuel from coal to gas. The emissions reductions following this dash for gas have been substantial, and emissions are projected to fall lower as the result of a further shift towards gas use. The drop in overall UK emissions has been caused almost entirely by the power sector; indeed, in 2000 the combined energy-related emissions from the non-power sectors were at the same level as in 1990 (see Figure 11.1).

The 'dash for gas' has delivered substantial savings that could bring UK emissions down close to the country's Kyoto target of −12.5%; however, as

---

[1] The author would like to thank Penny Tomlinson of Innogy for her help in reading this chapter and providing valuable input and guidance; industry and government colleagues were also very helpful. The opinions expressed in this paper are those of the author and do not necessarily reflect the position of the Association of Electricity Producers or CO2e.com.

[2] *In Trust for Tomorrow: Report of the Labour Party Policy Commission on the Environment* (London: Labour Party, 1994).

Figure 11.1: Sectoral CO_2 emissions in the UK, 1970–2000

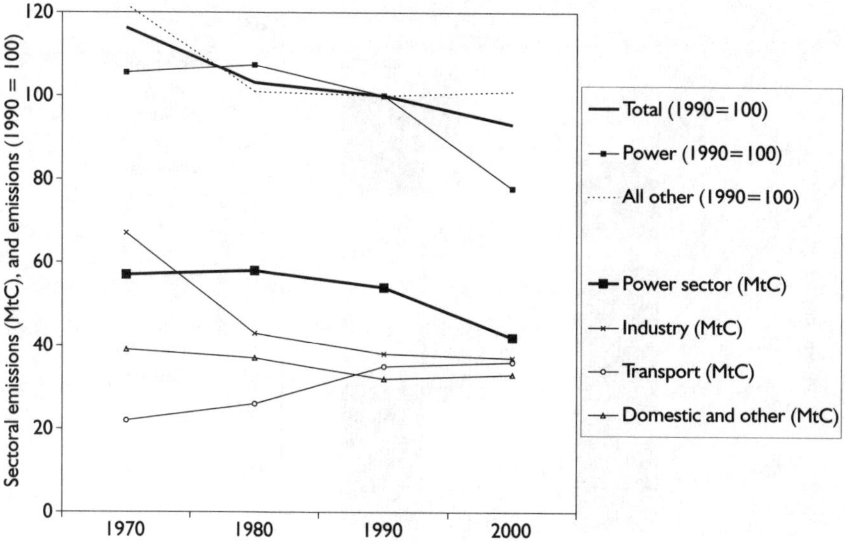

Source: *UK Energy in Brief* (London: DTI, July 2001); see www.dti.gov.uk/energy/index.htm.

noted earlier, the UK government set a more ambitious domestic CO_2 target of –20% for 2010. The government has backed up this target with additional measures, such as the Climate Change Levy, domestic emissions trading and involvement at the highest political level.

11.1 The electricity sector

11.1.1 Overview

The electricity sector of England and Wales was liberalized and privatized from 1989 onwards. At that time the sector was dominated by coal-fired power plants. After the 'dash for gas', by 2000, power production had increased by one-fifth compared with 1990 levels, while emissions decreased by one-fifth over the same period. The main reasons are that coal usage has more or less halved, and efficiency, driven by the market and new invest-ment, has increased. Figure 11.2 shows these trends.

The UK's second national communication to the FCCC in 1997 indicated the impact of market liberalization on emissions. This document set out a

Figure 11.2: Power sector emissions and fuel usage, 1990 and 2000

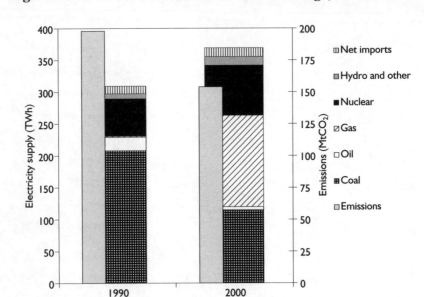

Source: *UK Energy in Brief* (London: DTI, July 2001); see www.dti.gov.uk/energy/index.htm.

series of measures under a climate programme aimed at achieving the FCCC goal of stabilizing emissions at 1990 levels by 2000, saving 7.7MtC. Other measures, predating this programme, produced reductions amounting to 7.6MtC; but market liberalization was estimated to lead to 17MtC of reductions through fuel-switching, and 2.9MtC of savings through increased efficiency in nuclear power plants.[3]

The Central Electricity Generating Board (CEGB), the monopolistic electricity company in existence before liberalization and privatization, was split into different companies. The National Grid Company took control over the transmission grid; other companies took on the generating business in 1990–1. Part of the nuclear power generation capacity was also privatized by the mid-1990s; the older nuclear plants were never privatized. Market shares have changed significantly since then, altering dramatically even in the last few years. These changes were encouraged by the regulator and effected through divestment and new entrants, and have increased competition substantially.

---

[3] *Climate Change: The UK Programme*, the UK's national communication to the Framework Convention on Climate Change (London: Stationery Office, Feb. 1997).

The large generating plants connected to the high-voltage network competed in the Electricity Pool of England and Wales, which decided the merit order and price half-hour by half-hour. Parallel to the Pool a market in risk-sharing contracts emerged. The Electricity Pool has now been replaced by the New Electricity Trading Arrangements (NETA), the impact of which is briefly described in section 11.1.2.

As the electricity industry continued to change shape during the 1990s, within this changing market the regulator, the Office of Gas and Electricity Markets (Ofgem) demanded lower prices as the result of competition,[4] leaving little room for environmental considerations. Ofgem's first environmental action plan illustrates the difficulty of incorporating environmental costs into prices.[5]

In 2000 the government introduced the new Utilities Act. This act has enhanced competition by separating distribution (owning and running the low-voltage network) and supply (retail). The industry faces substantial challenges posed by government policies: costs increase, taxes and regulations are introduced, and at the same time prices are expected to fall.

11.1.2   The New Electricity Trading Arrangements

In 1998 the government initiated a radical change in the England and Wales electricity market. The regulator had become increasingly frustrated by the processes of the self-governing Electricity Pool of England and Wales. There were also criticisms that the rules in the Pool led to players being able to manipulate prices. The Pool had just declared its intention to carry out a review of the market when the government announced its own review of the electricity trading arrangements (RETA). The resulting New Electricity Trading Arrangements, published by the Department of Trade and Industry (DTI) and Ofgem,[6] were developed by a consultation process; however, with very short consultation times, few industry suggestions were adopted.

Under NETA, generators have to predict their output not later than three and a half hours in advance of the time of generating. Any difference between predicted production and actual output is liable to a penalty fee. Less predictable or intermittent generation, such as run-of-river hydro or wind,

---

[4] Following privatization, the Office of Electricity Regulation (Offer) and the Office of Gas Regulation (Ofgas) were established. In June 1999 these amalgamated and became the Office of Gas and Electricity Markets (Ofgem).

[5] *Environmental Action Plan: A Discussion Paper* (London: Ofgem, July 2000).

[6] *The New Electricity Arrangements*, vols 1–3 (London: Ofgem, July 1999).

will therefore be worth less than more reliable base load. However, one problem for base-load production is that competition has driven down prices under NETA. In advance, the regulator and government suggested prices might drop by 10%. Price reductions, already starting in the last year of the Electricity Pool, have been substantial, but in the autumn of 2001 some large users suggested contract prices had begun to rise.

The degree to which prices might fall in the longer term is unclear; however, NETA certainly introduces increased risk into the market. It favours flexible, reliable technology. Managing the risk of plant failure is now core to the business of generation and trading electricity. Generating companies with portfolios of plant can manage failure risk by redistributing output among the remaining plant. Such uncertainties are affecting smaller generators proportionately more than larger ones, as smaller companies often have tighter margins and less opportunity to substitute output from different power stations. With NETA the predictability of output a few hours in advance is rewarded, increasing the competitiveness of coal and gas and putting the more changeable output from renewables and cogeneration at a great disadvantage. NETA has already discouraged further development of cogeneration capacity, and has badly affected renewables generators.

Although many renewables generators have not signed the Balancing and Settlement Code, as they are too small, they are still affected by NETA, for the companies with which they sign contracts are signatories to the code, and want to apply their balancing risks to their dealings with generators. Renewables generators initially asked for the option of 'consolidating' their power for trading purposes. The DTI and Ofgem agreed that this would be useful,[7] and at least five companies indicated they wished to provide such a service. However, it seems none has contracted a significant number of generators; small players do not see consolidation as the answer.

11.1.3 Markets outside England and Wales

England and Wales have one interconnected market for electricity. However, other parts of the UK have distinctly different power sectors. The sector in Northern Ireland is clearly separate from that on the 'mainland', and is not further described here. The Scottish market is also distinct from that of England and Wales at present, and is not at the heart of this case study, but is briefly outlined next.

---

[7] *The New Electricity Arrangements*, vols 1–3; *The New Electricity Trading Arrangements, Ofgem/DTI Conclusions Document* (London: Ofgem, Oct. 1999).

Scotland's electricity transmission network is owned and operated separately from the England and Wales network. An interconnector allows an average of 1,400MW of power to be transferred; this will rise to 2,200MW in 2002.[8] The flow is typically southwards, into England, driven by the market. There is also a new interconnector to Northern Ireland.

Scotland's electricity market has always been different from that of England and Wales. The network is owned by two companies: Scottish and Southern Energy, based in Perth, and Scottish Power, whose headquarters is in Glasgow. The electricity industry in Scotland was not split into disaggregated generation, transmission, distribution and supply companies as in England and Wales, but has remained vertically integrated. The market arrangements in Scotland are currently under review, with the goal of integrating the Scotland market with that of England and Wales. However, the issues raised are considerable and may require primary legislation, which is likely to delay change by several years.

Alongside the moves towards further integration of the markets, the newly devolved government bodies in Scotland and Wales are affecting political process and organization. Wales now has its own national assembly, which has only limited powers and no remit for energy but does consider environmental issues.[9] Since 1999, Scotland has had its own parliament, whose remit covers the environment and renewable energy, though not energy in general. The great majority of policies enacted in England and Wales are mirrored in Scotland, such as the Scottish Renewables Order, which reflects the NFFO (see section 11.6.1). The Scottish Executive also published its own specific consultation on renewable energy policy in Scotland.[10] Likewise, the Scottish Executive published its own climate change consultation.[11] While lobby,

---

[8] The actual amount depends on National Grid Company's system and its constraints. In summer, the wires are hotter and cannot carry as much capacity. In summer the limit could decline to 850MW, while in winter it could be as high as 1,850–1,900MW.

[9] The Welsh Assembly has commissioned a study on renewable resources in Wales, and is trying to develop an energy strategy for Wales. Civil servants work closely with the DTI.

[10] *The Renewables Obligation (Scotland)* (Edinburgh: Scottish Executive, Nov. 2000).

[11] *Scottish Climate Change Programme* (Edinburgh: Scottish Executive, Nov. 2000). However, the Kyoto targets are for the UK as a whole. The government does have powers to bind Scotland, Wales and Northern Ireland to this target, but it 'does not propose to use these powers at this stage because it is confident that significant emission reductions can be delivered through partnership with the devolved administrations'. See *Climate Change: The UK Programme* (London: DETR, Nov. 2000), p. 35, para. 4. Disaggregated emissions have been published since 1998 for Wales and Northern Ireland; it is hoped this will continue and that future publications will include disaggregated emissions for Scotland too.

focus and information groups can direct their attention on local MPs and committees, it is unclear whether greater regional involvement and accountability are an aid or a hindrance on issues such as planning permission. There are still cases, for example, where renewable energy projects gain local planning permission, only to be called in for further planning scrutiny at the regional level.

11.2 UK politics

The New Labour government inherited policies and the industrial legacy of those policies from the previous Conservative administration. The Conservative government had encouraged free markets and 'liberalization' of what had been nationalized industries. The electricity industry had become a prime example of this shift in philosophy. In 1979, when the Conservative government came to power, electricity was produced, transported and delivered to customers by the state-owned CEGB and, in England and Wales, the twelve regional electricity boards. When the Conservatives left government in 1997, the industry had completely changed:

- the companies had been privatized;
- around 90% of all electricity bought and sold went through a competitive exchange, known as the Electricity Pool of England and Wales;
- the fuel mix had completely changed; and
- a ground-breaking support mechanism for renewable energy projects was in place, which relied on developers bidding projects into a tender process.

At the same time, Sir Crispin Tickell, backed by David Pearce's *Blueprint for a Green Economy*,[12] had convinced Prime Minister Margaret Thatcher that the environment deserved at least a cursory glance. John Gummer MP, Minister for the Environment, took part in the Rio Conference in 1992 for the UK, and signed the UN FCCC.

The changes in the electricity industry (rather than government-driven environmental policy) led to CO_2 emissions being reduced by 22% in 2000 from 1990 levels, while electricity demand rose by 19%: a fall in carbon intensity per unit of output of 35% (see Figure 11.2).[13] CO_2 emissions from the

---

[12] David Pearce et al., *Blueprint for a Green Economy* (London: Earthscan, 1989).
[13] *UK Energy in Brief* (London: DTI, July 2001); see www.dti.gov.uk/energy/index.htm.

economy as a whole were 168MtC in 1990 and are projected to be 8% lower than this in 2000.[14] The government estimates that by 2010 UK emissions from all six GHGs will have dropped 15% from 212MtCe in 1990 to 180MtCe in 2010;[15] electricity generation will have provided 22MtCe (68%) of this reduction.[16]

However, the present government's reluctance to undertake action that could possibly raise domestic fuel prices is a particular obstacle. It mixes concerns about fuel poverty with environmental issues: 'For social policy reasons, the government is reluctant to introduce any policies that will raise fuel bills and so the use of economic instruments in the domestic sector is largely ruled out.'[17] Indeed, almost immediately after coming to power, the government reduced the rate at which value added tax (VAT) was applied to electricity to the minimum allowed rate under EU law (5%). The September 2000 'fuel crisis', with its demonstrations and protests about the high government taxes on petrol, emphasized this political sensitivity.[18]

After several consultation-laden, policy-packed years of Labour government a clear 'joined-up' strategy to tackle climate change is not apparent. One hastily conceived policy, that aims to be all things to all voters, has squared up badly with another well-meant but not sufficiently developed policy announcement or objective.

---

[14] *Climate Change: The UK Programme* (London: DETR, Nov. 2000), p. 6; see www.defra.gov.uk/environment/climatechange/index.htm.
[15] Ibid., p. 53, para. 4; see www.defra.gov.uk/environment/climatechange/index.htm.
[16] *Climate Change: The UK Programme* (2000), p. 54; see www.defra.gov.uk/environment/climatechange/index.htm. These figures include some policies in government projections (CCL, 10% renewable energy target, and the fuel duty escalator until 1999), but others, such as the NAs under the CCL and emissions trading, are not included.
[17] *Climate Change: The UK Programme* (2000), p. 103, para. 7; see www.defra.gov.uk/environment/climatechange/index.htm. See also *Fuel Poverty: The New HEES* (London: DETR, Aug. 1999): 'The commonly applied definition of a fuel poor household is one which needs to spend more than 10% of household income to achieve a satisfactory heating regime (21° C in the living room and 18° C in the other occupied rooms), with those needing to spend in excess of 20% regarded as being in the worst degree of difficulty. It is important to distinguish between the amount of income *actually* spent on heating and that *needed* to be spent. Given the competing pressures on low-income households, many do not spend the amount needed to stay warm.'
[18] See e.g. John V. Mitchell and Müge Dolun, *The Fuel Tax Protests in Europe, 2000–2001* (London: RIIA, Sept. 2001).

11.3 The climate change programme

11.3.1 Early days

The UK government prides itself on taking a lead on environmental issues. At The Hague in November 2000, its keenness to be seen internationally taking a leading role on environmental issues was exemplified by Deputy Prime Minister John Prescott's high-profile discussions and actions. In 1997, before the meeting in Kyoto, senior members of the government travelled the globe to build up momentum, expectation and commitment to the negotiating process. The Kyoto Protocol was agreed. The UK took a 12.5% reduction target under the EU's burden-sharing agreement. In addition, the government still holds on to its earlier domestic target: a 20% reduction in CO_2 by the same date.

In 1998, Sir (now Lord) Colin Marshall, then president of the Confederation of British Industry and chairman of British Airways, was asked to undertake a study for the government task force on the industrial use of energy. The task force's report, *Economic Instruments and the Business Use of Energy*, was first released as a consultation paper and later as a full publication.[19] However, consultations with industry are felt to have been too limited, because of time pressure.

About a tax on energy use, which later became the CCL, the report said:

My conclusion is that there probably is a role for a tax if businesses of all sizes and from all sectors are to contribute to improved energy efficiency and help meet the UK's emissions targets ... I recommend that: the revenues are recycled in full to business; consideration be given to special treatment of energy intensive industries; any measures are subject to detailed consultation about their design . . .

. . . in my view, there is a good case for trying to reflect, at least in broad terms, the carbon content of different fuels in the rates set in order to maximise the emissions savings resulting from the tax. (pp. 19, 21)

The report took a sympathetic view on emissions trading:

The issue over tradable permits is not so much whether they have a role in helping the UK to meet its target as how much and when. Trading is already on its way. A

---

[19] Government Task Force on the Industrial Use of Energy, chaired by Sir Colin Marshall, *Economic Instruments and the Business Use of Energy* (London: HM Treasury, Nov. 1998).

system of international greenhouse gas emissions trading is provided for in the Kyoto Protocol. (p. 11)

However, the report saw problems with a domestic ETS, concluding:

Though I think a statutory UK scheme will probably be unrealistic much in advance of 2008, I am convinced of the advantages which actual practical experience of trading before then would bring. I recommend that the government seriously consider a dry-run pilot with interested players as soon as possible, as a means of learning lessons for when an international scheme begins. (p. 16)

The 'Marshall report' lies at the basis of the UK's climate policies and the new 'Climate Change Programme' launched in 2000. In particular, the two policies on tax and emissions trading noted opposite, derived from the report, have been taken forward in the Climate Change Programme.

11.3.2 The climate policy package

After releasing a consultation document in spring 2000, the government published its final programme in November 2000, entitled *Climate Change: The UK Programme*.[20] In both publications there was a chapter devoted to energy supply. Both focused almost entirely on the electricity industry, describing many of the policies outlined in the present chapter.

The programme suggests that with implementation of the policy package outlined the UK is likely to reduce its GHG emissions by 23% from 1990 levels by 2010,[21] while projected CO_2 emissions would fall short of the domestic target of 20%, albeit only by 1%. This would lead to the UK delivering more than its share of the European target. If these emissions levels are reached, the programme will have accomplished its goal 'to make sure that the UK delivers its legally binding Kyoto target and moves towards its domestic goal'.[22]

---

[20] *Climate Change: The UK Programme* (2000), p. 103, para. 7; see www.defra.gov.uk/environment/climatechange/index.htm.

[21] Ibid., p. 7; see www.defra.gov.uk/environment/climatechange/index.htm: 'The quantified measures in this programme could reduce carbon dioxide emissions by about 19% below 1990 levels in 2010, representing significant progress towards the government's domestic goal. But there is much more that could be done, and the programme is designed to stimulate a wider response from all parts of society. This could reduce emissions still further and deliver the 20% goal.'

[22] *Climate Change: The UK Programme* (2000), p. 7; see www.defra.gov.uk/environment/climatechange/index.htm.

Less quantifiable is the aim to begin 'to prepare the UK for the fundamental changes that will be needed in the longer term to meet the challenge of climate change'.[23] The government is now giving further study to the longer-term goal, looking specifically at the possibilities for reducing emissions to 60% below 2000 levels by the mid-twenty-first century. Prime Minister Tony Blair said that 'it is time to re-awaken the environmental challenge as part of the core of British and international politics'.[24] He referred to the report from the Royal Commission on Environmental Pollution,[25] noting that it had concluded that 'the UK will have to cut the CO_2 we produce by 60% by 2050 if we are to slow down the pace of [climate] change'. He continued: 'If there is one immediate issue that could bring global disaster, it is the changes in our atmosphere.'[26]

The six key principles of the programme are that it should:

1 reflect the importance of tackling climate change by a positive response to the UK's domestic goal;
2 take a balanced approach, with all sectors and all parts of the UK playing their part;
3 safeguard, and where possible enhance, the UK's competitiveness, promote social inclusion and reduce harm to health;
4 focus on flexible and cost-effective policy options which will work together to form an integrated package;
5 take a long-term view, looking to targets beyond the Kyoto commitment period and considering the need for the UK to adapt to the impacts of climate change; and
6 be kept under review.[27]

---

[23] Ibid., p. 26; see www.defra.gov.uk/environment/climatechange/index.htm.
[24] Prime Minister's speech to the Green Alliance/CBI Conference on the Environment, Tuesday 24 Oct. 2000.
[25] Royal Commission on Environmental Pollution, 22nd Report, *Energy: The Changing Climate* (London: Stationery Office, June 2000).
[26] The DETR went further: *Climate Change: The UK Programme* (2000), p. 9; see www.defra.gov.uk/environment/climatechange/index.htm. 'Global emissions may need to be reduced by 60–70% if we are to avoid dangerous climate change. Developed countries may need to make a deeper reduction, perhaps by over 90%. This will require a major transformation in the way we generate and use energy – essentially a move away from fossil fuels to a low-carbon economy. We must therefore start to plan now for meeting our future energy needs in a world with tough emission reduction targets.'
[27] Ibid., p. 26; see www.defra.gov.uk/environment/climatechange/index.htm.

While some of the measures described in the Climate Change Programme, going beyond cost-effective measures, will increase costs for industry and consumers, the programme spells out the benefits of the policies and measures package:

- improved energy efficiency and lower costs for businesses and house-holders;
- more employment opportunities through the development of new, environmental technologies;
- a better transport system;
- better local air quality;
- less fuel poverty; and
- improved international competitiveness for the UK.[28]

The Climate Change Programme introduces a raft of measures that will reduce emissions. The projected 'business as usual' emissions are already 6% and 13% below 1990 levels in 2010, for CO_2 and the basket of GHG respectively.[29] As mentioned earlier, these extra measures would reduce emissions to 19% and 23% below 1990 levels. Table 11.1 sums up the most important policy measures; these will be dealt with in the following sections.

One of the elements of the Climate Change Programme is the establishment of the Carbon Trust. The trust is set up as an independent, non-profit-making company that will channel funds into low-carbon technology and information and education initiatives. Renewable energy projects can also benefit through grants and enhanced capital allowances. Actual savings facilitated through the Carbon Trust will depend on the final design and take-up, but the initial estimate was around 0.5MtC.[30] The trust will have an initial annual budget of £130m (€207m), recycling some of the CCL receipts.

---

[28] *Climate Change: The UK Programme* (2000); see www.defra.gov.uk/environment/climatechange/index.htm.

[29] The baseline emissions given in the climate change programme include the effects of the Climate Change Levy and the 10% renewable energy target; the baseline emissions reductions given are calculated by the editor to exclude the effects of these two key climate policies.

[30] *Climate Change: The UK Programme* (2000), p. 125; see www.defra.gov.uk/environment/climatechange/index.htm.

Table 11.1: Policy measures under the UK Climate Change
Programme

Sector	Policy measure	Emission reductions from business as usual (MtC)
Business	Climate change levy	2
	Climate change agreements	2.5
	CCL-related measures/carbon trust	0.5
Business	Emissions trading	At least 2
Energy	10% renewable energy target	2.5[a]
Domestic energy	Energy efficiency commitment for energy suppliers	2.6–3.7
Transport	EU car manufacturers' agreement	4
	All other measures	5.5–5.7
All	Reduction CCL and additional measures	19.75

[a] NFFO projects are assumed to be within the baseline, already reaching 5% market share by 2003 and continuing emission reductions of 2.5MtC by 2010.

Source: Department of the Environment, Transport and the Regions [now Department of the Environment and Rural Affairs], *Climate Change: The UK Programme* (London: DETR/DEFRA, Nov. 2000), Summary.

11.4   The Climate Change Levy

The Marshall report was embraced as justification for introducing a levy on business use of energy, which was known as the CCL. Even before its introduction in April 2001, environment minister Michael Meacher called it 'the government's favourite tax … (that's a joke)'.[31]

The CCL is a tax on energy use rather than on carbon. It was decided to collect the tax at the point of energy use, so that domestic users' energy consumption could be excluded. For electricity, this means electricity suppliers collect the levy when they bill non-domestic customers. The tax has a flat rate (currently 0.43p/kWh) on electricity.[32] After lobbying from industry, users of new renewable energy (excluding hydropower over 10MW) and 'good quality' (as defined by the government) CHP are exempt from the levy.

The aim of an environmental tax is to change behaviour for the benefit of the environment. The CCL makes energy more expensive, encouraging effi-

---

[31] The Rt Hon Michael Meacher MP, Minister for the Environment, 'The Road to COP-6 and Beyond', in *The Kyoto Protocol: The End of the Beginning?*, proceedings of the Chatham House Annual Climate Conference, London, 19–20 June 2000 (London: RIIA, 2000).

[32] Currently 0.15p/kWh (equivalent) on coal and gas, 0.07p/kWh on LPG; oil is not levied.

cient use. In an attempt to limit the financial impact of the tax on industry, the revenues of the levy are used to reduce employers' national insurance contributions on labour. As mentioned earlier, part of the funds raised has also been promised to low-carbon technologies, including energy efficiency and renewable energy projects through the Carbon Trust.

However, if the CCL is effective in changing behaviour, over time less tax revenue will be raised; therefore the multiple benefits sought through recycling of revenues would decrease as well. The aim of using less energy is at odds with providing funds for a reduction in national insurance payments and investment in energy efficiency and renewable energy.

For some energy users the CCL will not be important, because energy accounts for only a small percentage of their costs; for them, the reduction in national insurance could even reduce the overall tax burden. In general, employee-intensive industries and organizations with large payrolls, carrying out non-energy-intensive activities, will benefit financially from the new policy: service industries and government departments, for example.

However, energy-intensive businesses are very concerned about the CCL. These companies have the option to sign 'negotiated agreements' with government. Companies that are part of such an agreement to reduce energy use can receive an 80% reduction on their CCL rate. The agreements are expected to deliver savings of 2.5MtC per annum by 2010.[33] Details and an analysis of some forty agreements are available.[34]

The 'first wave' of negotiations included some fifteen sectors, but the number of agreements quickly rose to exceed forty. Because of the 80% rebate on the levy, if a large number of agreements are struck, the net revenue of the CCL could be dramatically lower than the initially estimated £1.75bn.

The CCLAs can be based on absolute or output-related energy use or carbon emissions. An absolute emissions target is the least favoured by industry; most CCLAs, at the time of writing, are based on energy efficiency targets.[35]

Further complexity arises because renewable energy and 'good quality' CHP are exempt from the CCL, but electricity from these sources still counts as energy use under the CCLAs, based on energy efficiency targets. It could, therefore, be cheaper for some companies to contract a large percentage of

---

[33] *Climate Change: The UK Programme* (2000), p. 124; see www.defra.gov.uk/environment/climatechange/index.htm.

[34] See www.defra.gov.uk/environment/ccl/index.htm.

[35] For more information, and access to an assessment of these negotiated agreements, see www.defra.gov.uk/environment/ccl/index.htm.

their electricity from renewable energy or CHP, on which they do not pay any levy, than sign a CCLA, which gives only an 80% reduction on the tax and still involves a company paying to implement energy efficiency measures.

11.5 Emissions trading

11.5.1 Introduction

The UK electricity industry is forward-looking. It knows about the Kyoto commitments and the UK domestic CO_2 target of –20%. It is aware of reports that reinforce the point that cuts in emissions will be called for in the future, and acknowledges that targets will tighten over time. Government documents are now referring to moving towards a 'low-carbon economy'.

The sector is also conscious of the CO_2 emissions reductions that it has made in the past decade: 22% between 1990 and 2000. Emissions are at the core of many of the electricity generators' businesses. Despite the large reductions in emissions already made, pressure is very likely, at some point, to be redirected on to the sector to contribute more reductions;[36] power generation makes up nearly 30% of UK CO_2 emissions.

With long lead-times – to bring new plant on line can take three to eight years, and plant can have a technical lifetime of up to forty years – the industry was looking for certainty about emissions. In 1994 several companies from the electricity and other sectors, far-sighted civil servants and the AEP began considering emissions trading as a means of minimizing the costs of reducing emissions. The companies were averse to a tax on electricity, which they did not believe would deliver an environmental goal, and as a group, they deliberated an alternative – an ETS.

Lord Marshall's November 1998 report notes that in reply to consultations, 'support for trading exceeded acceptance of a role for a tax only in the energy industries and the financial sector'. Government and other parts of industry warmed to the concept of emissions trading. Further cross-industry work on emissions trading was organized through a group set up by the

---

[36] Research for the UK climate change programme determined 'priority emissions reduction technologies'. Electricity production featured strongly; the list was 'carbon sequestration, coupled with engineered sequestration in geological formations; fuel cells; fuel cell feedstocks, particularly those that can be produced from non-fossil sources; battery technologies; photovoltaics, windpower, hydropower and biomass; transport integration; and integration of heat demand and sources.'

Advisory Committee on Business and the Environment (ACBE)[37] and the Confederation of British Industry (CBI)[38]. As in the AEP-facilitated work, this Emissions Trading Group (ETG) involved government departments in all discussions and others, such as NGOs, became involved over time. Stepping-stones of acceptance included prime ministerial endorsement of emissions trading,[39] and the chancellor's commitment of £30m to provide incentives for companies to become involved in a voluntary ETS.[40]

The Department of Environment, Transport and the Regions (DETR) held a consultation on an ETS from December 2000 to mid-January 2001.[41] It expected 'that the framework will be sufficiently well-established for some trading to be possible from April 2001'. The consultation also mentioned other points on the timeline: bids for the financial incentive by autumn 2001; rules of the scheme to be finalized and participation of companies confirmed by late autumn 2001; first compliance period to run from 1 January 2002 to 31 December 2002; achievement of targets to be verified and reported and first incentive paid by April 2003. However, the dates have slipped, with the auction now scheduled for February 2002, and the entry of participants in April, although the first year of the commitment period is still referred to as running from January 2002.[42]

The UK ETS registered its first – admittedly very small – deal in September 2001,[43] even before the market had officially started.

[37] ACBE is a cross-industry group, set up by ministers in the last Conservative government, to advise government on environmental issues. It is serviced by civil servants who participate in its meetings.

[38] The CBI is the UK's umbrella trade association for industry. Its direct company membership employs 4 million people, and its trade association membership represents 6 million. In addition to its central London office, it has thirteen regional offices and a European office in Brussels.

[39] Prime Minister's speech to the Green Alliance/CBI Conference on the Environment, Tuesday 24 Oct. 2000.

[40] The Treasury's *Spending Review 2000: New Public Spending Plans 2001–2004* (London: HMSO, July 2000) announced the availability of £30m for the domestic trading scheme for 2003/4. The government has now committed £215m over five years before corporation tax, or £30m annually after tax.

[41] *A Greenhouse Gas Emissions Trading Scheme for the United Kingdom: Consultation Document* (London: DETR, Nov. 2000).

[42] UK Emissions Trading Scheme Auction Guidance, DEFRA ETS (02) 02, see www.defra.gov.uk/environment/climatechange/trading/auction.htm

[43] Reuters (UK), 'UK Emissions Trading Scheme Registers First Deal', 24 Sept. 2001; see www.planetark.org.

11.5.2   Interactions

The ETS and the CCL both focus on the same products: coal, oil, gas and electricity.[44] Implementing two instruments aimed at the same goal is economically not efficient, but politically this could be acceptable. However, there have been immediate practical repercussions on the design of the ETS, as industry players and government representatives have attempted to dovetail two very different policies.

During their negotiations with government, energy-intensive users emphasized that they should be allowed to 'trade' allowances to meet their CCLAs. Although a separate trading scheme could have been set up for this purpose, government and industry decided to incorporate such trading within the ETS being designed by the ETG.

The interface between the ETS and the CCLAs   In a 'classical' ETS, generators would be responsible for emissions produced in electricity generation. The caps they would take on could influence the price of electricity; generators could buy quotas, reduce emissions or stimulate demand reductions. The inclusion of generators is logical as it places caps on the source of the emissions, on the emitters, who can most effectively control the emissions. However, the CCLAs have opened a Pandora's box.

First, complications arose because the great majority of the CCLAs are based on energy per unit output; this could mean that absolute emissions rise despite meeting a CCLA target. In contrast, an ETS is concerned about absolute reductions in GHG emissions. Solutions for the interaction of the two exist, but they add complexity to what should be a simple mechanism.

Another potential concern, for government and participants, has been how a complicated ETS would be viewed by non-UK players. The complexities of incorporating energy efficiency targets from the CCLAs into an ETS said to be focused on reducing GHG emissions might be bewildering. It could also undermine confidence in the UK's carbon 'currency' in the pre-2008 period. As a solution, the number of permits from those companies with efficiency targets sold into the absolute part of the ETS needed to be limited. The ETG proposed a 'gateway' mechanism that acts like a valve, regulating the number of permits from companies with efficiency targets. The 'gateway' allows trades in both directions, but transfers from the efficiency target sector are not allowed to be higher than transfers from the sector with absolute caps.

---

[44] The CCL is applied to electricity and the CCLAs include energy efficiency reductions related to electricity.

A second complication came about because the CCLAs include electricity use. Solutions exist to address this problem too. The concerns focused on the 'allocation' of permits in the ETS related to emissions in electricity. In theory, three situations are possible: users only have responsibility; generators have responsibility (as in a 'classical' ETS); or both have responsibility. If both users and generators have responsibility over emissions related to electricity, there would be 'double counting' of emissions; this might be acceptable to government, or could be eliminated by some instruments.[45]

The ETG set up a working group specifically to consider how electricity should be treated in the ETS. The format of the CCLAs influenced the working group's discussions. Users who had not signed CCLAs, but who wished to participate directly in the ETS, also lobbied for the inclusion of their indirect emissions related to the electricity they consumed, as in the CCLAs.

In addition to the discussion about responsibility for carbon in electricity and the related potential 'double counting', an issue that has been called 'discrepancy' also needed to be thought through. This would happen whether or not generators were involved in such an ETS. (It is distinct from double counting, although double counting could aggravate it.) The current trading, transmission, metering and billing systems for electricity do not differentiate among sources of electricity, other than a few systems noting renewable sources.[46] Users do not know whether the electricity they consume is generated by, say, coal, gas or nuclear fuel; nor can they know how much carbon has been emitted to produce the electricity they use. In the CCLAs a fixed factor is used that assumes how much CO_2 was emitted to produce the electricity users are consuming.[47] The same factor is used in the ETS and renewable energy obligations (see section 11.6). However, the real emissions factor of the electricity used is probably different.

Financial incentives in a voluntary scheme   The voluntary nature of the proposed ETS, combined with the incentives on offer, add further complexities.

---

[45] For example, a factor could be applied to the permits that related to the 'double counted' element to deflate the error that would otherwise occur between allowed emissions and permits.

[46] The new renewable obligation that should start in spring 2002 will encourage suppliers to monitor the amount of electricity they sell from renewable sources of power. The CCL acts as a similar driver. There has been discussion about whether an 'ingredient labelling' system could be established, to indicate all sources of power used in electricity. There is disagreement about the ease or difficulty of running such a scheme, particularly under the NETA.

[47] The emissions factor 0.43kgCO$_2$/kWh has been set.

The chancellor's incentives have been set at £30m after tax for the year 2003/4, and are to continue for five years. In a 'bidding process' companies will offer possible reductions in GHG emissions with a price attached. A clearing mechanism is aimed at producing the most efficient outcome. Again, however, there is more than one aim: the government wants to have cost-effective emissions reductions, but is also interested in enticing a good number of companies into the scheme. The government has decided to balance these two aims by setting a maximum percentage (10%) of the incentive to be given to any one company.[48]

Through capping and trading emissions, the ETS should be encouraging the cheapest emissions reductions in the economy to influence the market value of reductions. In a mandatory ETS all players have the same incentive of extending the scope of the scheme to involve those companies whose reduction activities cost least. However, the government's financial incentive could be counterproductive. Firms bidding against each other for part of the incentive could create a perverse incentive. Companies could want to exclude valid competitors for the incentive funds. The £30m will be on offer for five years, and companies will bid for reductions and incentives over that five-year period.

Generators' involvement   It is anticipated that much of the commercial and industrial sector will not volunteer to join the ETS with absolute caps, leaving the electricity they use uncapped; electricity for the domestic and commercial sectors is also uncapped in the government's climate change programme. Theoretically, including generators in the ETS would have helped capture much more electricity, and thus carbon, under regulated emissions caps. This is true for a classical ETS, but the UK ETS is not a classical scheme.

How generators are brought into an ETS is very important to the sector as a whole. The level at which caps are set, for example, affects not only those companies that produce GHGs, but also those that do not. The price of electricity from nuclear and renewable sources benefits from any associated price increases attracted to their competitors' use of fuel.

The nature of the product leads to it making more sense for generators to join an ETS en masse. If they did not, perverse situations could arise. For example, if one generator volunteered to take a cap, and its prices rose, consumers would choose (or be forced to choose) other generators' cheaper

---

[48] *Framework for the UK Emissions Trading Scheme* (London: DEFRA, 14 Aug. 2001); see www.defra.gov.uk/environment/climatechange/trading/index.htm.

non-capped electricity. Also, if a generator chose not to generate in order to meet its cap, consumers would take power from elsewhere. In both scenarios, emissions from the sector would not necessarily fall.

As the electricity sector has relatively high emissions, other potential participants in the ETS were keen to know from the outset of the scheme how and when generators might be involved, even if they were to join the scheme after the starting date.

The DETR's consultation document asked several questions about how electricity should be treated in an ETS.[49] In parallel, the government asked the AEP to facilitate high-level discussions between government and generators on these issues. Any discussions between the government and the generators were bound to take account of the government's range of policies for energy, which value, among other things, diversity in fuel sources.

Initially, the involvement of generators in the ETS is limited. End-users have responsibility for emissions in electricity. Generators can enter the scheme as direct participants only in respect of their own energy usage (such as the energy usage of their headquarters) or by taking the responsibility for emissions of others (though this option might be of more interest to supply companies than to generators). Generators can also enter as 'project participants' – the national equivalent of JI projects (see overleaf). It is anticipated that projects will involve CHP plants, energy efficiency improvements on existing sites, or newly built installations not covered under the renewables obligation (see section 11.6). However, the Prime Minister announced in 2001 that the Performance and Innovation Unit (PIU), linked to the Cabinet Office and as such cutting across government departments, would conduct a review of energy policy for Great Britain, which would be ' ... set within the context of meeting the challenge of global warming, while ensuring secure, diverse and reliable energy supplies at a competitive price'. As the chapter went to press the PIU reported to government.[50] The consequences of the energy review could lead to a revision of the generators' involvement,[51] which would bring sharply into focus the relative importance of diversity and the position of coal in the fuel mix.

---

[49] *Greenhouse Gas Emissions Trading Scheme for the United Kingdom.*

[50] www.cabinet-office.gov.uk/innovation/reports/reports.shtml, February 2002. The study is likely to draw attention to some of the policy conflicts inherent in statements such as the Prime Minister's above.

[51] 'There is a general caveat applying to generation projects: the findings of the Government's energy review may have a bearing on whether they are allowed within the Scheme.' See *Framework for the UK Emissions Trading Scheme*, www.defra.gov.uk/environment/climatechange/trading/index.htm.

Projects The proposals for the UK ETS include opportunities for projects that reduce emissions to participate in the trading scheme.[52] Verified reductions could contribute to a company's 'carbon permit' account. As mentioned, generators will be able, where appropriate and within the agreed rules, to develop carbon offset projects.

There is, however, potential for further confusion here, and the rules for these projects will need to be considered to ensure that those who invest in reducing GHG emissions from what they otherwise would have been then own the emission credits thus created. The rules for project credits will need to be developed in conjunction with policy measures such as the UK renewable obligation targets (and the trading of those obligations), green certificate trading (developed Europe-wide), exemption from the CCL for renewable electricity and 'good quality' CHP, and energy efficiency measures such as energy efficiency commitments (EECs) and the CCLAs.[53]

In the short and medium term the ETS will not include generators as core participants, even though generators have made the greatest contribution towards reducing the country's GHG emissions. It was their past action that brought UK emissions below 1990 levels in 2000 and has helped give confidence to the government that the UK's 2010 emission targets will be met. In this climate, the government's concerns about fuel diversity and fuel poverty have dominated concerns about the environment.

Over time the political climate will change. Negotiations about steeper emission targets will have started; fuel poverty should be less prevalent; the Kyoto compliance period will be about to start; and international trading should have developed.[54] European and international trading systems are likely to include generators as emitters. EC legislation will allow CCLAs only for a maximum of five to ten years. The ETS will be thoroughly reviewed in 2005, and the government believes that the gateway should be

---

[52] These projects will be similar to JI or projects under the CDM, where credits are created without a cap, from a projected baseline.

[53] The 'exchange rate' between a renewable obligation and carbon permit has now been set at $0.43\text{kgCO}_2/\text{kWh}$. *Framework for the UK Emissions Trading Scheme*; see www.defra.gov.uk/environment/climatechange/trading/index.htm.

[54] The government intends to permit use of the Kyoto Mechanisms. *Climate Change: The UK Programme* (2000), p. 28, para. 12; see www.defra.gov.uk/environment/climatechange/index.htm. 'The government proposes to include any credits generated through the Kyoto mechanisms in its assessment of the UK's progress towards its domestic goal. However, it is confident that the strength of the climate change programme will ensure that the UK does not fall foul of any restrictions on the use of the mechanisms (the so-called 'concrete ceiling') which might be agreed internationally.'

closed by 1 January 2008.[55] Therefore 2007 could see the introduction of a more classical ETS.[56]

When that happens, and the interface with other policies is re-examined, there will also need to be consideration of how imported electricity, in particular from France, will be treated.

11.5.3 The Climate Change Projects Office

ACBE's working group on climate change worked with government to ensure the establishment of a Climate Change Projects Office in the UK. This office has been running since spring 2001 and its remit includes facilitating projects internationally, which can be validated under JI or the CDM. It sits between the Department of Environment, Food and Rural Affairs (DEFRA, successor to DETR) and the DTI, and will liaise with other departments such as the Department for International Development (DfID).

11.6 The renewables obligation

The UK has pursued renewable energy development for many years. Initially, the government used the NFFO; in spring 2002 the new Renewables Obligation is to be put in place.

11.6.1 The Non-Fossil Fuel Obligation

From 1990, the UK government introduced, with some success, several rounds of bidding for renewable energy contracts. These rounds were known in England and Wales as the NFFO, in Scotland as the Scottish Renewables Order (SRO) and in Northern Ireland as the Northern Ireland NFFO. With

---

[55] *Framework for the UK Emissions Trading Scheme*; see www.defra.gov.uk/environment/climatechange/trading/index.htm.

[56] The UK climate change programme refers to the 'Voluntary reduction targets through first stage of an Emissions Trading Scheme . . . Potential for carbon savings from a successful scheme: at least 2MtC' (p. 125). The 'voluntary' is explained as 'with the financial incentive in place, a successful trading scheme has the potential to deliver savings of at least 2MtC per annum by 2010' (p. 77). This was written before the final rules and generators' involvement had been decided. It also says: 'As the only recognised currency within the international trading community will be absolute units of carbon, it is the government's long term objective to move to a domestic trading scheme that is based *exclusively* on absolute targets by 2008' (p. 77, para. 37).

each round of bidding, prices declined and contracted capacity rose. These NFFO rounds stimulated the development of many different technologies through the award of contracts with technology-specific prices. The most successful technologies are those using landfill gas, municipal and industrial waste, and wind.

However, of the 3,271MW of the total capacity in England and Wales awarded contracts, so far only 818MW has been built and come online.[57] One of the greatest obstacles that developers face is gaining planning permission. The government is focusing its attention on improving this planning process. Planning now dovetails into the devolved, regional and local governments' remits, as they develop their agendas on sustainable development.

One of the main complaints about NFFO by project developers was the uncertainty surrounding the rounds. The timings of the NFFO rounds were not clear. NFFO orders in England and Wales were called in 1990, 1991, 1994, 1997 and 1998. It was also unclear what technologies were allowed, and what the total and technology-specific sizes would be. Thus the process was very uncertain for firms, often small, that needed continuous cashflow to keep their workforce employed.

Liberalized markets do allow for some internalization of environmental benefits and additional costs. For several years electricity companies have been offering green tariffs. Customers can select particular options, such as a renewables mix, exclusion of particular technologies, or payment into ring-fenced funds to be used for investing in new renewable energy plant. In 1999, following an industry–NGO initiative, government encouraged the Energy Savings Trust (an independent, part-government-funded body) to validate companies' green tariffs.[58] Most of the endorsed tariffs are slightly more expensive than conventional tariffs, and the take-up has not been extensive.[59]

---

[57] Data as on 31 Dec. 2000: *Energy Trends* (London: DTI, June 2001); see www.dti.gov.uk/energy/index.htm.

[58] There might be difficulties endorsing green tariffs that charge a premium price once the new renewables obligation is in place. The obligation plus an additional green tariff could be seen as double charging, unless the tariff would ensure capacity over and above the level of the obligation.

[59] The website www.greenprices.com indicates that domestic take-up of renewable energy in 2000 was a fraction of 1% of electricity consumption. The CCL exemption means take-up by industrial players is rising sharply. A note from the (UK) Green Ministers Official Working Group encourages government departments to consider buying renewable energy to 'set an example to others in reducing carbon emissions and contribute to the government's proposals to ensure 10% of electricity is supplied from renewable sources by 2010'. See *Renewable Energy – Setting an Example to Others* (London: DETR, 26 Jan. 2001).

11.6.2   Tradable Renewable Obligation Certificates

The policy chosen by the government to replace the NFFO and SRO is more market-driven than the tender-like process of the NFFOs.[60] The new policy places an obligation on electricity suppliers to ensure that a minimum percentage of the power they sell comes from renewable energy sources. The Utilities Act of July 2000, contains the basic rules. The DTI published a consultation paper on the workings of the policy; at the time of writing the details are still being finalized.[61]

Renewable Obligation Certificates (ROCs) are awarded to the power production from accredited generators. Nearly all renewable energy sources are counted towards this obligation; only production from existing large hydro plants (over 20MW) and waste incineration will not get accredited.[62] As long as the power is sold on the UK market, producers that are currently under NFFO contracts will be subject to a special transitional regime, whereby they still receive the guaranteed NFFO prices, and the Non-Fossil Purchasing Agency (NFPA) will sell the ROCs and output into the market.

These ROCs can be traded separately from the electricity produced. This should help ensure that both the electricity and the ROCs are purchased by whoever values the commodity most. It is likely the electricity will be bought locally, where the 'embedded benefits' will have greatest value.

Suppliers can fulfil their obligations by producing or buying renewable energy directly, buying ROCs from a generator or other supplier, or by paying the buy-out price, which is set at 3p/kWh (adjusted for inflation). The industry's regulatory body, Ofgem, will ensure that suppliers fulfil their obligations.

A crucial aspect, from the industry's perspective, is the greater policy certainty of the new renewables obligation, compared with NFFO and SRO. Apart from increasing job security, greater certainty about the policy framework can lead to better rates being offered by financiers for loans, and so facilitate cheaper projects. The anticipated size of the obligation, growing over time, will be stated at the policy's outset. Figure 11.3 gives an overview of generation from renewables in recent years and the new targets. The DTI's consultation paper suggests a long-term view of twenty-five years.

---

[60] *New and Renewable Energy: Prospects for the 21st Century.*

[61] Ibid.

[62] At the time of writing, it is proposed to exclude *existing* hydro plants over 20MW and the incineration of waste; biomass and other treatment of waste from plant and animal material will not be excluded. See *New and Renewable Energy: Prospects for the 21st Century.*

Figure 11.3: Renewables generation and the renewables obligation in the UK

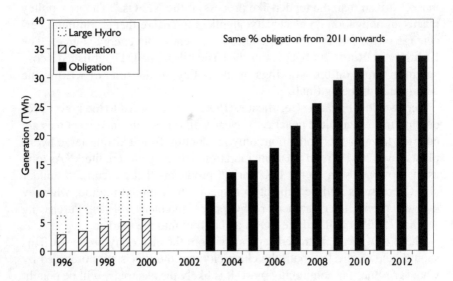

Source: Generation: *Digest of United Kingdom Statistics 2001* (London: DTI); see www.dti.gov.uk.
Obligation: *New and Renewable Energy: Prospects for the 21st Century: The Renewables
Obligation Statutory Consultation* (London: DTI, Aug. 2001); see www.dti.gov.uk.

Notes: Past generation is given by calendar year, the obligation is given for the financial year
ending on 1 April.

Despite the greater policy certainty of some aspects of the new policy,
renewables generators have to face other new market uncertainties. Under
NFFO, the contracts with generators were for fifteen years with indexed
prices.[63] Under the new obligation, neither the contract length nor a price
will be guaranteed. Renewables generators know only that the annual obligation is increasing (see Figure 11.3) and that the penalty for failing to meet
the obligation is £30/MWh, which will be paid back to the holders of ROCs.

As mentioned in section 11.2, the government is concerned about the fuel
poor. This is a key element in its justification for introducing the 'buy-out'
option for suppliers, which will cap the price increase that consumers may

---

[63] The earlier orders gave contracts until 1998, when full competition in the supply side
of the industry was scheduled. These shorter contracts gave higher prices and a move
to 15-year contracts from NFFO-3 was agreed as beneficial for government and
generators.

have to pay.[64] The buy-out enables suppliers to pay an agreed amount if they fail to fulfil the obligation that is imposed on them. This buy-out price level, therefore, will directly influence the amount of renewable energy that is installed, and the technologies that are viable.

The efficacy of the buy-out option as a tool to protect the fuel poor is weak. If there is an environmental need to bring more renewable energy online, then associated costs, incorporating what had previously been environmental externalities, will have to be paid. If a minority cannot afford these costs, then they should be assisted with targeted measures, rather than the additional costs being capped for all consumers.

Funds from the buy-out option will be returned to compliant suppliers. The prospect of a fine from one company going to its rival should act as a strong deterrent. Compliant suppliers will receive funds that reduce the cost to them of meeting the obligation. The cost of compliance will be equal to the cost of the renewable energy bought, minus any receipts from the buy-out fund. This benefit could feed through either to the prices for renewable generators or to lower costs for customers – or both. The recycle value in the early years of the obligation, when there is unlikely to be enough renewable electricity to meet the obligations, might be around (or indeed well above) 1p/kWh. In principle, this would cap the price paid for ROCs at 4p/kWh.[65]

The percentage obligation will favour cheaper projects. The government therefore announced just over £100m (€160m) funding for what are currently the more expensive technologies – offshore wind and biomass. A sum of £39m (€62m) will be available over a period of three years for capital grants for offshore wind, and £12m (€19m) for biomass, both from the CCL's funds; a further £50m (€80m) is made available for these two technologies from the New Opportunities Fund, which hands out lottery funds. The PIU's review involved a 'comprehensive study into the future of renewable energy, with a view to increasing substantially our long-term investment',[66] as part of its

---

[64] 'Fuel poverty remains an issue for too many families and individuals in the UK . . . Ensuring that electricity prices do not rise by an excessive amount as a result of our drive to encourage renewables had therefore been an important part of our decision making process.' See *New and Renewable Energy: Prospects for the 21st Century*.

[65] Rob Driver, 'ROCs: Ready to roll', *Wind Directions*, Sept. 2001. This article also says that 'the recycle value could remain well above 1p/kWh until 2010'.

[66] See Prime Minister's speech to the Green Alliance/CBI Conference on the Environment, Tuesday 24 Oct. 2000. As the book went to press, the PIU's report to Government was produced, and recommended that the government's target for renewable

wider review of energy policy. In March 2001 the Prime Minister announced a further £100m, with additional capital grants for offshore wind, energy crops and other schemes. This brings the total support for renewable energy, including ongoing grants from the DTI for research and development of renewables and stimulation of PV, to about £260m (€420m) over the next three years.[67]

The Renewables Obligation will link into and overlap with other policies. Through the obligation, the market will be placing a value on the 'greenness' and fuel diversity provided by renewable energy. The exemption from the CCL will also be placing a value on renewables, as will green certificate trading across Europe.[68] Emissions trading will be placing a value on renewable energy's zero or minimal carbon content. Currently, renewable certificates can be used to contribute to emissions reductions, using the exchange rate of $0.43 kgCO_2/kWh$, but not vice versa. Market systems will need to be developed that are capable of tracking (and possibly assigning) ownership of these attributes. Double counting of value may be acceptable in a policy arena, but industry needs certainty that the value is allocated to those who invest.

11.6.3   Embedded generation

Electricity production connected to the local network, the distribution network at 132kV or lower voltages, is called embedded generation. Most renewable energy (excluding some large hydro power plants) is embedded generation. The costs and price structure of using electricity networks, both distribution and transmission networks, are very important to the economics of embedded generation, as they make the purchase of power from local embedded generators attractive for suppliers. This 'embedded benefit' is reflected in a price premium.

Decisions about cost structures can prove crucial to potential developers of new, small plants: connection charges can amount to millions of pounds.

---

[66] (cont)
energy should be increased to 20% by 2020. www.cabinet-office.gov.uk/innovation/2002/energy/report/index.htm.
[67] The Cabinet Office's Performance and Innovation Unit, *Renewable Energy in the UK: Building for the Future of the Environment* (London, PIU, November 2001); see www.cabinet-office.gov.uk/innovation/2001/energy/renewener.shtml.
[68] Whether carbon is implicitly valued in green certificates across Europe is currently under discussion, with different countries having differing views. One concern is the effect on the potential market of excluding the carbon value.

The crucial question is: who pays for what cost of the connection? A 'shallow' connection fee charges only the costs of the physical link-up of the new plant to the existing network. A 'deep' connection fee also charges (some of) the costs for the necessary reinforcements upstream from the new connection.

In March 2000 the DTI and Ofgem set up a working group, consisting of industry and government representatives, to consider embedded generation issues. It published its initial report for consultation in January 2001.[69] Helen Liddell, then Minister for Energy, said: 'It is vital that we help developers and operators of environmentally friendly embedded plants such as CHP and renewables gain fair access to the distribution network at fair prices. This report makes a significant step on the road to achieving that. I am impressed by the degree of consensus reached given the wide range of interests involved in the Group.'[70]

The working group recommended the use of 'shallow' network tariffs and additional incentives for the distribution network operators to facilitate competition in generation and supply. It also recommended a new review of tariffs, which would take into account the inherent contribution of embedded generation to the distribution networks.[71] However, as mentioned on page 228, the effects of NETA have been to worsen the market position for many smaller-scale generators, in particular those with unpredictable output.

11.7 Cogeneration

As for renewables, the government has set an explicit target for the contribution of CHP to electricity production. The target has been set at just over double the current installed capacity, at 10GWe by 2010; in 2000, 4.6MWe was installed in the UK.[72]

'Good quality' CHP is exempted from CCL payments. Additionally, enhanced capital allowances for new CHP plants are available, through

---

[69] Ofgem/DETR/DTI, *Embedded Generation Working Group, Report into Network Access Issues: A Consultation Document from the Joint Government–Industry Working Group on Embedded Generation* (London: DTI, 12 Jan. 2001). A response to comments received was published in May 2001; see www.dti.gov.uk.

[70] DTI press release, 'Liddell Welcomes Progress on Better Deal for Greener Generators', P/2001/29 (London: DTI, 17 Jan. 2001).

[71] *Embedded Generation Working Group Report into Network Access Issues.*

[72] *UK Energy in Brief* (London: DTI, July 2001); see www.dti.gov.uk/energy/index.htm.

the Carbon Trust, recycling funds from the CCL to low-carbon technologies.[73]

However, as noted on page 228, NETA have not had a positive effect on the market position of CHP. Innogy announced it had halted further expansion of its CHP business, partly because 'NETA has created problems for small plant'.[74]

11.8 Demand-side efficiency

The Gas Act 1986 and the Electricity Act 1989 gave powers to the regulatory bodies Ofgas and Offer to set Energy Efficiency Standards of Performance (EESOPs). While the gas regulator chose not to take up these powers, the electricity regulator did. Offer imposed a requirement on electricity suppliers that they should undertake environmentally beneficial activities to a specified value. The cost of the last performance standards, EESOP-3, was set at £1.20 per customer per fuel. The supply companies were required to report their activities to the regulator.

The Utilities Act 2000 reinforced these powers with the EECs,[75] due to run from 2002 to 2005. The act specifies that both gas and electricity are included in the provision, and that the targets are to be measured in energy terms, rather than being converted into a monetary value per customer. However, an indicative cap on expenses for this programme has been set, at £3.60 per customer.

Previous schemes focused their attention mainly on 'low-income' customers, to target fuel poverty, with a dual purpose of reducing energy use and improving living conditions. Much of the action taken by the utilities did not reduce demand, but rather increased comfort levels. However, the introduction of EECs has three objectives: first, to make a significant contribution to meeting the Kyoto targets; second, to reduce fuel costs for customers; and third, to give particular help to lower-income customers and reduce fuel poverty.[76] Table 11.2 gives an overview of some of the demand-side programmes.

The Climate Change Programme stated:

---

[73] Capital allowances are offset as expenditure against profit for tax reasons. Power plants would normally be allowed to be offset over twenty years; enhanced capital allowances enable all the allowance to be offset in year one, which helps cashflow.

[74] Reuters (UK), 'UK Innogy Halts CHP Power Expansion', 21 Sept. 2001; see www.planetark.org.

[75] Formerly EESOP-4.

[76] *Energy Efficiency Commitment 2002–2005: Consultation Proposals* (London: DEFRA, 17 Aug. 2001); see www.defra.gov.uk.

Table 11.2: Demand-side programmes in the UK

Name	Information
Energy Efficiency Standards of Performance (EESOPs)	This scheme started in 1994 and aims to help households, in particular those on low income, to use less energy. Power companies have the obligation to achieve a set amount of energy savings or increased comfort at a maximum price on delivered energy. The performance is tradable.
Energy Efficiency Commitment 2002–5 (EEC)	Consultation proposal launched on 17 August 2001. Replacing EESOP–4, EEC aims to save 64TWh (0.4MtC) annually. The performance is tradable, and surplus can be traded in the ETS.
New Home Energy Efficiency Scheme (HEES)	This scheme aims to improve heating and insulation of housing for the most vulnerable households. Should deliver 0.2MtC under the Climate Change Programme.
Energy efficiency marketing campaign	Run by the Energy Saving Trust.
Energy efficiency offices	Energy efficiency offices throughout the country give free advice to domestic customers.
Energy efficiency incentive schemes	Run by the Energy Saving Trust.
Energy Efficiency Best Practice Programme	Advice to building professionals, managers of housing associations and local authorities.
Reform of building regulations	Should deliver 1.3MtC under the Climate Change Programme.
'Are you doing your bit?' campaign	Advertising campaign.
Carbon trust	Energy efficiency measures under the CCL package should deliver 0.5MtC by 2010.

Extensive discussion of the potential costs and benefits of energy efficiency has confirmed that a range of simple measures could save up to 2.7–3.8MtC per year by 2010, with a substantial net saving for consumers and major financial and health benefits for low-income householders in particular. With the energy efficiency priorities of those on low incomes addressed first, the government aims to work towards this total carbon saving figure by 2010, taking into account the experience of the EEC 2002–2005 scheme.[77]

---

[77] *Climate Change: The UK Programme* (2000), p. 106; see www.defra.gov.uk/environment/climatechange/index.htm.

11.9 Further regulation

Two further factors that could influence GHG emissions and the fuel mix of power generation in the UK are the IPPC Directive and the existing Large Combustion Plant Directive (LCPD), which the European Parliament recently reopened for discussion. The UK government has assured industry that it 'intends to ensure that the energy efficiency requirements of IPPC are applied in a way that is complementary to the climate change agreements and emissions trading'.[78]

The discussion about the LCPD suggests a twofold tightening of emissions limits. Existing EC limits have been reflected in discussions between government and industry and in the resulting limits on emissions of sulphur and nitrogen oxides in the UK. Further tightening of these limits could be hard to integrate with the government's keenness for coal-fired power plants to keep a substantial share in the market, for reasons of diversity of supply.

11.10 Conclusions

A mix of pragmatism, realism and free-market experience has produced a situation and set of policies which make the UK relatively well-placed in the move towards a 'low-carbon economy'.

In the early 1990s, the developers of new power plants responded to the regulatory and economic climate when they built gas-fired power stations. Environmental issues were part of that political climate, and would have been factored into investment decisions that were to last forty years. The resultant less carbon-intensive fuel mix in the electricity sector has given the UK government confidence that it will meet its international targets for emissions reduction to such an extent that it has set its own, more challenging, aspirational target. If the privatization of the electricity industry had led to a more environmentally damaging industry, the government might not have been encouraged to consider further market-based policy instruments to respond to the threat of climate change. But it didn't, and it has.

Where industry and government have worked together the resulting policy has met with wider approval than when a policy has been imposed. Contrast the ETS and the Renewables Obligation on the one hand with the CCL on the other. The environmental contribution of these policies cannot yet be determined. However, there is greater certainty about how many emissions the

---

[78] Ibid., p. 78, para. 49.

ETS and the Renewables Obligation will prevent, as these policies, more strongly supported by industry, both exercise more direct constraints on business activity than the CCL.

Despite its unpopularity, there are perhaps two roles that the CCL has played. First, it has helped catch the attention of end users of energy. Developing a link between an energy tax and the absolute capping of emissions, through the ETS, has reinforced the point that the CCL is an initial measure relating to society's concerns about the greenhouse effect. Carbon is not as central a component to end users' businesses as it is to electricity generators' or oil companies'; the CCL provides a signal to end users that action will be taken, over the long term, to reduce emissions of GHGs. The link between the CCL and the ETS demonstrates the levy's second role: it allows the economy and the environment to benefit from some of the potential reductions in GHG emissions that end users can make.

The government asserts that, in the longer term, a move to a low-carbon economy is needed. The policies that are being put in place will not deliver such an economy. At the moment, the government's commitment to emissions reductions in the electricity sector is clearly no stronger than its desire for diversity in the fuel mix. At some point, however, the need for larger carbon reductions could threaten the position of fossil fuels, particularly coal, in that mix.

The programme now in place consists of a raft of suboptimal policies. Inconsistencies in the climate change programme are partly due to the government's relatively early commitment to the CCL on business energy use, and the consequent problems of consistency with, for example, emissions trading objectives and renewable energy objectives. However, another government objective, reduction of fuel poverty, is also partly to blame, since this leads to its refusal to accept higher energy prices for domestic consumers. Additionally, the NETA have significantly dented prospects for renewables and cogeneration.

The Climate Change Programme recognizes that current policies 'begin to prepare the UK for the fundamental changes that will be needed in the longer term to meet the challenge of climate change'.[79] The document acknowledges that the policies described might have a limited impact by 2010, but, looking further ahead, believes that 'The direction of the energy supply sector beyond 2010 will be critical to the UK's ability to make the deeper emission cuts needed in the longer term.'[80]

---

[79] Ibid., p. 24.
[80] Ibid, p. 59.

That direction of the energy sector is based on competitive markets; and environmental policy too is likely to follow that route, increasingly capturing environmental value in those markets.

Part III
Interactions, implications and conclusions

12 National climate policies in Europe

Chapters 12–14 form the conclusions of this book. This chapter summarizes the case studies of Part II. It draws out the lessons learned in the different countries, and the interactions between the policies applied and the structure of the power market. Chapter 13 analyses the big questions that this book raises, including the interaction between environmental and in particular climate policies and the liberalization of the electricity market; and it considers how pressing is the need for harmonization or convergence of European policies. Chapter 14 sets the broad conclusions of this book.

This chapter summarizes the case studies by applying the same structure used in Chapter 4, focusing in turn on:

- energy efficiency improvements;
- fuel-switching to lower-carbon fuels;
- fiscal instruments increasing the cost of carbon;
- increasing the share of renewable energy; and
- the introduction of emissions trading.

The discussion focuses on the relative importance of these elements in national climate policies and looks at the instruments used.

12.1 Energy efficiency improvements

There is scope for substantial energy efficiency improvements in all countries of the EU. The ECCP has identified energy-saving measures that account for emissions reductions of over $400MtCO_2$ annually, enough to cover all the reductions required to comply with the Kyoto targets.[1] These savings occur in different sectors and as a result of implementation of different instruments.

Working group III of the ECCP, on energy consumption, identified $220MtCO_2$ of savings at zero or low ($<€20/tCO_2$) costs and an additional $85MtCO_2$ from new rules for more energy-efficient end-use equipment. The $220MtCO_2$ savings come from a raft of measures including the new directive on the energy

[1] See European Commission, *European Climate Change Programme – Report June 2001* (Brussels: CEC, June 2001).

performance of buildings, energy services and additional use of CHP. The ECCP study estimates that the first 150MtCO$_2$ can be saved at zero or negative cost.

More efficient end-use equipment could save emissions up to 85MtCO$_2$, a quarter of the required EU reductions. Most of the proposed programmes, agreements and directives are scheduled to be implemented by 2003. Savings in industrial processes have been identified of up to 100MtCO$_2$ through long-term agreements, the IPPC directive, etc.

In the energy supply sector, around 100MtCO$_2$ could be reduced at low costs (<€20/tCO$_2$). This estimate includes 63MtCO$_2$ due to fuel-switching from clean coal to natural gas, which is mainly the result of the liberalization of the electricity and gas markets rather than climate policies. Many more savings can be made at higher costs (an extra 100MtCO$_2$ at €20–100/tCO$_2$).

12.1.1   End-use efficiency

The focus on end-use efficiency has been weak in many countries, partly because of the difficulties of DSM experienced in the past, partly because the ongoing liberalization process sets difficult conditions for such policies. The EU is taking the lead in the standards for end-use equipment, reducing impacts on competitiveness. At the same time, national efforts in some countries are continuing.

Long-term policies in Denmark have focused mainly on the energy performance of buildings, in particular heating demands. As a result, an extensive heat network exists in most Danish towns.

In Germany and the Netherlands household demand is mainly targeted through ecological taxes and campaigns such as that for '100,000 solar roofs' in Germany. Energy conservation is expected to deliver 18% of the reductions required in the Netherlands, but part of this will be due to the use of CHP.

In France, electricity has a very high share in total energy use, including in space heating and other thermal uses. However, this heating demand causes a distinctive winter peak in consumption, as summer cooling is not widespread. The French tariffs now include a 'time of use' component, aiming to reduce peaks in the load curve when conventional thermal plants are used for generation.

The Italian regulator has introduced DSM-friendly tariffs that limit revenues per customer, rather than per unit of electricity sold. These measures are expected to deliver about a quarter of the reductions required, around 25MtCO$_2$ in the commitment period.

The UK policy for domestic energy demand management is intertwined with concern for fuel poverty. A raft of measures is in place and is being renewed as part of the climate programme. The new tradable energy efficiency commitments for energy suppliers and various building standards could make the largest impact. Projects reducing demand can also be used to meet commitments under the ETS, using a fixed 'exchange rate'.

End-use efficiency is not a very popular focus for energy and climate policies. However, at both the European and the national levels some measures are in place. Substantial emissions reductions can be achieved through various measures, such as taxes, 'time of use' tariffs and efficiency standards.

12.1.2   Generation efficiency

The liberalized market is expected to bring higher efficiencies to some power markets, in particular through investment in new, highly efficient plants. In Denmark, a special programme is under way to increase the efficiency of coal-fired power plants, possibly to 55%. The French sector aims to reduce transmission and fuel-cycle energy use, which together make up nearly 10% of electricity use. In Italy, ENEL's divestment comes with detailed plans for mandatory upgrading of the generation stock, which could deliver substantial savings. In the tradition of voluntary agreements with government, Dutch industry promises to 'be among the best in the world'. In the UK, since the opening of the market, nuclear generation has increased its operating efficiency and saved nearly 3MtC.

12.1.3   Cogeneration

The Danish electricity market is highly integrated with the heat market, through the existence of many heat supply grids: three-quarters of electricity production is from CHP. This situation has developed thanks to decades of consistent policy.

Electricité de France has the obligation to buy electricity from small-scale CHP, which has stimulated growth in this sector. There are also incentives to switch from conventional coal or oil-fired plant to gas or CHP in the climate programme. However, some of the power could displace nuclear generation and therefore emissions reductions achieved are likely to be modest.

In much of the rest of the EU cogeneration is in trouble. The share of CHP has grown substantially in most countries in the last decade, but now new market rules or increased competition are affecting its profitability. In the

UK, 'good quality' CHP is exempted from the climate levy, but CHP is still badly affected by the new trading arrangements. In the Netherlands, CHP is also exempted from energy taxes, and a quota system may be introduced, but the previous incentives have been scrapped as unfair competition. The German government has already had to reach an agreement with industry and raise the feed-in tariff to guarantee the expansion of CHP, as was foreseen in the baseline emission forecasts, but market conditions are adverse and actual developments would fall far short of previous expectations.

12.2   Fuel-switching to lower-carbon fuels

As a result of the electricity liberalization, and changes in regulations concerning the use of natural gas in power plants, the UK's electricity sector switched en masse from coal to gas as the preferred fuel. In the decade after liberalization the use of natural gas increased from only 0.5% to 39%, almost entirely due to switching out of coal. Emissions dropped by more than a fifth, while production increased by nearly a fifth. The fall in emissions was mainly caused by fuel-switching (over $60MtCO_2$), but also partly by increased efficiency of the nuclear generators (just over $10MtCO_2$).

The UK example is not fully applicable to all other European countries that liberalize their markets because they already have a substantial share of natural gas usage in their power sectors. Still, the ECCP estimates that $63MtCO_2$ will be saved due to fuel switching, and $25MtCO_2$ through other measures driven by the liberalization of the markets. These savings will only have low costs ($<€20/tCO_2$). Additional efficiency savings can be made at higher costs.

Denmark

Despite a rapid decline in the share of coal in the electricity sector, from just over 80% in 1980 and over 90% in 1990, over 50% of the Danish electricity still comes from coal-fired power plants.[2] The focus of Danish efforts to lessen carbon intensity has therefore been on increasing the efficiency of coal-fired power, but also on introducing renewables, including biomass. The newly introduced emissions caps could lead to significant levels of fuel-switching to natural gas; the quotas are unlikely to lead to significant switching to renewable energy technologies. There is, however, no clear push towards any fuel.

---

[2] www.ens.dk.

France

France has only a very small share of fossil-fuel-fired power plants, accounting for about 10% of production. However, 60% of the thermal capacity is fuelled by coal and 15% by fuel oil. A complete replacement of the older coal- and oil-fired plants by CCGT and CHP could reduce emissions by about 4MtC, which would make up about a quarter of the French Kyoto commitments. However, at the current carbon tax rates proposed, only part of this substitution will take place, reducing emissions by 1.5MtC.

Germany

The fuel mix in Germany is expected to change quite dramatically in the next twenty years. By 2020 the share of nuclear power is expected to have decreased from 31% to 9% – a decline anticipated even before the phase-out was agreed. At the same time, natural gas will become more important, with its share rising from 9% now to 20% in 2020. Renewables, in particular wind power, will grow substantially, but remain relatively small.

Cut-throat price competition in the first years of liberalization has reduced investment in new power plants. However, CCGTs are expected to play a more important role in the future market, due to their flexibility and the slow reduction of coal subsidies. The additional use of CCGT, promoted through the national climate plan, is expected to reduce emissions by 15–20MtCO$_2$. Other energy sector policies are aimed at renewables, CHP and energy services.

Italy

In Italy, high-carbon heavy fuel oil is the most important fuel used in power generation. With old capital stock in need of investment, the power sector could generate substantial emissions reductions during the liberalization process, aided by the progressive carbon tax. The divestment of ENEL's production capacity, to reduce its market share to the stipulated maximum of 50%, goes hand in hand with investment and refurbishment plans for the plants sold. These investment plans include measures such as early retirements, substantial refurbishment or retrofitting for natural gas. The ENEL plants earmarked for sell-off must represent the overall structure of ENEL in geographical and technological spread. If, therefore, the new entrants buying these plants must follow detailed investment and refurbishment plans, then so should ENEL, to level the playing field. Upgrading the stock ENEL sells already promises to deliver substantial savings; upgrading the rest of ENEL's plant would reduce emissions much further.

The Netherlands

The Dutch power sector is already heavily dependent on natural gas. Gas accounts for close to 70% of the country's electricity generation, and this share is unlikely to shrink in the near future. Indeed, as part of the Dutch climate programme, emissions from coal-fired power plants are limited to the levels that would pertain if they were fuelled by natural gas. However, this does not mean that all existing coal-fired power plants will indeed switch to using natural gas. Other options are available, such as capturing carbon in sinks, cofiring biomass, or retiring of some of the current plants and replacing them with highly efficient combined cycles. JI and CDM projects could also potentially be used for meeting this emissions cap.

UK

As indicated earlier, the UK fuel mix has already changed substantially from the levels in 1990, when natural gas had a share of only 0.5%. Its current share of nearly 40% is expected to increase even further, bringing the UK's emissions close to the 12.5% target.

Overview

The case-study countries are all expecting an increase in the use of natural gas in the electricity sector, limiting emissions growth. Denmark and the UK have not introduced specific measures to catalyse this fuel-switching in order to reap greater emissions reductions; however, increases are still expected. The other countries have introduced targeted measures that are expected to deliver substantial parts of their domestic commitments.

12.3   Fiscal instruments increasing the cost of carbon

The Belgian presidency of the EU in the second half of 2001 has put a harmonized energy tax back on the table. Both the Commission and many member states believe that a harmonized energy tax is an important step towards meeting the Kyoto targets. However, some countries have reservations. In September 2001, the finance ministers agreed on a procedure for exploring the possibility of harmonization further, either by consensus or by 'reinforced cooperation' among the willing member states.[3]

Denmark

In Denmark, the introduction of energy taxes coincided with the sharp fall in oil prices in 1986. Recently, energy taxes have been supplemented with green taxes on domestic and industrial consumers. However, tax levels for industry are lower. Fuels for power generation are not taxed, but electricity consumption is.

France

As part of the French climate programme the general tax on polluting activities was extended to energy consumption. The government will implement the tax at both production and consumption levels, adding a price signal according to carbon content to the producers' costs, and moderating demand through a general tax on electricity usage. The tax level for 2010 has been set at a preliminary level of €278/tCO$_2$, but will start in the shorter term at a level just below €100/tCO$_2$. The carbon tax is expected to reduce emissions by 6.7MtC per year, and in the electricity sector alone by 1.5MtC per year, nearly 10% of the total reductions in the national programme.

Germany

Despite ecological tax reform, in Germany coal production is still subsidized, and lignite plants (in the new *Länder*) have received subsidies for modernization. However, taxation on fossil fuels has increased in the last few years and will increase further; the revenues arising are used to reduce social security payments. Public transport and industry receive discounts on the taxes; industry pays 20% of the general tax increases. The tax reform is projected to save 20MtCO$_2$ by 2010.

Italy

Italy has a progressive carbon tax on energy supply. The tax is implemented to modify the fuel mix in favour of lower-carbon fuels and to encourage

---

[3] Joe Kirwin, 'EU Finance Ministers Table Decision on Harmonised Energy Tax until December', *International Environment Reporter*, vol. 24, no. 20, 26 Sept. 2001, p. 817.

greater efficiency. The rates are set to increase annually until 2005, when revenues could be nearly €6bn, over €400m of which would come from the electricity generation sector. Tax revenues are recycled through cuts in social security payments and other taxes. The cost of coal-fired power could increase by as much as 40% due to the tax, while the increases for oil and gas are much lower at 6% and 3%. In total, the carbon tax is expected to reduce emissions by 12MtCO$_2$, or 12% of the domestic target.

The Netherlands

In the Netherlands, an ecotax was introduced as part of a general 'greening' of the tax system. This tax is levied on all consumers of gas and electricity. However, the tax is heavily regressive, with lower tax rates on the higher consumption levels and a nil rate on the highest category consumption. Until 2001, the first small part of consumption was excluded from the tax, for social reasons. Electricity (and gas) from renewable energy sources is exempted from the tax, and this exemption is used as an incentive for voluntary demand for 'green' energy.

The previously existing tax on fuel inputs into power generation has been cancelled as a negotiating concession to the coal plant owners, but also for competitiveness reasons. The ecotax rates were subsequently increased.

UK

The UK first outlined the CCL in the April 1999 budget. The levy has been introduced from April 2001. The CCL has become the centrepoint of the UK's climate policy, to which most other related policies are linked in some form or other.

The levy is applied on industrial consumers of energy. For political reasons domestic energy consumption has not been included in the CCL. Industry pays a tax on the use of gas, coal and electricity. Power generators are exempted from the levy for the fuel used. The levy of the tax is substantial, equal to £3–10/tCO$_2$.

Energy-intensive industry was concerned about the impact of the tax, and was allowed to negotiated agreements with government to reduce energy use in return for an 80% discount on the tax. These CCLAs are now negotiated with over forty sectors, and projected emissions savings (2.5MtCO$_2$) exceed those from the levy itself (2MtCO$_2$). The targets in the agreements, often output-related, can now be used as the basis for entering the ETS.

Overview

Energy and environmental taxes exist in most European countries, in some cases forming a substantial part of the climate programme. Tax levels, in particular for industry, are initially set at moderate levels, mainly for competitiveness reasons. Nevertheless, domestic carbon and energy taxes are expected to achieve results by changing the fuel mix or reducing demand. A European effort to establish a coordinated energy tax may reduce the problems. New taxes or increased tax rates are generally recycled through lowering of social security payments.

12.4 Renewable energy

Renewable energy could deliver substantial emissions reductions. Indeed, if the EU renewables directive's 12% target is reached, this may save $330MtCO_2$ in emissions, which equates to the total reductions required to meet the Kyoto commitments. According to the calculations of the ECCP, nearly 40% of this target could be met through low-cost options. The directive has set differentiated targets for penetration of renewables in the electricity sector in all the member states, adding up to 22% of power production; nearly half of this comes from already existing large hydro plants. However, the compromise directive fails to harmonize support systems for the member states.

Denmark

The Danish government has long been committed to various renewable energy sources. As early as the 1981 energy plan, the government aimed to increase the use of renewables (wind and biogas) to 10% of electricity. This target share of renewables was met; and, at the same time, partly because of continued long-term support on the domestic market, a large export sector was created, with Danish wind turbine manufacturers dominating the world market.

The target share of renewable energy has now been set at 29% in 2010 in the European renewables directive. The Danish government intends to meet its target by introducing a green certificates market. Initially, a fixed price band has been set for these certificates. The minimum price of 0.10DKK (1.3e) per kWh has been set to support the renewables generators; the maximum of 0.27DKK (3.6e) per kWh will protect customers from excessive costs. The Commission has approved the gradual phase-in of a renewables obligations system with trading.

France

Currently, a substantial share of electricity (abour 14%) is produced by hydropower plants. This share will have to increase to comply with the EU renewables directive target of 21%. The NCP also proposes new objectives for additional renewables generation. However, when renewables replace nuclear power, no emissions savings are made.

The most recent renewables support programme (Eole 2005) is based on a tender procedure, which might be more difficult to run in the context of a more liberalized market. The implementation of a green certificates system, to bring the cheapest options to the French market, is being investigated. A Europe-wide system of green certificates could bring substantial investment into the French renewables sector, since it has many attractive sites.

Germany

The German target in the renewables directive is a tripling of the 1997 share of renewables in electricity production. This increase in the use of renewables would also save a substantial amount of GHG emissions.

The main instrument for stimulating renewable energy generation is the feed-in law, giving a relatively high price per kilowatt hour (as a percentage of historic retail prices). However, the dramatic fall in electricity prices reduced the price paid for renewables, potentially harming their future development. A new feed-in law was agreed in 2000 to solve this and other problems. The European Commission approved the new law, and the European Court of Justice also ruled in favour. The feed-in prices paid are now fixed at relatively high levels; the feed-in tariff for hydro (between 0.5 and 5.0MW), for example, is 6.65e/kWh; other tariffs are generally higher.

Additional programmes and campaigns are also being implemented. The '100,000 solar roofs' programme, for example, started in 1999 and has already subsidized about 25,000 solar roofs with a total capacity of 100MWp. This and other programmes often give direct subsidies or low-interest loans to stimulate investment. Recycled funds from the ecological tax reforms are mostly used.

Many different 'green power' tariffs currently exist in Germany. The systems range from 'rebranding' existing power capacity to promising that all power will be covered by new and additional renewable sources.

Italy

The Italian renewables target for 2010 is to produce a quarter of electricity from renewable sources. In 1999, hydropower represented more than 16% of generation; geothermal and other renewables accounted for 2.5%. Some additional renewables therefore need to be implemented to reach the target, but this would also account for nearly 20% of meeting the Kyoto emissions target.

The NCP uses a mix of instruments, including fiscal, flexible and other, that is compatible with market liberalization and the relative low energy intensity of the Italian economy. The instruments are aimed at changing the fuel mix and increasing the efficiency of the thermal plants. The implementation of the progressive carbon tax has already stimulated the use of low-carbon or carbon-free sources of electricity. But a targeted renewables policy also exists.

Increased target levels for different renewable sources are set. The greatest increases are expected to come from biomass, hydro, wind, geothermal, energy from waste and solar energy. In total the emissions savings could add up to $18MtCO_2$ for renewables in electricity production. Before liberalization, favourable feed-in tariffs were granted, as well as capital grants. However, the incentive system has changed with the introduction of liberalization.

Generators with production or imports over 100GWh – which means most generators – will have the obligation to produce 2% renewable power. This obligation can be complied with through trading in green certificates. These certificates are granted only for renewable power produced from installations built after 1999. However, certificates can also be traded internationally, subject to some sort of reciprocity clause. Failure to meet the obligation can lead to restricted access to the power pool.

Further incentives are also given, for example, through allowing 'green tariffs', increasing the feed-in tariffs for small-scale renewables that do not qualify for green certificates, and incentives to increase capacity when relicensing hydro plants.

The Netherlands

The share of renewables in the Dutch power generation sector is very small, about 3.5%. However, the new target for 2010 is set at 9%, which could deliver 16% of the required domestic emissions savings. Various fiscal and regulatory instruments are currently used, including accelerated depreciation of green investments and an easing of planning procedures. However, the government has hitherto been unwilling to set obligations.

The government is promoting voluntary demand by lowering the prices of renewables relative to 'normal' electricity. The market for 'green customers' has been liberalized in 2001, while other customers have to wait another two years. The main incentive for voluntary demand is the difference in levels of ecotax; for renewables the level is zero. The difference between the tariff on 'normal' electricity and the nil tariff for renewables is substantial, but the recent ecotax increases have fuelled inflation. The government has implemented a green certificates scheme to validate renewable energy in this voluntary market. However, the electricity law also includes the possibility to mandate minimum levels of renewables for energy consumers, which could be met through the green certificates system already in place. Similar obligations can also be mandated for gas and heat customers.

UK

Despite its large potential, the UK has a very small percentage of renewably generated electricity, only 1.7% in 1997. The target level for 2010 has been set at 10%, requiring a substantial increase. The NFFO, involving several rounds of competitive tenders for renewable capacity, was successful in increasing the supply and lowering the cost of renewables. However, a new, more market-driven and more predictable approach has been taken by introducing an obligation to supply a minimum level of renewables. The government set rising annual targets; renewable schemes under the old NFFO system count towards the target, but do not qualify for tradable certificates as this would lead to double benefits for these schemes.

A failure to comply with the obligation will lead to penalty payments, which are recycled back to suppliers that have met their obligations. The penalty level is set at 3p/kWh (4.8e/kWh), but the recycling value could add another 1p to the maximum costs for competitive renewable projects. The system has also quantified the link with emissions trading, giving $0.43kgCO_2$ per kilowatt hour over the renewables obligations.

Overview

Renewables obligations and markets in certificates do now exist in Denmark, Italy and the UK. The obligations will lead to meeting the European renewables directive targets, and will contribute significantly to reducing emissions. The Netherlands is still using a voluntary-based system, but has the regulations in place to mandate a share for renewables in consumption of electricity, gas and even heat. Germany and France use the tried, tested and highly successful feed-in tariffs and tenders, respectively.

12.5 Emissions trading

All six countries studied, and the European Commission, are looking at ways of implementing the mechanisms of the Kyoto Protocol. However, there are not necessarily many similarities across the schemes. Some countries are actively looking to implement a domestic trading system or have already done so. Other countries are simply looking for ways to make the Kyoto mechanisms compatible with domestic policies, for example, by allowing industry to claim credit for JI or CDM projects to meet domestic targets.

National governments, in pursuit of their own (European bubble) target, are therefore proposing emissions reductions policies, including emissions trading. The national approaches to the market mechanisms in the Kyoto Protocol are diverse, depending on national perceptions, stringency of the target and policies already in place. The national proposals were discussed in detail in the case studies; this section outlines some of the key differences among the various schemes.

Denmark

Denmark was the first EU country to implement a compulsory ETS. This scheme was set up relatively quickly after Kyoto, and the Emissions Quota Act entered into force in 2001. The Danish scheme consists only of the electricity sector, including all auto-producers above a threshold. In 2000, the number of allowances was set at $23MtCO_2$, around one-third of total Danish emissions, and reduced by 1Mt annually until 2003, when the initial phase ends. As a counterbalance for the possible loss of competitiveness in the Nordic power market, the Danish Quota Act included a price cap, at a penalty rate of €5.38(DKK40)/tCO_2 . This price cap is important for the Danish sector, which functions as a swing producer in the Nordpool electricity market; a dry year in Norway leads to substantial power exports from Denmark. The reason for the initial low level of the penalty is the competitiveness of the Danish sector in the liberalized market, and the asymmetry of emissions regulations in other north-west European countries. Despite the quota act entering into force, trading has not yet started, partly because of the limited number of participants inside Denmark, partly due to the absence of compatible schemes across the border, and therefore the lack of trading partners.

France

In France, the electricity sector is virtually carbon-free, and the Kyoto mechanisms are not seen as key measures for reducing emissions. Most of the French measures include taxes and subsidies that stimulate lower-emission technologies. JI and the CDM could still be used by French companies. Indeed, EdF has been very interested in JI and CDM projects, in particular where these projects would involve their nuclear expertise. The Bonn Agreement, discouraging the use of nuclear in JI and the CDM, has reduced the potential participation of the French electricity industry.

Germany

German companies have been involved with the AIJ pilot phase from the beginning, even thought the number of projects officially recognized has been low. More projects are planned or already under way. Germany is involved with the EU emissions trading proposals, and a domestic emissions trading scheme is under discussion. Despite positive noises from the environment minister and one power company, most industry, including the other power companies, favours the existing voluntary agreements over hard emission caps. An initiative for the introduction of CHP quota trading was also abandoned after comments and promises by industry.

The Netherlands

The government of the Netherlands has set very clear targets for the amount of emissions that will be covered through the Kyoto mechanisms: 50% of the required reductions. Half of the reductions are to be met through domestic measures, such as efficiency improvements, fuel-switching, and so on; the other half would be met by the government buying allowances on the international market. Accordingly, the government has started a process of ERUPT. The first tender has finished and contracts are signed for projects involving emissions reduction investments in other Annex I countries (JI). Preparations for further tenders are under way at the time of writing, which might also include CDM-type projects in developing countries. The ERUPT scheme is paid for entirely by the government. The tender process is open for bids from

Dutch and foreign industry to execute the emissions reduction projects within a certain price range per delivered tonne of emission reduction. The Dutch climate programme does not include absolute caps for the industry on which to base emissions trading; but it does prescribe that the industry's energy efficiency shall be 'among the best in the world'. It is possible that industry will also use the mechanisms to meet some of their domestic targets ('to be among the best in the world' and reducing emissions from coal-fired power stations). A national CO_2 emissions trading committee is analysing the possibility of introducing emissions trading.

UK

The United Kingdom is home to one of the most pro-emissions trading communities in Europe since the idea was first floated. Government, business and NGOs were looking at the issue even before Kyoto, and the business sector reconfirmed its preference for market-based mechanisms over carbon taxes when the government was investigating climate policies after COP-3. Lord Marshall investigated the government's options in the business sector and recommended both a tax and a pilot phase for emissions trading; soon thereafter, the government launched the climate change levy. Partly because of this, industry set up the ETG, which promoted the idea of emissions trading as preferable to taxes with backing from key companies. After a very inclusive debate – the ETG included industry and government representatives and had regular discussions with NGOs – the ETG proposal was welcomed by government and incorporated in further policy work. The CCL urged industry to take these steps quickly.

However, this background has also made the ETS more complicated. Some targets are based on sectoral energy efficiency agreements, for which the participants receive a discount on the levy. Other participants will be tempted in with extra money from a £30m auction. Also, the levy excluded fuel inputs for the power sector, which effectively excludes them from emissions trading. The CCL agreements include indirect emissions from industry, i.e. the emissions of the power sector related to the electricity used, whereas caps in other systems are normally based on direct emissions.

The scheme will commence on 1 January 2002, including possible links with the project mechanisms and international emissions market. Government and industry are worried about the complexity of the system and its impacts on interest from international actors. There are also worries about the compatibility with the European proposal.

Overview

Italy and France are currently not looking to implement an ETS in the power sector. France has very low carbon emissions, and Italy might hit the target by a 'dash for gas' and improved efficiency as a consequence of liberalization.

Germany and the Netherlands have a history of 'voluntary' agreements between government and industry, mostly based on flexible targets rather than emissions caps. These agreements are ill-suited to serve a basis for emissions trading. However, the Netherlands in particular is very active in the field of the Kyoto mechanisms – not a domestic system – and Dutch industry may be using these mechanisms to meet the requirements of its agreements.

Denmark and the UK have both implemented domestic systems. Denmark's system is for the power sector alone, whereas the UK system excludes this sector. The Danish system has an explicit buy-out clause at a reasonably low carbon price (€5.38/tCO$_2$). The UK system, for industry excluding the power sector, has a more implicit cap – participants can revert back to paying the climate change levy (equivalent to €5–16/tCO$_2$ depending on the fuel). Both systems are intended to have commitment periods starting many years before the Kyoto period. The Danish caps are fixed, but the UK caps are mostly based on efficiency targets (emissions per unit of output). It is the intention for both systems to become fully compatible with the international ETS of Kyoto.

12.6 Conclusions

The six case studies set out in Part II of *Climate Change and Power* show that European countries are using different instruments to reach similar goals. The case studies also show that the relative importance of various goals differs between countries. Many of the differences can be explained in terms of the market situation in the respective countries, or historical policy experience. Although there is a considerable degree of similarity in many of the policies, they can affect the market differently and have widely different results in emission reductions.

13 Reconciling climate change and the market

The process of electricity liberalization in Europe and concerns about climate change clash. Whereas the liberalization of energy markets aims to reduce regulation in favour of market forces, climate policies add a new dimension of regulation that could potentially limit the newly freed market. In particular, the demand for emissions reductions on the one hand and, on the other, increased demand, partly due to the expected lower prices, seem to be on collision course. Liberalization could also possibly lead to a worsening of environmental standards under market pressure for cost-cutting; however, there is no evidence to date of this actually happening.

The two policies clash head-on in some circumstances. The introduction of new plant from independent power producers, for example, would increase the share of fossil fuels (and therefore emissions) in the French power sector. In Germany, the share of efficient and low-emitting cogeneration had reached around 10%; but the fall in prices since the opening-up of the market in 1998 has made many of these plants uneconomic.

At the same time, liberalization in the UK has been a happy accident in climate policy terms. The power sector there has reduced emissions by over 20% since liberalization as a result of new investment, increased efficiency and a switch to the use of natural gas. A similar 'happy accident' is waiting to happen in Italy, where the opening of the market will bring in the necessary investments for (early) replacement, refuelling and refurbishment of old, inefficient generating stock. Total emissions from the sector, which is still heavily dependent on oil-fired plants, will decline substantially when this happens.

This chapter aims to describe how the liberalized market for electricity and climate change objectives can be reconciled. This is particularly important in the light of the fact that the power sector is expected to be delivering more reductions than other sectors of the economy – more than the –8% reduction of the EU bubble – mostly to make up for the fast emissions growth in the transport sector. Industry and the energy sector, whose business-as-usual emissions are already declining, are expected to deliver even more reductions, ending up with a total more than double the European target. Transport, however, has sharply rising emissions and its 'cost-effective' reductions are very small.[1]

---

[1] Jos Delbeke, 'The EU Internal Implementation: Could Europe Do It?', paper presented to the conference 'Delivering Kyoto: Can Europe Do It?' at the RIIA, London, 1–2 Oct. 2001.

This chapter first explains the liberalization process and the consequent relative convergence of the European power sectors; other energy sector regulation, such as the renewables directive, also aim to harmonize the sectors. It then goes on to describe the action taken in some countries, noting that different targets and different national circumstances have led to the use of different economic instruments without causing problems for competitiveness. The various sectors' attitudes towards emissions trading are also important, with, for example, UK companies at the forefront of the action and German companies heavily opposed to any cap on their emissions. Then it looks briefly at various situations in the light of convergence, situations in which it is best that the EU takes a leading role. Finally, the chapter moves on to look at trading mechanisms as the best way to reconcile the electricity market with climate objectives, without the necessity for fully fledged harmonization in the first commitment period.

13.1 The electricity market

13.1.1 Liberalization

After pioneering work by some member states, the European Commission has taken the lead in liberalizing the European electricity sectors. As one of the fundamental building blocks for the economy, creating a competitive internal market for electricity (and gas) was seen as essential to achieve a fully integrated market with a level playing field throughout Europe. The Commission set the liberalization process in motion in all member states by the electricity directive in 1996. All member states were given minimum levels of opening of the market, including those that still had state-run monopolies, such as France. The key regulation for opening the market is TPA, giving access to the network – and therefore to the market – to third parties, i.e. customers and suppliers other than the owner of the network or local monopoly utility.

The liberalization process was designed to create a more level playing field for industry and other energy users in the whole of the EU. It has also created a new competitive market, in which the existing utilities compete with one another and with new entrants. It was believed that market forces would drive down prices, and indeed they have done so in most countries. This would increase the international competitiveness of European industry, and in particular of energy-intensive industry.

Government has retreated from involvement through direct regulation; in some countries, government has also withdrawn from direct ownership, privatizing the utilities. However, this process is going faster in some countries than in others, and privatization is not a necessary ingredient of the liberalization process.

In general, since the directive came into force, market prices for power have declined; competition, cross-border trades, takeovers and mergers have increased substantially across Europe. However, competition remains limited in some cases by the still partial opening of the market only to the largest industrial users, the dominant position of the former monopoly supplier, the unwillingness of customers to switch suppliers, and market barriers such as restricted market access for new entrants or competitors.

13.1.2 Energy market convergence

The Commission aimed to achieve a single market for electricity with the implementation of the liberalization directive. To some extend this has happened. Cross-border trading and takeovers have already led to substantial convergence of the markets. Power pools that operate across borders also further integrate the markets. The Amsterdam Power Exchange, for example, has Belgian, German and other foreign participants with their own special pricing area. However, within even the longer-established Nordic power market the national markets remain diverse, with Norwegian hydropower, Swedish nuclear power, Finish peat, and Danish CHP and coal. These differences depend on national circumstances that the linking of markets cannot influence. Price convergence does occur, depending on interconnection capacity and constraints.

Interconnection capacity is now expected to increase, which would lead to further evening-out of price differences, in particular for the large industrial consumers on the high-voltage grids. With increased cross-border competition there is an increased need for harmonizing the regulations so as to reduce cost differences of regulation. This issue is of particular interest for the smaller, highly integrated power sectors, such as those of Denmark and the Netherlands, but much less urgent for the larger countries.

In general, the European Commission proposes policy when the aim can only, or much better, be achieved through harmonized regulation at the European level. Accordingly, the Commission has proposed some new regulation for the power markets. The new renewables directive and the green paper on energy security, among others, have harmonized energy policy aims to some extent in the EU countries. However, even the renewables directive does not harmonize absolute levels or required increases of renewables generation; nor does it harmonize the support systems. It does, however, give the Commission the opportunity to propose harmonization four years after the directive enters into force if this is seen to be necessary.

It is important to note that the EU's analysis of the 'cost-effective' emissions reduction potential assumes that substantially more reductions will take place in the energy sector than in the economy as a whole. This is because of the speed with which emissions are rising in particular from transport, but also from other sectors.[2] The power sector is reluctant to subsidize emissions in other sectors.

13.2   Climate differences

13.2.1   Different circumstances, different instruments

EU countries differ greatly with respect to climate change policy. The EU burden-sharing agreement acknowledged this difference by differentiating the targets between the countries very widely. The overall target of −8% from 1990 levels was redistributed on a basis of willingness to pay and ability to reduce. As a result, some of the richer member states took on very steep targets of −21% (even −28% for Luxembourg), while the cohesion countries were allowed substantial increases in emissions. Elements in the rationale behind the varied targets included current emissions levels, expected emissions growth, policies in place and economic impact.

While member states differ greatly in targets and already existing policies, it is not unlikely that different economic instruments will be chosen to deliver the emissions control necessary to comply with the targets. This is not necessarily a problem. Differences already exist and, as long as the cost associated with these climate-related instruments is not very high, will not be greatly amplified. Only if costs were excessively high in some countries would this become more important than existing differences. This, however, does mean that tougher targets in subsequent commitment periods could require a closer convergence of policy instruments to minimize impacts on competitiveness.

Many European countries have already developed national climate policy programmes that will deliver all or most of the reductions needed for their 'bubble' target. Although these national programmes have not yet been fully implemented, countries were aiming to implement these programmes even without further convergence or harmonization of measures. This is because

---

[2] Ibid.

most countries have been able to identify policies at relatively low cost that do not undermine their economies' competitiveness.

The Netherlands has proposed measures to reduce emissions by half of the required amount domestically, while the other half will come from other countries, using the Kyoto mechanisms. This choice has been made for both domestic (competitiveness) and international (strategic) reasons. The domestic measures, were they to fail, are backed up by an additional set of measures. Despite competitiveness concerns, even the first raft of measures include draconian policies such as the limiting of coal-fired power plants to the emissions that would pertain if they were fired by natural gas; however, this policy was agreed upon by industry under pressure from the lifting of the fuel input tax – as a consequence of which the tax on consumers has been increased. The availability and relatively small expected share of coal in the commitment period make this policy possible in the Netherlands; it would be unthinkable in other countries.

In contrast to the Dutch approach, the UK's concern for the fuel poor has led the Labour government to implement a tax on business use of energy, contrary to the common approach of taxing domestic consumers and exempting or reducing the tax on industry and in particular energy-intensive industry. At the same time, the UK's climate programme is set to deliver a substantial reduction below its Kyoto target. While the use of the Kyoto mechanisms is anticipated, they will not primarily be used to meet the target. Again, this is possible in the circumstances in the UK without adversely affecting international competitiveness, but would be impossible elsewhere.

However, some policies would indeed be easier implemented if harmonized throughout Europe.

13.2.2 Need for convergence

The countries studied have remained loyal to their traditional regulatory systems. In Germany and the Netherlands, (voluntary) agreements are playing an important role in reducing emissions. In France and Italy, more direct control on, for example, the demand side is used. In Denmark, longer-term strategies have been used in the past to stimulate CHP and wind, and these are continued alongside the introduction of emissions caps on the power sector. And finally, in the UK, both a tax and a trading mechanism are introduced.

Of great importance for the choice and execution of the national climate policy instruments are the different national circumstances. The French rules have to take into account that most of the country's power is produced by non-carbon-emitting nuclear power plants. The Danish rules can build on the existence of many (small) district heating systems.

Several suboptimal decisions were made in countries of the case studies. These decisions were partly driven by policies or the lack of policies in the other European countries. The abolition of fuel taxes in the Netherlands, for example, happened (partly) because of the lack of fuel taxes in the neighbouring countries. However, it is now explained as a carrot used to obtain the emissions agreement with coal-fired power plant operators. At the same time, energy-intensive industries have always been exempted from paying energy taxes or have been given large discounts for competitiveness reasons. In general, policies were bound by market considerations and anxieties about competitiveness.

At least some degree of convergence among climate policies across the EU countries should happen. The EU, together with the fifteen member states, is a party to the Kyoto Protocol. The countries and the EU also have to submit their instruments for ratification to the UNFCCC at the same time, because of the EU bubble agreement under Article 4 of the Protocol.

Convergence would help mitigate some of the problems leading to suboptimal or even divergent policies (UK emissions trading, for example, excludes the power sector directly but includes it as producer of indirect emissions via power *users*, while the Danish system includes only this sector). A single market throughout Europe would also improve the chances of industry agreeing with policies that impact on it and its competitiveness. The same or very similar instruments would reduce competitive (dis)advantages between countries. Indeed, a further integrating market would automatically lead to a convergence of national circumstances, national (climate and other) policies, and less diverse future emissions targets.

However, these (convergent) policies would still need to take national circumstances and existing policies into account. Existing agreements between government and industry, and existing taxes or other regulations, should not necessarily be overthrown by new harmonized European policies.

Europe has taken up the challenge of further convergence on several more difficult electricity market policies. In particular, the new energy efficiency regulations for appliances would be impossible for member states to implement on their own. Indeed, member states have been very reluctant to take measures on the energy demand side, despite a very large potential for emissions reductions. The new directive on energy efficiency of buildings is also further harmonizing standards in Europe.

Another area which should be a primary target for EU-wide regulation is energy taxes. The Belgian presidency has once again opened the discussions on harmonized energy taxes across Europe. However, it is very hard to get agreement from the member states, who find European taxation in infringement on their sovereignty. The relatively large differences in energy taxes across countries could also pose difficulties, with low-tax countries unwilling to shoulder a higher burden, and high-tax countries unwilling to lose revenues.

There is no direct problem with different levels of energy taxes if they are levied on consumption. Taxes on energy at the point of the final consumption, independent of how and where it is generated, does not discriminate among fossil fuels, non-fossil fuels and imports. This form of taxation stimulates energy savings, without regard for emissions. There are only minor problems with this kind of taxation in the country that imposes the tax: it is possible that imports would be taxed twice, depending on the regime in the exporting country.

However, the most effective taxes from a climate perspective differentiate among the fuels used for generation. Also taxes on the generators could change behaviour and therefore emissions through fuel-switching, this is due to the relative size and avoidability of the tax for generators compared with final energy consumers. Unfortunately, fuel-input taxes are unsustainable in an open and relatively interconnected market such as that in Europe. A country with input taxes disadvantages its power industry in export markets, as well as in the domestic market, where it has to fight untaxed imports.

13.3   Carbon market mechanisms

13.3.1   The new climate policies

The new market environment of the electricity sector has led to the development of many new policy instruments that work under market conditions, in particular those that use market forces in order to achieve policy goals.

However, the classic direct regulation is still important in all European countries, especially in those countries that have liberalized their markets least and in the captive customer markets. Even in the UK, with the longest-established liberalized electricity market, a 'carbon' tax is implemented including further regulation such as agreements based on discounts and exemptions; various regulations are also proposed on the energy demand side. Also, the German mainly regulatory approach seems at odds with its highly competitive power market.

The new policy instruments use market forces to address the problem and reach the goal. The UK's NFFO was an early version of such a market-based mechanism. However, the newer economic instruments build on the Protocol's mechanisms – emissions trading, JI and the CDM. National or sectoral emissions trading schemes have been set up. Renewable energy obligations can now also be traded in several countries. Energy efficiency, cogeneration and other targets have often been made tradable in the new competitive market.

These market mechanisms fit better than any other kind of instrument with the new market for power. Yet the national sectors' attitudes towards them are diverse, with UK companies having promoted emissions trading since 1994 and German companies still heavily opposed to it in 2001. The cap and trade approach delivers the environmental goal with certainty, while allowing the greatest possible flexibility to the companies on how to meet the goals. Whereas a tax would principally aim to reduce demand of the high-carbon fuels, emissions trading allows for continuing use with emissions reductions elsewhere if that proves to be cheaper. Emissions trading also builds upon the trading knowledge and culture. It provides a mechanism for industry to value emissions and emissions reductions, to factor in opportunity costs and to receive credit/value for action. While it provides incentives to reduce emissions, it also allows cheaper reduction options – even if they are in different sectors or countries – to be used first.

- In Denmark, power sector emissions have been capped, with the possibility of trading the quota among companies. The Danish system started in 2001; however, few trades are expected, because of the limited number of players, the distribution of the players and the buy-out clause at DKK40 (€5.38) per tonne of CO_2. A tradable system for green certificates has also been introduced in Denmark. Again, this system has a price cap (3.6e/kWh), but also has a minimum price (1.3e/kWh).
- In France, the renewables support system could be replaced by a green certificates trading system now that the EU directive on renewables has laid the foundations. Indeed, France has very attractive possibilities for producing energy from renewable sources, and could become a large supplier on the European market.
- In Germany, resentment and misunderstanding surround any trading mechanism. Emissions trading is rejected by industry, because it requires caps which would replace the existing (voluntary) agreements. Renewables are supported heavily with the German feed-in law, which was changed

after the market prices for electricity fell through the floor, halting their dependence on retail prices and giving fixed tariffs instead. The CHP quota system, too, which would have been very innovative, was not supported by industry; government is nevertheless keeping the option in reserve.

- In the Italian power sector the target will be met mainly through improved efficiency and fuel-switching as a consequence of the liberalization process. Most of the plans are already laid out in the ENEL divestment process. However, for renewables a system has been developed with renewables obligations that are tradable. Interestingly, special rules have been developed for international trading of certificates.
- The Dutch government has approached emissions and renewables in a different way. Emissions trading could be one of the ways Dutch utilities will be able to comply with their agreements on emissions, in particular the emissions of coal-fired power plants. However, government will be the main actor on the emissions trading market, buying 50% of the Kyoto obligation on the international market. The first trades have taken place under the ERUPT programme, which is basically a form of JI. Further rounds of ERUPT are to be called and will include CDM-type projects. Renewables certificates can be traded to meet (initially voluntary) demand for green power, but other support mechanisms such as feed-in prices still exist and a system setting obligatory targets is ready if voluntary demand is inadequate. The Dutch utilities have already been active on the international green certificates market.
- The UK industry took the initiative on emissions trading very early; the power sector was already engaged in 1994, before Kyoto. After the introduction of the CCL, industry responded quickly with the establishment of the ETG, proposing a UK emissions trading scheme as an alternative. The scheme has now been endorsed by government. Participation is voluntary, with government paying a financial incentive (on delivery of the reductions), or based on the climate change agreements. In effect, two markets exist, linked through the so-called 'gateway': an emissions trading market with fixed-cap participants, and a market where energy efficiency targets can be traded. On renewables, the government has recently introduced the renewables obligation certificates; these may be traded, as may the obligations for energy efficiency improvements.

13.3.2   *The need for convergence in Europe*

Essentially, an ETS is a domestic policy, using market mechanisms for distributing and minimizing costs nationally; but larger coverage, including other countries, would make further cost savings. Indeed, the EU green paper on emissions trading estimates that the savings of a Union-wide scheme rather than separate national schemes could be €1.7bn, or 20% of the costs.

If Europe, with its highly interconnected economy, fails to make its emissions markets compatible, how could it expect to be able to trade with economies as different as Japan or Russia, where more economic savings are to be made?

Divergent emissions trading models could create problems concerning the internal market and compatibility. On the internal market, different schemes could introduce as yet non-existent distortions on the relatively level playing field, while also complicating trading arrangements when sectors are not treated the same across systems. By creating different rules, systems could become incompatible or not recognize each others' reductions. The compartmentalization of emissions trading might also increase the prices and transaction costs.

With the advance of international climate policy and the realization that GHG emissions have a detrimental effect on the climate, carbon has become a scarce resource for the markets. The European Commission and the EU member states have already realized that energy is of primary importance and therefore needed to be harmonized in the internal market. A similar argument can be advanced for emissions (or reductions) and the need to harmonize the emissions market.

However, whether a mandatory EU-wide scheme with fixed quota allocation rules across the Union is needed is another question.[3] Some form of harmonization of emissions trading markets – requiring compatibility or recognition of each others' allowances – is essential for European-wide operating industries. This would itself have the positive effect of lowering costs.

The EU argues that an EU-wide scheme would strengthen commitment and raise the Union's international political credibility. Despite being more acceptable to industries operating across the Union, this is clearly no reason to abandon all national efforts, many of which involve hard-won concessions from industry in favour of the (long-term) national policy, in favour of the

---

[3] The EU proposal for an emissions trading directive does not promote full harmonization on all issues; allocations would be left to the member states.

EU scheme. Commitment and international credibility should undoubtedly be derived from the national policies too.

The proposed harmonization of the ETS and emission allocations could possibly reduce the competitiveness impacts on the affected industries. However, 'diverse domestic policies, institutions and standards are generally compatible with gainful trade.'[4] As long as minimum standards are met, therefore, harmonization might not be necessary. Indeed, with widely different marginal abatement costs, domestic targets ranging from –28% to +27%, and the environment very differently valued, even full harmonization could still affect competitive advantage. Indeed, as long as cross-border trades are recognized by government and backed up by a parallel transfer of assigned amounts, and as long as member states are in compliance with their targets, even efficiency target trading systems, such as the UK system, should not pose a problem.

Allocation rules for emissions quotas would already be subject to state aid scrutiny, and do not need further harmonization. Whereas grandfathering of emission allowances increases the (investor) value of a company, it does not necessarily change the pricing strategy on the carbon market, as explained in Chapter 4; so theoretically there is no need for harmonization. Industry will be wary after the recent experience with the auctioning of 3G mobile phone licences, leaving many telecom companies in financial trouble. The business responses to the EU proposal, indeed, stressed their wish for a high degree of harmonization.[5] The new EU scheme proposed harmonization only to the extent that no auction of allowances will take place in the initial phase, not on the actual allocation, which is left to the member states.

Full harmonization of emissions trading in Europe, therefore, is not necessary. In the long term, with international mechanisms, markets will converge. However, circumstances in countries are different and need to be taken into account.

• In Germany and the Netherlands, agreements between government and industry have been made that could help these countries meet their targets, while not putting an absolute cap on industry's emissions. Despite its enthusiasm for trading, the Dutch government does not want to break the agreement in order to cap industries and implement a trading scheme.

---

[4] Laurent Viguier, *Fair Trade and Harmonization of Climate Change Policies in Europe*, MIT JPSPGC report no. 66, Sept. 2000.
[5] Peter Vis, *Green Paper on Greenhouse Gas Emissions Trading within European Union: Summary of Submissions*, 14 May 2001.

- In the UK, the trading system is voluntary and has to work around the existing CCL and its negotiated agreement. This complicates the trading system, but fits with national policy. With the system close to kick-off, the newly proposed mandatory EU system is seen as a competitor, and a reason for the domestic market to fail.
- In Denmark, a trading system already exists, but for various reasons includes only the power sector. The sector's market position is weakened compared with the hydro-based generators in the Nordic market (not all of them in the EU), but the price cap limits this impact. An EU-wide carbon market would not solve the competitiveness problem for Danish power generators.

A system with mandatory participation, even if the allocations are not fully harmonized, as the EU is proposing, would not fit the member states' priorities or the Commission's competence. Indeed, it would unnecessarily infringe the rights of the member states; also, an EU emissions market would not mean that competitiveness is unaffected because the burden-sharing targets are so diverse. Coordinated national trading schemes are able to take account of national circumstances, while setting some necessary common rules. Central coordination of national systems – of those countries that *want* to start trading – can limit divergence between the schemes, set minimum financial penalties (to stop 'eco-dumping' in the country with the lowest non-compliance penalties), and increase learning.

13.3.3   No need for harmonization

The EU and its fifteen member states will have to submit their instrument for ratification and implementation plans for the Kyoto Protocol at about the same time. This will require some coordination of climate policy development across Europe. Coordination is also needed to prevent the emergence of incompatible policies in different countries. However, heavy-handed harmonization of climate policies is not necessary in the short term, for the first commitment period targets.

Existing policies in some of the countries (mainly Germany and the UK) are already leading them towards meeting the Kyoto or burden-sharing targets. For other countries, radical new policies will have to be developed because their emissions are projected to be substantially above their targets (the Dutch government, for example, aims to buy half of the required reductions from abroad). Existing policies and national circumstances in these countries, as well as policies in other European countries, will have to be taken into account in designing the new policies.

The proposed European emissions trading system includes mandatory coverage of most industry in all EU countries. This would allow nearly all industry to trade allowances, reduce market distortions and lead to close convergence of emissions allocations in the EU. However, in Germany and the Netherlands long-term agreements between government and industry have been signed in which industry agrees to reduce emissions, or increase energy efficiency, without being subject to a quantified cap. These existing agreements work, despite sometimes tough standards, usually because substantial concessions were given, such as promises that industry would not be taxed or capped. Also in the UK, the new agreements based on the climate change levy, for which industry receives an 80% discount on the tax, are mostly based on intensity targets rather than hard caps. Not all industry is willing or ready to forgo the flexibility of these agreements, and the accompanying concessions by governments, in order to take on caps and take part in emissions trading.

Convergence of climate policies throughout the EU would be long-term aim, and would strengthen the EU's position in the climate negotiations. A further convergence and rationalization of the burden-sharing arrangements could be a necessary step towards agreement on more demanding second commitment period emissions reductions. However, heavy-handed harmonization is unnecessary for the first commitment period:

- National circumstances and existing regulation or allocations have to be taken into account. A European harmonized system is unlikely to be able to account for all these national circumstances, leading to real competitive advantages and disadvantages. A EU-wide system will also fail to take account of existing policies in the various countries, which potentially leads to clashing or ineffective policies, or ending (proven) national policies.
- In some cases, an existing emissions allocation has been allowed under the state aid rules. It is questionable whether harmonization and competitiveness arguments can be used to overthrow these existing 'rights'. Actually, the new EU state aid regulation allows special environmental rules for the duration of ten years; this could be used to allow allocations on a national basis until the first commitment period, with a harmonized system taking over during or after 2008–12. Of course, any new allocation should still meet the minimum requirements for state aid.

- As shown in Chapter 4, the allocation of allowances is unlikely to make much difference in the market. The theory of perfect markets even disputes the competitiveness impacts of grandfathering compared with full auctioning of permits (or new entrants) on the basis of opportunity costs. The obligatory state aid procedures, as well as learning from and copying of neighbouring countries' systems, will keep differences to a minimum. Even when taking the financial position and equity into account, and using an economic theory of non-perfect capital markets, the impact of allocations on competitiveness in Europe will be minimal.
- Heavy-handed harmonization of emissions allocations could lead to the complete unravelling of the burden-sharing agreement. Although the EU proposal does not include such allocation rules – stating only that no auctioning will take place in the initial phase – close linking of the systems, some general EU guidelines for allocations and learning from neighbours will lead to close convergence of the allocations and could lead to incompatibilities with the burden-sharing targets. The national emissions allocation in the EU was agreed, not on the basis of harmonized allocations or rational economic rules, but as an act of political will. Many wealthier countries, and those that had already made great reductions, agreed to reduce their emissions below the EU 8% target, while substantial increases were allowed for the cohesion countries. Much of the present agreement is based on political will, willingness to pay and national circumstances.
- The differences in the EU countries' systems can be considered a strength as well as a weakness. Diverse climate policies could lead to more learning by doing, and maybe to increased possibilities for emissions trading (as long as countries recognize each other's quotas). The UK's market, for example, could start earlier and lessons could be learned for other European countries. The Danish system could also bring experience to the wider European market.

Some form of coordination of European policies is clearly required. A further integration of the European markets and further convergence of the liberalized electricity markets demand such coordination. However, in the short term complete harmonization could lead to an unravelling of the burden-sharing agreement. Concerns about a level playing field are warranted, but as long as the state aid rules are observed national policies should not pose a problem. One exception to the rule could be the existence of fuel input taxes in some countries and their absence in others, where sufficient interconnection capacity exists. To date, national circumstances differ substantially, but from this starting position industry and government policy can converge over the longer term.

In the short term, with existing policies and relatively modest targets, the impacts on the industry's competitiveness will be limited. At the same time, abandoning existing policies and measures in favour of a harmonized European scheme could lead to political capital being lost, and the existing relatively level playing field being distorted. Company policies based on the already-agreed national schemes would become uncompetitive or obsolete. Thus, the economic argument for a single market for emissions is weak.

The sectoral and GHG coverage, and specific sectoral allocations, can also be harmonized. Allocations cannot currently be harmonized for the reasons spelled out earlier, but in particular because of the political nature of the burden-sharing agreement. However, the European proposal includes harmonized coverage of sectors and gases. The gas coverage could be useful for international recognition of the emissions allowances traded; as long as they are exchangeable with assigned amounts of the country of origin, no problems should arise. The harmonized sectoral coverage would reduce any cross-border competitiveness problems, as well as problems between sectors; this will be needed when targets get tougher in the subsequent commitment periods. However, mandatory sectoral coverage is unnecessary if sectors are required under existing regulation to make reductions similar to those in other countries, and emissions reduction commitments are spread throughout the sectors in the economy.

13.4 Conclusions

European countries and the European Commission are working to implement climate change policies necessary to ratify the Kyoto Protocol and to reduce their emissions to the levels agreed in Kyoto and under the European burden-sharing agreement. In many cases, the policies proposed or already implemented have similarities throughout Europe, but sometimes the economic instruments used differ. Despite a patchwork of policies, national power industries are responding to these climate policies and the notion of a 'carbon-constrained' future. Currently the industry's responses, for the most part, take the forms of actively engaging in the national and European policy debate, cooperating in pilot studies and making investments in renewable energy sources.

To date, power markets in Europe remain rather diverse; the relative strength of the emissions targets varies widely, as does existing national legislation.

The impact of the Kyoto-related policies on the competitiveness of individual companies in the national power sectors is still relatively small. The existence of differences among national policies on Kyoto, therefore, are of only limited influence on the European-wide market. Some of these differences might persist for some time, due to national circumstances and policy histories. However, convergence is taking place in respect of some policies, in particular the market-based policies such as emissions trading and renewable obligations with trading of certificates. This is attributable in part to the active involvement of internationally operating industry, learning from other countries and the active involvement of the European Commission.

With further integration and faster liberalization over the coming decade leading to further convergence in power markets, the Commission and national governments still have time to resolve some of the differences that would cause competitiveness problems. With national governments already having invested political capital in national schemes and policies, the EU must play its role in setting standards and guaranteeing Europe-wide – and broader international – recognition of efforts, mainly those resulting in certificates, credits and permits. While harmonization could bring substantial benefits, these could be outweighed by the wasted political capital invested in the existing national policies and domestic trading schemes. Some industry concessions agreed under traditional methods of regulation might be impossible to capture under harmonized emissions trading.

The current plans for a European ETS would harmonize some elements that are helpful for the recognition of trades internationally, including gas coverage, measurement and verification methods. This level of harmonization would be useful and welcome to all parties. However, the proposed mandatory sectoral coverage, though theoretically attractive, is unnecessary if sectors are required under existing regulation to make reductions similar to those in other countries. Mandatory coverage of sectors is likely to give rise to opposition from those countries that have already implemented policies covering these sectors.

The EU has an important role to play in long-term convergence of the national policies and ETSs, in particular in the light of the time limits that have been set for state aid: ten years for environmental regulations. In the longer term, after 2012, when tougher targets will have to be agreed, further convergence, including rationalization of the burden-sharing and industry allocations, will be required to ease negotiations and reduce impacts on competitiveness.

The process of electricity liberalization and concerns about climate change clash. This book has described the clash of policies and processes on these two themes. On the one hand, liberalization of the power market could lead to a reduced emphasis on environmental regulation with detrimental effects on the environment. On the other hand, market forces reward efficiency of production, reducing waste, and could be used to great advantage in pursuing environmental goals.

However, after ten years of international negotiations leading to the UN FCCC, the Kyoto Protocol and now to the Marrakesh Accords, it is undeniable that the future is 'carbon-constrained'. GHG emissions, in every sector and in every country, will have to be reduced in the long term; in the shorter term only the industrialized countries are affected, albeit with flexibility through using offsets, such as emissions trading and sinks.

14.1 Climate change and economic policy instruments

The Kyoto Protocol has set out GHG emission targets for all industrialized countries. However, the protocol allowed these targets to be met in the most economically efficient way, through the use of various flexibilities. These flexibilities include in particular the basket of gases and the inclusion of 'sinks', and the Kyoto mechanisms, emissions trading, joint implementation and the clean development mechanisms. It is thus possible to meet the emissions targets through reductions in gases other than carbon dioxide, the planting of forests or changes in land use, and various forms of action overseas.

The Kyoto mechanisms allow parties to use emissions reductions from investments in projects elsewhere to be counted for emissions reductions at home. Indeed, these mechanisms have become intrinsic to the Kyoto Protocol, and the further development of the protocol since Kyoto up to the Bonn Agreement and the Marrakesh Accords has highlighted the emphasis on these novel mechanisms. Emissions trading (domestically and with the economies in transition) is expected to reduce the costs of meeting the targets by a substantial amount. JI (also with the EITs) and, in particular, the CDM (for environmentally friendly investments in developing countries) are expected to reduce costs even further. The expected global costs, using all flexibility, amount to no more than $10–20bn dollars annually; less if the United States is not taking any action. Industry and some countries that are expecting particularly high costs for meeting the agreed targets are looking forward to the use of these mechanisms.

The EU has taken on a joint target of –8% from 1990 levels, with the understanding that this target is redistributed among the member states. The European 'bubble' targets are very wide-ranging around this overall European goal. Germany and the United Kingdom in particular have taken on a large share of the reductions, far greater than that of the EU as a whole. Some other parties, in particular the cohesion countries that are in a different stage in their development path, have been given growth targets.

Not only is the EU bubble important for setting the country targets; the European policy framework is also a very important determinant for domestic climate policy. Four key policies areas are of interest and are explained in this book: electricity liberalization, the renewables directive, energy security and the ECCP.

The European Commission has taken the lead in liberalizing the European power market, after initial pioneering work by some member states. The 'single energy market' is of great importance for the Commission, promoting the competitiveness of Europe and European industry and creating a level playing field in the EU-15. The result of the liberalization directive has been a reduction in prices, an increase in trades and the decline of government influence. With a continuing growth in electricity demand, this could lead to substantial increases of emissions from this sector. However, one of the clauses included in the directive allows governments to prioritize some kinds of generation for environmental (or specific other) reasons, and this provision could be used for promoting renewables. Despite an obvious clash between the power companies' fight for market share and increased demand and Kyoto's emissions reduction targets, the market can also be a key driver for lower emissions. In the UK, increased efficiency and use of natural gas has led to sectoral emissions reductions of around 20% within a decade. A similar efficiency increase and 'dash for gas' could happen in Italy, where ENEL is instructed to sell off and upgrade a large part of its capacity. However, in Germany efficient cogeneration plant has suffered from low prices, and in France any new merchant plant is likely to increase overall emissions by replacing nuclear capacity.

In 2000 the Commission launched a paper on energy security in the EU. This paper acts as an umbrella policy for most of the Union's other energy and energy-related environmental agreements. In principle, market liberalization, renewables and climate change are all part of energy security policy. The key conclusions from this exercise are a renewed interest in energy efficiency, a reduction in emissions and diversification of energy sources, including from renewables and possibly nuclear.

The European renewables directive prescribes percentages of the electricity supply that will have to be supplied by renewable energy in 2010 in every country of the EU. The percentages are wide-ranging, depending on the current levels, possibilities and willingness to pay of the countries. Despite starting out as an idealized system of green certificates throughout the Union, the directive now allows current support systems to be continued for several years. The Commission has the facility to propose a harmonized support system four years after the entry into force of the directive, if that is deemed necessary. So far, this has led to the establishment of various green certificates schemes, sometimes linked, and in other countries renewal of existing feed-in tariffs.

The ECCP consists of various proposed policies, particularly in the field of energy efficiency and emissions trading. Key to the European scheme is the recognition that action needs to be taken. Emissions from the EU as a whole have declined by 4% from 1990 levels, half of the Kyoto commitment. However, these reductions have come for a large extent from 'lucky accidents', such as the UK's dash for gas and the German 'wall fall profits'. Without further policies, emissions in the EU could increase substantially, possibly even to 8% *above* 1990 levels. All countries of the Union, including those with substantial growth targets, will have to start taking action to limit and reduce emissions.

The climate change programme promotes increased shares for renewables and CHP power, the incorporation of environmental considerations in the further liberalization of the markets, the establishment of an energy services market for smaller users, and increased efficiency of electrical equipment, industrial processes, buildings and infrastructure. A harmonized carbon tax and research into the capturing of CO_2 are also proposed. However, of most importance is the establishment of a European ETS. This scheme would include the power sector – unlike the UK scheme – and harmonize industry participation across Europe. Allocations of emissions allowances will be subject to guidelines and state aid rules, but only the requirement to allocate the allowances to industry for free in the initial period (before 2008) will be harmonized. However, the next year or two of negotiations will show whether the mandatory top-down European scheme will survive or incorporate the existing domestic schemes.

Three classes of economic instruments are identified in this book: regulatory, fiscal and flexible. Regulatory instruments include minimum standards, prescribed technologies, planning and market structure. These could therefore include market liberalization and minimum levels of renewables and cogeneration. Fiscal instruments include energy or carbon taxes and feed-in tariffs. Flexible instruments include voluntary agreements and trading systems, in particular emissions trading. However, emissions caps without the trading option should be classed as a regulatory instrument.

Government policy on climate change and the power industry's response focus on five areas:

1   Improved energy efficiency could bring about substantial emissions reductions. While some of the efficiency investments might be costly, reduced energy costs could make many investments economic. The focus in many sectors is on supply-side efficiency, both through more efficient plants which are also more competitive in a liberalized market, and through cogeneration, in particular for industrial use. End-use efficiency also features in governmental climate plans, but is hard to reconcile with the market in the traditional sense.

2   An increased share of natural gas would lower the carbon content of the power sector, and has already brought emissions in the UK down by 20%. Where available, natural gas is the fuel of choice in liberalized electricity markets. The new CCGT plants combine very high efficiency with flexibility in building and operation. Most European countries have relatively easy access to natural gas for their power sectors; however, some countries already have substantial shares of gas and could choose not to increase this share further for energy security and diversity reasons.

3   An increased share of renewables in the generation portfolio would also help reduce the carbon content of the sector. When renewables replace fossil-fuel generation, their use will reduce GHG emissions; however, in France's power sector the large-scale use of non-emitting nuclear power introduces an additional layer of complexity. Member states are encouraging the use of renewables for environmental and diversity reasons, and often for socio-economic reasons as well (employment, local industry and reduced imports of fuels). The European renewables directive is the central policy, encouraging a doubling of the share of renewables. However, many member states have their own support systems through subsidies, feed-in tariffs, etc.

4   The introduction of energy/carbon taxes shifts costs from goods (employment) to bads (energy use/emissions). The taxes increase the

costs of energy and are aimed at reducing its use and the resulting emissions. Although the tax rates to date are often too low compared with the overall energy costs to produce much impact on demand, the taxes could be increased if results fail to materialize. The best results for GHG emissions would be achieved if the tax rates were dependent on carbon content of fuel.

5 The introduction of an ETS has been under discussion in several countries and is proposed by the European Commission for EU-wide implementation. Of course, such a trading scheme works only with emission caps for the industry involved, giving a certainty to the government policy outcome in terms of emissions that none of the other measures can give. Indeed, this approach gives both the highest certainty of emissions levels and the greatest flexibility in how to reach emissions targets and therefore keep costs down. However, some of the other measures have side-benefits, such as diversity of energy supply, which are important for policymakers.

Many countries will put in place a combination of policies that will result in a mixture of responses by generators and end users.

14.2 Case studies of European electricity sectors

This book has described and analysed the climate policy regimes in the electricity sectors in six different EU member states. The case studies were chosen to reflect a wider range of sectors and countries than just these six, and possibly even wider than just European countries. The six countries studied were Denmark, France, Germany, Italy, the Netherlands and the UK. These countries represent the four largest power sectors in Europe, as well as one medium (Netherlands) and one small (Denmark) sector. This selection of six also represents very different fuel and technology bases: from nearly exclusively nuclear to largely coal or natural gas, from large central power plants to small CHP plants. The countries also range from completely liberalized to still largely operating as a monopolistic sector.

Denmark has a small power sector, which is nearly completely open for competition from outside, with interconnections to the Nordic market and the European market through Germany. The sector is heavily based on coal-fired power plants, many of which use CHP technology, making the sector heavily interwoven with heat demand. The sector also has an increasing share of natural gas and renewables, mainly straw cofiring and wind power.

The Danish policy towards climate change has focused on a long-term effort to increase supply and demand efficiency and infrastructure. A power-sector-only ETS has been established in Denmark with relatively stringent caps. However, for competitiveness reasons, a low buy-out price has been established to cap the costs on domestic producers and to maintain competitiveness compared with other generators in the Nordic market. Similarly, the proposed renewables obligation market includes a buy-out clause, but also a minimum price level for continued support.

In France, where carbon emissions in the power sector are low, the emphasis of climate policy is on other sectors. However, further liberalization could jeopardize the emissions target, because new merchant plant, almost certainly fossil-fuel-based, would increase emissions. The plans have to focus on gains in the small share of fossil-fuel plants, by increasing generation efficiency and the share of natural gas. There is also a focus on reducing peak demand, when the most inefficient fossil-fuel plants have to be used; this would also reduce the need for new plant. Additionally, the potential for the use of renewables is very large and the European drive to double generation could provide a market. However, where renewables replace nuclear generation, or increase the required back-up from fossil-fuel plants, emissions might not be reduced.

The German liberalization has prompted a dramatic cut in electricity prices, reducing the economic viability of both renewables and CHP plants. Indeed, the established share of CHP was under threat and the government has had to increase its support to avoid closures. Government and industry reached a deal to increase the use of cogeneration, as was projected in the national climate plan, in return for stronger and long-term support from government. The support system for renewables was based on the retail price of power and, consequently, had to be redesigned to avoid making renewables uneconomic as prices fell. The government fixed feed-in tariffs independent of market prices, thereby restraining the operation of market forces. Despite the cut-throat competition in the Germany market, the long-established culture of long-term (voluntary) agreements prevails over market forces in the effort to reduce emissions.

The Italian power sector will change dramatically when ENEL's divestment has been followed through. Government has set a maximum market share of any generator before further opening up of the market can take place. It is agreed that ENEL will sell off a substantial amount of its capacity, which should be representative of ENEL as a whole in fuel, technology and age structure. These divestments come with a full investment plan, including refurbishment, refuelling and early closures. The Italian liberalization could therefore bring most of the emissions reductions required. However, important measures have also been taken on DSM-friendly end-use tariffs and renewable obligations and feed-in tariffs. The most important measure is probably the combination of progressive carbon taxes, increasing the price of coal-fired electricity by 40% and oil and gas by 6% and 3%, and the further introduction of market forces.

The Dutch power sector is already dominated by low-carbon natural gas, and has a relatively high share of CHP, reducing the potential for easy emissions reductions. However, fiscal measures are in place to encourage further switching to gas and CHP. The fuel-input tax has been scrapped and added to the ecotax on the demand side in return for commitments from coal-fired power producers to reduce emissions to the levels that would apply if gas were used. The Dutch ecotax exempts CHP and renewables, stimulating voluntary demand, but with systems in place to set quotas if demand languishes. Building on the long-term agreements with industry, the government has chosen to enter the emissions trading market itself with the aim of achieving half of the Dutch commitment abroad.

The UK power industry has already achieved emissions reductions of about 20% below 1990 levels since liberalization and opening of the gas market. The sector realized the importance of climate change policy for its core business early on, and has been working on emissions trading since 1994. However, the UK ETS excludes the direct emissions of the power sector, placing the responsibility for these emissions indirectly on electricity consumers. This could be one of the key incompatibilities between the UK and mainland European ETSs, in particular the EU's proposal. However, other measures have also been taken in the power sector to reduce emissions, despite fears for the fuel poor, a great problem in British political eyes. These measures include the new renewables obligations, with annual targets set that rise rapidly from the current 2% to 10% in 2010. To reduce the price impact on domestic customers a buy-out clause has been introduced. The CCL encourages energy efficiency by raising the price, the associated negotiated agreements, and exemptions for 'good quality CHP'.

14.3 Interactions and implications

The six countries studied have all taken measures to reduce emissions. The national programmes, together with the European Commission's climate change programme, will lead to emissions declining further towards to Kyoto target of –8%. However, while the domestic programmes have many elements in common, they are not necessarily implementing the same measures.

The countries studied have remained loyal to their traditional regulatory systems. In Germany and the Netherlands, for example, agreements define the role for industry up to the commitment period; in Denmark the longer-term perspective is continued with a focus on energy efficiency, infrastructure and emissions caps. Different national circumstances drive the choice of national climate policy instruments. The French rules, for example, have to take into account that most of the country's power is produced by non-carbon-emitting nuclear power plants. The Danish rules can build on the existence of many (small) district heating systems.

However, several suboptimal decisions were made in countries of the case studies, partly driven by policies or the lack of policies in the other countries. The abolition of fuel taxes in the Netherlands, for example, happened (partly) because of the lack of fuel taxes in the neighbouring countries. Tax exemptions for energy-intensive industry are also given for competitiveness reasons, even if they are given in return for energy efficiency agreements. In general, policies were bound by market considerations and competitiveness concerns. Therefore, at least some degree of convergence among climate policies across the EU countries should happen. This could mitigate some of the problems leading to suboptimal or divergent policies, and improve the chances of industry agreeing with policies that impact on them and their competitiveness. A further integrating market would automatically lead to a convergence of national circumstances, national (climate and other) policies, and less diverse future emission targets.

Because the Union is a party to the Kyoto Protocol, and wants to use the 'bubble' to redistribute the target among the member states, the EU and its fifteen member states will have to submit their instruments for ratification of the protocol at about the same time. This requires coordination of climate policy development across Europe, in particular considering the tight deadline of the Johannesburg meeting in September 2002. However, heavy-handed harmonization of climate policies is not necessary.

Action is being taken across the member states that will reduce emissions. Some countries have measures in place already that will reduce emissions to their burden-sharing target by 2010. The measures already taken and proposed by these countries do not threaten competitiveness and do not require full harmonization in the EU. The current NCPs have been built in cooperation with industry, and much political capital (from government and industry) has been invested in these programmes. It would be unwise to discard this work and risk an unravelling of the national agreements by imposing new and sometimes opposite or incompatible harmonized rules.

Although a much further convergence of climate policies throughout the EU would be a long-term aim, and would strengthen the EU's position in the climate negotiations, full harmonization is unnecessary for the first commitment period, for the following reasons:

- National circumstances and existing regulation or allocations are different. Existing agreements with industry in Germany and the Netherlands, for example, would be put in jeopardy if these industries had to be given emissions allocations.
- It is questionable whether harmonization and competitiveness arguments can be used to overthrow existing emission 'rights' or allocations.
- As shown in Chapter 4, the allocation of allowances is unlikely to make much difference in the market, because competitiveness concerns will be taken into account and competitors will also have to reduce or limit emissions.
- Full harmonization of emissions allocations would lead to the complete unravelling of the burden-sharing agreement, because the agreement was based not on rational economic rules but on political will.
- The differences in the EU countries' systems can be considered a strength rather than a weakness, increasing the possibilities for learning by doing.

However, further convergence and even harmonization could be required when emissions reduction targets become more demanding in the second, third and further commitment periods. These further targets might well have to be more rational and less political to succeed, giving more scope for such convergence across EU member states or an even wider group of countries.

Some form of coordination of European policies would clearly be beneficial, including some common requirements and minimum standards on emissions trading. Further integration of the European markets and further convergence of the liberalized electricity markets demand such coordination. However, in the short term a complete harmonization would seriously undermine the burden-sharing agreement. Concerns about a level playing field are warranted, but as long as the state aid rules are observed national policies should not pose a problem. The one exception to this rule could be the existence of fuel input taxes in some countries and their absence in others, while sufficient interconnection capacity exists. To date, national circumstances differ substantially, but from this starting position industry and government policy can converge over the longer term.

14.4   Conclusions

The European countries studied in this book, and the European Commission, are working towards climate change policies that will bring about the emissions reductions set out at Kyoto and in the European burden-sharing agreement. However, despite substantial overlap the national policies are diverse. These differences among national policies do not matter at the moment, when markets also remain rather diverse, emissions targets are wide-ranging and existing national legislation is disparate. Due to national circumstances and policy histories, some of these differences are likely to exist for some time. However, some policies are converging, in particular the market-based policies such as emissions trading and renewables obligations with trading of certificates. This is partly due to the active involvement of internationally operating industry and the learning from other countries.

There is a clear role for the European Commission and national governments to resolve these differences when markets converge due to further integration and further liberalization. With national governments already having invested political capital in national schemes and policies, the EU must play its role in setting standards and guaranteeing European-wide – and wider international – recognition of earlier national efforts, mainly those resulting in certificates, credits and permits.

The future of the electricity sector is 'carbon-constrained', and emissions will have to be reduced. Any long-term investment decision must take this reality into consideration, despite market pressures focusing on the near term. Even in the short term, to meet the Kyoto Protocol targets, it is most likely that the power sector will have to do more than its share.

Appendix 1
Key articles of the Framework Convention and Kyoto Protocol

United Nations Framework Convention on Climate Change

Article 2   Objective

The ultimate objective of this Convention and any related legal instruments that the Conference of the Parties may adopt is to achieve, in accordance with the relevant provisions of the Convention, stabilization of greenhouse gas concentrations in the atmosphere at a level that would prevent dangerous anthropogenic interference with the climate system. Such a level should be achieved within a time-frame sufficient to allow ecosystems to adapt naturally to climate change, to ensure that food production is not threatened and to enable economic development to proceed in a sustainable manner.

Article 4   Commitments

2. The developed country Parties and other Parties included in Annex I commit themselves specifically as provided for in the following:

(a) Each of these Parties shall adopt national policies and take corresponding measures on the mitigation of climate change, by limiting its anthropogenic emissions of greenhouse gases and protecting and enhancing its greenhouse gas sinks and reservoirs ... These Parties may implement such policies and measures jointly with other Parties and may assist other Parties in contributing to the achievement of the objective of the Convention and, in particular, that of this subparagraph[.]

Kyoto Protocol to the United Nations Framework Convention on Climate Change

Article 2   Policies and Measures

1. Each Party included in Annex I, in achieving its quantified emission limitation and reduction commitments under Article 3, in order to promote sustainable development, shall:

(a) Implement and/or further elaborate policies and measures in accordance with its national circumstances, such as:

(i)   Enhancement of energy efficiency in relevant sectors of the national economy; [...]

(iv)   Research on, and promotion, development and increased use of, new and renewable forms of energy, of carbon dioxide sequestration technologies and of advanced and innovative environmentally sound technologies;

(v)   Progressive reduction or phasing out of market imperfections, fiscal incentives, tax and duty exemptions and subsidies in all greenhouse gas emitting sectors that run counter to the objective of the Convention and application of market instruments;

(vi)   Encouragement of appropriate reforms in relevant sectors aimed at promoting policies and measures which limit or reduce emissions of greenhouse gases not controlled by the Montreal Protocol; [...]

(viii) Limitation and/or reduction of methane emissions through recovery and use in waste management, as well as in the production, transport and distribution of energy;

(b) Cooperate with other such Parties to enhance the individual and combined effectiveness of their policies and measures adopted under this Article, pursuant to Article 4, paragraph 2(e)(i), of the Convention. To this end, these Parties shall take steps to share their experience and exchange information on such policies and measures, including developing ways of improving their comparability, transparency and effectiveness. The Conference of the Parties serving as the meeting of the Parties to this Protocol shall, at its first session or as soon as practicable thereafter, consider ways to facilitate such cooperation, taking into account all relevant information.

2. The Parties included in Annex I shall pursue limitation or reduction of emissions of greenhouse gases not controlled by the Montreal Protocol from aviation and marine bunker fuels, working through the International Civil Aviation Organization and the International Maritime Organization, respectively.

3. The Parties included in Annex I shall strive to implement policies and measures under this Article in such a way as to minimize adverse effects, including the adverse effects of climate change, effects on international trade, and social, environmental and economic impacts on other Parties, especially developing country Parties and in particular those identified in Article 4, paragraphs 8 and 9, of the Convention, taking into account Article 3 of the Convention. The Conference of the Parties serving as the meeting of the Parties to this Protocol may take further action, as appropriate, to promote the implementation of the provisions of this paragraph.

Article 3   Quantified Emission Limitation and Reduction Commitments

1. The Parties included in Annex I shall, individually or jointly, ensure that their aggregate anthropogenic carbon dioxide equivalent emissions of the greenhouse gases listed in Annex A do not exceed their assigned amounts, calculated pursuant to their

quantified emission limitation and reduction commitments inscribed in Annex B and in accordance with the provisions of this Article, with a view to reducing their overall emissions of such gases by at least 5 per cent below 1990 levels in the commitment period 2008 to 2012.

2. Each Party included in Annex I shall, by 2005, have made demonstrable progress in achieving its commitments under this Protocol.

3. The net changes in greenhouse gas emissions by sources and removals by sinks resulting from direct human-induced land-use change and forestry activities, limited to afforestation, reforestation and deforestation since 1990, measured as verifiable changes in carbon stocks in each commitment period, shall be used to meet the commitments under this Article of each Party included in Annex I. The greenhouse gas emissions by sources and removals by sinks associated with those activities shall be reported in a transparent and verifiable manner and reviewed in accordance with Articles 7 and 8.

4. [...] The Conference of the Parties serving as the meeting of the Parties to this Protocol shall, at its first session or as soon as practicable thereafter, decide upon modalities, rules and guidelines as to how, and which, additional human-induced activities related to changes in greenhouse gas emissions by sources and removals by sinks in the agricultural soils and the land-use change and forestry categories shall be added to, or subtracted from, the assigned amounts for Parties included in Annex I [...]. Such a decision shall apply in the second and subsequent commitment periods. A Party may choose to apply such a decision on these additional human-induced activities for its first commitment period, provided that these activities have taken place since 1990.

5. The Parties included in Annex I undergoing the process of transition to a market economy whose base year or period was established pursuant to decision 9/CP.2 of the Conference of the Parties at its second session shall use that base year or period for the implementation of their commitments under this Article. [...]

6. Taking into account Article 4, paragraph 6, of the Convention, in the implementation of their commitments under this Protocol other than those under this Article, a certain degree of flexibility shall be allowed by the Conference of the Parties serving as the meeting of the Parties to this Protocol to the Parties included in Annex I undergoing the process of transition to a market economy.

7. In the first quantified emission limitation and reduction commitment period, from 2008 to 2012, the assigned amount for each Party included in Annex I shall be equal to the percentage inscribed for it in Annex B of its aggregate anthropogenic carbon dioxide equivalent emissions of the greenhouse gases listed in Annex A in 1990, or the base year or period determined in accordance with paragraph 5 above, multiplied

by five. Those Parties included in Annex I for whom land-use change and forestry constituted a net source of greenhouse gas emissions in 1990 shall include in their 1990 emissions base year or period the aggregate anthropogenic carbon dioxide equivalent emissions by sources minus removals by sinks in 1990 from land-use change for the purposes of calculating their assigned amount.

8. Any Party included in Annex I may use 1995 as its base year for hydrofluoro-carbons, perfluorocarbons and sulphur hexafluoride, for the purposes of the calculation referred to in paragraph 7 above.

9. Commitments for subsequent periods for Parties included in Annex I shall be established in amendments to Annex B to this Protocol, which shall be adopted in accordance with the provisions of Article 21, paragraph 7. The Conference of the Parties serving as the meeting of the Parties to this Protocol shall initiate the consideration of such commitments at least seven years before the end of the first commitment period referred to in paragraph 1 above.

10. Any emission reduction units, or any part of an assigned amount, which a Party acquires from another Party in accordance with the provisions of Article 6 or of Article 17 shall be added to the assigned amount for the acquiring Party.

11. Any emission reduction units, or any part of an assigned amount, which a Party transfers to another Party in accordance with the provisions of Article 6 or of Article 17 shall be subtracted from the assigned amount for the transferring Party.

12. Any certified emission reductions which a Party acquires from another Party in accordance with the provisions of Article 12 shall be added to the assigned amount for the acquiring Party.

13. If the emissions of a Party included in Annex I in a commitment period are less than its assigned amount under this Article, this difference shall, on request of that Party, be added to the assigned amount for that Party for subsequent commitment periods.

14. Each Party included in Annex I shall strive to implement the commitments mentioned in paragraph 1 above in such a way as to minimize adverse social, environmental and economic impacts on developing country Parties, particularly those identified in Article 4, paragraphs 8 and 9, of the Convention. [...]

Article 4   Joint Fulfilment of Commitments

1. Any Parties included in Annex I that have reached an agreement to fulfil their commitments under Article 3 jointly, shall be deemed to have met those commitments

provided that their total combined aggregate anthropogenic carbon dioxide equivalent emissions of the greenhouse gases listed in Annex A do not exceed their assigned amounts calculated pursuant to their quantified emission limitation and reduction commitments inscribed in Annex B and in accordance with the provisions of Article 3. The respective emission level allocated to each of the Parties to the agreement shall be set out in that agreement.

2. The Parties to any such agreement shall notify the secretariat of the terms of the agreement on the date of deposit of their instruments of ratification, acceptance or approval of this Protocol, or accession thereto. The secretariat shall in turn inform the Parties and signatories to the Convention of the terms of the agreement.

3. Any such agreement shall remain in operation for the duration of the commitment period specified in Article 3, paragraph 7.

4. If Parties acting jointly do so in the framework of, and together with, a regional economic integration organization, any alteration in the composition of the organization after adoption of this Protocol shall not affect existing commitments under this Protocol. Any alteration in the composition of the organization shall only apply for the purposes of those commitments under Article 3 that are adopted subsequent to that alteration.

5. In the event of failure by the Parties to such an agreement to achieve their total combined level of emission reductions, each Party to that agreement shall be responsible for its own level of emissions set out in the agreement.

6. If Parties acting jointly do so in the framework of, and together with, a regional economic integration organization which is itself a Party to this Protocol, each member State of that regional economic integration organization individually, and together with the regional economic integration organization acting in accordance with Article 24, shall, in the event of failure to achieve the total combined level of emission reductions, be responsible for its level of emissions as notified in accordance with this Article.

Article 6   Transfer and Acquisition of Emission Reduction Units (Joint Implementation)

1. For the purpose of meeting its commitments under Article 3, any Party included in Annex I may transfer to, or acquire from, any other such Party emission reduction units resulting from projects aimed at reducing anthropogenic emissions by sources or enhancing anthropogenic removals by sinks of greenhouse gases in any sector of the economy, provided that:

(a) Any such project has the approval of the Parties involved;
(b) Any such project provides a reduction in emissions by sources, or an enhancement of removals by sinks, that is additional to any that would otherwise occur;
(c) It does not acquire any emission reduction units if it is not in compliance with its obligations under Articles 5 and 7; and
(d) The acquisition of emission reduction units shall be supplemental to domestic actions for the purposes of meeting commitments under Article 3.

2. The Conference of the Parties serving as the meeting of the Parties to this Protocol may, at its first session or as soon as practicable thereafter, further elaborate guidelines for the implementation of this Article, including for verification and reporting.

3. A Party included in Annex I may authorize legal entities to participate, under its responsibility, in actions leading to the generation, transfer or acquisition under this Article of emission reduction units.

4. If a question of implementation by a Party included in Annex I of the requirements referred to in this Article is identified in accordance with the relevant provisions of Article 8, transfers and acquisitions of emission reduction units may continue to be made after the question has been identified, provided that any such units may not be used by a Party to meet its commitments under Article 3 until any issue of compliance is resolved.

Article 12   Clean Development Mechanism

1. A clean development mechanism is hereby defined.

2. The purpose of the clean development mechanism shall be to assist Parties not included in Annex I in achieving sustainable development and in contributing to the ultimate objective of the Convention, and to assist Parties included in Annex I in achieving compliance with their quantified emission limitation and reduction commitments under Article 3.

3. Under the clean development mechanism:

(a) Parties not included in Annex I will benefit from project activities resulting in certified emission reductions; and
(b) Parties included in Annex I may use the certified emission reductions accruing from such project activities to contribute to compliance with part of their quantified emission limitation and reduction commitments under Article 3, as determined by the Conference of the Parties serving as the meeting of the Parties to this Protocol.

4. The clean development mechanism shall be subject to the authority and guidance of the Conference of the Parties serving as the meeting of the Parties to this Protocol and be supervised by an executive board of the clean development mechanism.

5. Emission reductions resulting from each project activity shall be certified by operational entities to be designated by the Conference of the Parties serving as the meeting of the Parties to this Protocol, on the basis of:

(a) Voluntary participation approved by each Party involved;
(b) Real, measurable, and long-term benefits related to the mitigation of climate change; and
(c) Reductions in emissions that are additional to any that would occur in the absence of the certified project activity.

[...]

8. The Conference of the Parties serving as the meeting of the Parties to this Protocol shall ensure that a share of the proceeds from certified project activities is used to cover administrative expenses as well as to assist developing country Parties that are particularly vulnerable to the adverse effects of climate change to meet the costs of adaptation.

9. Participation under the clean development mechanism, including in activities mentioned in paragraph 3(a) above and in the acquisition of certified emission reductions, may involve private and/or public entities, and is to be subject to whatever guidance may be provided by the executive board of the clean development mechanism.

10. Certified emission reductions obtained during the period from the year 2000 up to the beginning of the first commitment period can be used to assist in achieving compliance in the first commitment period.

Article 17   Emissions Trading

The Conference of the Parties shall define the relevant principles, modalities, rules and guidelines, in particular for verification, reporting and accountability for emissions trading. The Parties included in Annex B may participate in emissions trading for the purposes of fulfilling their commitments under Article 3. Any such trading shall be supplemental to domestic actions for the purpose of meeting quantified emission limitation and reduction commitments under that Article.

Appendix 2
Some issues from the Bonn Agreement (Decision 5/CP.6)

'The Conference of the Parties, ...
1 *Decides* to adopt the agreements contained in the annex to this decision as core elements for the implementation of the Buenos Aires Plan of Action; ...'

The Bonn Agreement was the result of negotiations within four groups focusing on separate core decisions. The agreement separates the decisions under eight headings:

I Funding under the Convention

The COP agreed that there is need for new and additional funding through the Global Environment Facility (GEF), a special climate change fund and bilateral and multilateral channels. (This additional funding is deliberately attached to the convention rather than the protocol, so as to accommodate those parties that will not ratify Kyoto.) The 'special climate change fund' is set up to fund activities (not funded by the GEF) that focus on adaptation, technology transfer, energy, transport and other sectors, and diversification of economies of fossil-fuel-exporting countries. The 'least developed countries fund' will support work on, inter alia, adaptation.

II Funding under the Kyoto Protocol

The COP agreed to establish the adaptation fund under the Kyoto Protocol, mentioned in Article 12 on the CDM. The fund will support adaptation programmes for developing countries that are parties to the Kyoto Protocol and will be funded through the 2% adaptation levy on the CDM.

III Development and transfer of technologies

The COP agreed to establish an Expert Group on Technology Transfer.

IV Adverse effects

The COP agreed to fund adaptation measures through the funds mentioned in I and II.

V Article 3.14 of the Kyoto Protocol

The COP recognized that minimizing the impact of implementation measures is a concern for both Annex I and non-Annex I parties, and that Annex I parties commit to take these impacts into account fully. The COP/MOP[1] shall request of Annex I parties that they report on the implementation of Article 3.14. The facilitative branch of the compliance committee will consider the reports.

VI The Kyoto mechanisms

Only parties that have accepted the agreement on compliance (see VIII below) are eligible to take part in the Kyoto mechanisms. A party is also required to comply with various reporting requirements of the Kyoto Protocol.

Joint implementation

On JI projects, the COP agreed to discourage (rather than exclude) nuclear projects ('Parties included in Annex I are to refrain from using emission reduction units generated from nuclear facilities'), and to establish a supervisory committee for emission reduction units.

CDM

On the CDM, the COP agreed to establish the CDM board at COP-7 to facilitate a prompt start. The adaptation levy on CDM projects will be 2% of the CERs generated. Using the same language as under JI, nuclear projects are strongly discouraged. COP-8 will develop simplified procedures for small-scale, energy efficiency and renewable energy projects. Afforestation and reforestation are the only LULUCF projects allowed under the CDM.

Emissions trading

The compliance reserve is 90% of assigned amounts, or equivalent to the most recent inventory.

VII Land-use, land-use change and forestry (LULUCF)

The COP affirms that the treatment of LULUCF should be based on 'sound science', and try to exclude business-as-usual carbon stock (growth). Virtually all sources of

---

[1] The Conference of the Parties serving as meeting of the parties to the Kyoto Protocol, i.e. when the protocol has entered into force.

LULUCF can be included, up to a maximum set by Appendix Z (and balancing any possible debit from Article 3.3 sinks), with individually negotiated caps. LULUCF activities in JI projects count towards the Appendix Z cap. LULUCF activities in the CDM are limited to 1% of base year emissions times 5 (for each year of the commitment period); only afforestation and reforestation are allowed under the CDM. Appendix Z gives particularly generous caps to Japan and Canada.

VIII Compliance

The COP agreed to set up two branches of the compliance committee. The facilitative branch will promote compliance and give early warnings for potential non-compliance. The enforcement branch will apply consequences for those parties that fail to comply with the protocol. The penalties for non-compliance are: the access emissions will be deducted at a penalty rate of 30% from the second commitment period target; a compliance plan will have to be developed; no emissions allowances can be sold; and payments to repair damage to the environment will be made. There will be an appeal process to the COP/MOP. A separate legal instrument on compliance should be adopted.